7/22/13
$25.99
BoT
AS-14
Bio
8/13

D1005872

J. Paul Getty with twins Martine *(left)* and Jutta Zacher at the infamous "Cocaine" shoot. (AP Images)

UNCOMMON
YOUTH

UNCOMMON YOUTH

The Gilded Life and Tragic Times of J. Paul Getty III

CHARLES FOX

ST. MARTIN'S PRESS NEW YORK

www.stmartins.com

Design by Steven Seighman

Title-page photo courtesy of AP Images

Library of Congress Cataloging-in-Publication Data

Fox, Charles.
  Uncommon youth : the gilded life and tragic times of J. Paul Getty III / by Charles Fox.—First edition.
     pages cm
  ISBN 978-1-250-01821-2 (hardcover)
  ISBN 978-1-250-01822-9 (e-book)
  1. Getty, Paul, 1956—Kidnapping, 1973. 2. Getty, J. Paul (Jean Paul), 1892–1976—Family. 3. Kidnapping—Italy—Case studies. 4. Children of the rich—United States—Biography. I. Title.
  HV6604.I82G484 2013
  364.15'4092—dc23
  [B]

2013002631

St. Martin's Press books may be purchased for educational, business, or promotional use. For information on bulk purchases, please contact Macmillan Corporate and Premium Sales Department at 1-800-221-7945 extension 5442 or write specialmarkets@macmillan.com.

First Edition: May 2013

10 9 8 7 6 5 4 3 2 1

Let me tell you about the very rich. They are different from you and me. They possess and enjoy early, and it does something to them, makes them soft where we are hard, and cynical where we are trustful, in a way that, unless you were born rich, it is very difficult to understand.

—F. Scott Fitzgerald, *The Great Gatsby*

CAST OF CHARACTERS

Getty Family

J. Paul Getty III: (aka Paul, Little Paul, young Paul) Grandson to J. Paul Getty

J. Paul Getty: (aka Old Paul) The grandfather, the oil magnate

J. Paul Getty II: (aka Big Paul) Father to Little Paul, son to Old Paul

Gail Harris Getty: (aka Gail Harris Jeffries) Mother to Little Paul, first wife to Big Paul

Martine Zacher: Little Paul's girlfriend, and later wife

Victoria Brooke: Big Paul's mistress, and later third wife

Talitha Pol: Big Paul's second wife and Victoria's close friend

Gordon Getty: Big Paul's younger brother

Sarah C. Getty: Old Paul's mother

Balthazar Getty: Son of Little Paul and Martine

Tara Gabriel Galaxy Gramophone Getty: Son of Big Paul and Talitha

The Kidnappers: (Fifty, the Chipmunk, Piccolo, VB1, VB2)

James Fletcher Chace: (aka Chace) Troubleshooter hired by Old Paul to investigate kidnapping of Little Paul

Giovanni Iacovoni: Gail's Roman lawyer

Nicolette Meers: Housekeeper for Big Paul in Morocco

Marcello Crisi: Little Paul's best friend and roommate in Rome

Jutta Winkelmann: Martine Zacher's twin sister

Others

Byron: Getty driver in London

Jerry Cherchio: Big Paul's friend and owner of the Luau Club in Rome

Ciambellone: The Roman coke dealer

"Cockney Pauline": London LSD supplier

D. O. Cozzi: Writer and social anthropologist, a San Francisco expatriate who has lived in Italy for fifty years

Ed Daley: Owner of World Airways

George d'Almeida: American in Rome, friend of Gail and Big Paul

Luigi Della Ratta: (aka Lou) Gail's boyfriend

Derek: Big Paul's London minder

Derek: Old Paul's manservant

Danielle Devret: Rome go-go dancer and sometimes girlfriend of Little Paul

Capt. Martino Elisco: Commander of the *carabinieri* (one of Italy's two police forces), in Lagonegro

Jack Forrester: Old Paul's best friend

George and Aileen Harris: Gail's parents

Iovinella: *squadra mobile* (Rome police)

Lang Jeffries: Gail's second husband

Fiona Lewis: Victoria's close friend in London

Martin McInnis: Family lawyer in San Francisco

Mario: Big Paul's Roman chauffeur and minder, suspected of using the kidnapping to extort money, but nothing was proved

Dr. Fernando Masone: Head of *squadra mobile* (Rome police)

Ann Rork: Big Paul and Gordon's mother, Old Paul's third wife

Dado Ruspoli: Big Paul's friend

Lord Christopher Thynne: Social peer to Big Paul, Talitha, and Victoria

Jack Zajac: American sculptor in Rome, friend of Gail and Big Paul

UNCOMMON YOUTH

PROLOGUE

Los Angeles, 2001

As things turned out, it was the last time we met. Soon after our visit, Paul and his mother/custodian, Gail, took their entourage and moved back to Europe, never to return. I imagine they went in Uncle Gordon's 747.

On this, our final visit, Véro, James, and I came down from the north through Death Valley. This time of year the desert was in bloom.

Paul was living up on the hill opposite the Hollywood Bowl in a luxurious cottage hideaway, said to have been formerly occupied by a senior CIA operative. A wheelchair van like my own was parked opposite a ramp leading to the living room. John, one of Paul's minders, came out to help unload me. He told us that Paul was out back.

We went through the living room into a garden with a swimming pool. Paul was reclined on his wheelchair in the deep shade of a magnolia, long legs stretched out before him, bedroom slippers on lolling feet, thin freckled arms secured on the armrests by black velvet ribbons about the wrists. We joined him. John invited Véro and James to go swimming and led them into the house to change, leaving the two of us side by side on our chairs.

In the buzz of the afternoon heat, a solitary bird repeated a plaintive note. Water trickled on jasmine-scented air. I looked up and watched a pale liquid fire dancing on the underside of the magnolia leaves, the sun reflected off the surface of the pool. A hummingbird hovered before a fuchsia. Through mists of steam, a clearing of crabgrass gave way to birds of paradise, frangipani, and black bamboo screening the door in the fence that led back out into the street. It was a mirage, this place.

From within the house a woman's voice called out in Spanish. A man answered and there was laughter. They were, I supposed, preparing lunch. This was their place now. It was a good life, steady work. They would never know the nature of the man for whom they worked any more than museum curators know that of the creators of the artifacts they preserve.

I watched the steam rise off the water. He liked the water warm, I no longer enjoyed it; the paralyzed body bobs like a cork. The sensation is strange, the lack of control frightening.

Led by John, Véro, my wife, and James, my son, reemerged from the house laughing, cajoling. Véro and James plunged into the pool. I watched them swim, heard their laughter. When they'd had enough, they went back into the house. The ruffled water slowly slackened.

I could turn my head enough to see Paul reclined in effigy beside me, blank eyes staring fixedly ahead, nose rising up like the dorsal on a sailfish, shock of red hair cut short. He'd had no wish to conceal the swirl of scar tissue around the hole and pale patch of skin exposed by the missing ear. I watched his face for a sign of recognition, a flicker that would move us forward. There was none. When we had first met, his flame had been dazzling. The hotter he had burned, the more he had sought. He had trod where you dared not, done what made you wonder. That's how his father had been, the late John Paul Getty II, the man who had kindled his fire and then left him to burn until all that remained was stillness and silence.

Where was Paul at this moment? In the halls of memory, waiting for the sound of a familiar voice? Was he, too, prey to clouds of claustrophobia? What to say? I couldn't carry on the way his mother, Gail, did each morning, chattering cheerfully over the speakerphone, her optimistic voice floating into his bedroom. But encouraged by the thought of her effort, I broke the silence: "We just came from Zabriskie Point. Do you remember that film, *Zabriskie Point*?"

There came the sound of voices. They were coming back from the house. They had changed, wet hair gleamed. Martine was with them. She was fifty now, slight, gentle, hair cut short, her pretty face become beautiful. John came to stand behind Paul, putting hands upon his shoulders. A small smile, easily mistaken for a grimace, appeared on Paul's face.

"I was just telling Paul that we came from Zabriskie Point." I spoke to John. "Who directed *Zabriskie Point*?" Before John could reply, Paul's mouth opened and uttered a series of clicks, almost a stammer, unintelligible to me.

"What's he saying?"

"He's saying 'A.'"

"Of course. A for Antonioni."

So Paul was in there, listening. Some assume that, being diminished, I cannot think for myself. I was doing the same with him. What did he make of us, this Paul? As if to cover up the thought, I breezed on. "Not one of his better films. Pamela Jane"—at the mention of her name, Paul's mouth spasmed into a rictus grin that seemed to draw back his head and stiffen his whole body—"she sends her love. We all miss you up north. You should come up and visit us, stay with me. The house is ramped. It would be easy."

John was shaking his head. "Too many memories."

Once more Paul began uttering small, indecipherable clicks. Again I looked up at John. "What's he saying?"

John stared steadfastly at me. "He says he wants you to write his story."

It was a shock. I'd thought all that was long behind us. John was looking down on Paul once more. Paul's mouth had resumed its grin. There was nothing more, just the echo of those words.

Martine stooped to kiss my cheek. "Hello." The world was moving on.

"How are you, my dear?"

Before she could reply, James announced, "Véro and I are going to shoot pool." They went off together back toward the house.

Martine stroked Paul's head. She turned back to me. "Paul wants me to come live here, but I have my life in Germany." She carried on about her life there and her children, but I didn't follow.

When she paused, John said, "It's getting hot, let's go in." He turned Paul's chair and led the way across the tiles toward the house and the ramp leading to the living room. Martine pushed me after them. I asked her, "Are you in touch with Marcello?"

From behind me I heard her say, "Marcello died. He was really sick. He needed a liver transplant or something. Strange character, Marcello. I didn't trust him one bit."

As we came into a patch of shade, I asked her to stop. John and Paul were disappearing into the house. I told Martine, "Paul just asked me to write his story."

She came around to stand before me. Her smile was wistful. "What did you tell him?"

"Nothing."

She gave me a look. "Jutta and I are very defensive about Paul; he is part of us. We don't want to shed any bad light on him."

"That may be rather difficult. It's why I didn't write the book in the first place."

Again there was that wistful smile, almost apologetic, and a tiny shrug. "You must remember, we were coming out of the sixties, a very ecstatic time. It was a period where we went very deep into ourselves to defeat the shadow world."

Carl Jung, G. I. Gurdjieff, Timothy Leary, Carlos Castaneda, and Oscar Ichazo were arrayed before me.

She hesitated and then said softly, "Sometimes I think he paid for all of us."

Without saying more she went around behind me and pushed me on into the house. Odd how Paul's words made me feel, once more confronted by a truth I'd thought best left untold. The living room was cool, reflecting Gail's easy elegance, its walls hung with large, contemporary oils, light and luminous. The others stood about talking among themselves.

Martine turned my chair to face the nearest painting. "The artist is Paul's favorite."

James appeared in the living-room doorway. "I'm going to take Véro to see a friend of hers." The cook, a cheerful woman dressed in a business suit, came out to tell us what we were having for dinner.

That night we ate around a candlelit table. Paul and Martine's son, Balthazar, was supposed to be there, but he didn't appear, the prerogative of a son. Our talk was inevitably about Paul or things surrounding him. It was self-conscious talk, but we were pleased to be together once more. It wasn't easy to know what to say around Paul that would naturally include him, a silent partner in the conversation. As we did our best, Paul, through Martine, once more asked that I write his story.

Véro and I slept in the guest bedroom, beyond Paul's. From down the corridor I could hear a woman's voice talking softly to Paul—the night nurse who would stay with him until dawn.

We ate breakfast with Paul in the garden. Martine hadn't stayed the night. Late that morning we said our farewells. John came with us to help load me aboard the van. We left Paul in the shade of the magnolia where we had found him.

James backed into the lane and we were on our way, charged with Paul's request. At least I was. *He wants you to write his story.* What had made Paul ask again—why now? Perhaps I'd been wrong to think there was no benefit to him in telling it, that it was best to leave the skeletons in the closet. In either case, as his friend I'd had no stomach for the task.

Why had he waited so long?

From up on the hillside, the tall Spanish mansion once owned by silent-film star Pola Negri, now by Gail, stared down on us, over twin stone staircases spilling steeply through a desert garden to where tree foliage covered Little Paul's exquisite cottage, a truffle hidden beyond the road beneath a canopy of green. Gail had not appeared. I imagined her behind the blank windows of the house up on the hill, watching. She had always watched over her son's life. Someday, I thought to myself as we started off down the hill, the desert will reclaim this place.

We turned north on the San Diego Freeway, drifting out of the San Fernando Valley, where aging stuntmen waited beside their fiberglass stagecoaches for the Western to return. The highway climbed alongside the aqueduct into the Tehachapi Mountains. As it flattened out, stretches of a winding, narrow, crumbling abandoned road appeared on the opposite wall of the canyon. Paul's grandfather, the original John Paul Getty, must have driven that road, on his way to his big strike in the Kettleman Hills. He always drove Cadillacs, the aristocrat of American automobiles. The Gettys of Gettysburg think of themselves as American aristocrats. Old Paul had made a fortune larger than that of any other private citizen on the planet, on the confidence of his judgment. Whatever had happened to his grandson in Rome had to do with this same confidence, the Getty hubris. That had been his undoing.

It was as we came down the north face of the Grapevine onto the floor of the San Joaquin Valley that I made up my mind to do as he asked and write his story. When we got home I would put other work aside and assemble a team of amanuenses, get out the box of transcripts that had been collecting dust all these years in one cupboard or another, and tell the story that he no longer could. Given what little time remains, there is something to be said for living those days again.

1.
—

It began for me on San Francisco's Telegraph Hill the morning of Friday, July 13, 1973. I walked down Green Street to the Chinese grocery at the corner and bought things for breakfast and a copy of the *San Francisco Chronicle*. Its front-page headlines brought the news that Nixon had been hospitalized with viral pneumonia, Perón was going to be reelected in Argentina, and right below that:

YOUNG GETTY VANISHES—"KIDNAP" CALL
ROME

J. Paul Getty III, 16-year-old grandson of the American oil billionaire, has been missing from home for two days and may have been kidnapped, Rome police said Friday.

The youth's mother . . . said the caller did not specify any amount of ransom. He did not call again, she told police. Police did not rule out the possibility of a hoax, and Mrs. Getty commented: "I think the phone call was some sort of joke."

It was a small story, interesting. The rich and famous sell magazines, but it was going to be too fast-moving for *True* ("The Man's Magazine"), with its ninety-day lead time. *True* magazine was then my principal source of income as a freelance writer. It was essentially a Midwestern "book." When you went into the Midwest and people there heard you were from *True* magazine, they shook your hand, even if you had long hair. It was a stretch for them, but they did it.

Five days later I was in New York to see my editor about an assignment in London and read in *The New York Times*:

MOTHER OF GETTY'S SON IN TOUCH WITH KIDNAPPER

The mother of J. Paul Getty III said today that her 16-year-old son had definitely been in touch with her and that "We are ready to negotiate his release . . . We have asked police not to interfere and we are now asking the press to help us. We want them to carry the message that the contact has been made and the family is ready."

So the drama was settling down, as I thought. *True*'s editors agreed. On the flight to London I picked up a copy of *Newsweek*. Inside was a photograph.

Paul's hair was cut short, long face dominated by the straight nose, eyes close, concentrated, and astute, from a well-known face, his grandfather's face, the face of the world's richest citizen. This boy was a Getty all right. This story was clearly gathering momentum too quickly for us at *True*.

After my assignment was wrapped, I drove down to the Black Mountains in Wales to see my mother. She ushered me in, put on the kettle, and as she did so, said, "I've been saving some clippings for you on this Getty boy business. I thought it might be an interesting story for your magazine." She handed me three clippings—all from

London's *Daily Mail,* July 13, 14, and 20. On July 13 the *Mail* claimed that Gail, the mother, had reportedly said, "I beg on my knees that the life of my child will not be endangered." Asked if ransom had been demanded, she said, "I can't tell you now. It was all so peculiar." On July 14 the *Mail* reported that police believe that Getty is "more likely to be in the hands of a bewitching French-woman than ransom-seeking gangsters. According to his hippy friends, Getty has fallen in love with Danielle Devret, a twenty-five-year-old 'blond Go-Go dancer with honey-gold skin' and . . . has run away with her." Detectives were searching the chic Italian haunts of Amalfi, Positano, Gaeta, and San Felice. On July 20 the *Mail* reported that the police were now "going to investigate the financial situation of Mrs. Gail Getty Jeffries."

So the story really was flaring up.

My mother told me, "I've asked my newsagent to set aside papers for me while you're here, in case there's more. The *Mail* and the *Telegraph* are covering the story."

On the weekend I drove back up to London.

When I telephoned my editor in New York to tell him the assignment was in the mail, he said, "While you're there I want you to go down to Rome and find out what's happened to this Getty boy. Has he been kidnapped, or is he staging a hoax?"

"That's the super-rich. I don't know any of those people."

"You'd be surprised," he said.

Owen Summers, veteran crime reporter for the *Daily Express,* suggested I talk with the paparazzi in Rome. "The king of the paparazzi," Summers told me, "is a Russian émigré with a name like Crochenkov. Ask any hotel doorman, and he'll tell you where to find him. Crochenkov will know what's going on, if anybody does. You may have to slip him a quid or two."

Looking among my London friends, I made contact with Olivier Bertrand, a Chelsea antiques dealer. He was a friend of the missing boy's father, J. Paul Getty Jr., who also lived in Chelsea. Getty Jr. was forty and had once been a leading figure in society but was now a recluse. His second wife, Talitha Pol, renowned for her beauty, had been the stepgranddaughter of Augustus John. She had died in Rome, and though the circumstances of her death were hazy, the coroner had listed an overdose of heroin as being the cause. Possession of heroin carries a mandatory seven-year prison sentence in Italy and, whatever the details, Paul Jr. had left Italy and taken refuge in London rather than answer to Italian magistrates. Olivier agreed to try to arrange a meeting. He said Paul Getty Jr. had retreated to No. 26 Cheyne Walk, known as Queen's or Tudor House, once owned by the pre-Raphaelite artist Dante Gabriel Rossetti. He had bought the house for Talitha in 1964, as a wedding gift. Bertrand agreed to try to get me an interview.

A couple of days later he called back. "Charles, I had a long talk with Paul. I know absolutely everything, and can tell you absolutely nothing other than that Paul said he won't talk to you. I'm awfully sorry. But look, try getting hold of the photographer who took the nude pictures of Little Paul that *Playmen* magazine, a sort of Italian *Playboy,* ran in its August issue. I can give you the name of his agent in Milan."

I made contact with the photographer, but the phone number he had for Little Paul was no longer in use. However, I found the photograph.

One afternoon, I met a contact in the Chelsea Potter and after a fruitless encounter was standing outside the Chelsea Public Baths on the King's Road, wondering what on earth to do, when an African-violet Testarossa Ferrari pulled out of the traffic and stopped before me at the curb. At the wheel sat Harri Peccinotti, a fashionable London photographer I'd once worked with. He leaned across the empty passenger seat looking up at me, bronzed aquiline face, wispy Solzhenitsyn beard, black Viet Cong pajamas. "Get in."

I did, grateful to have somewhere to go. In doing so I fell, like Alice down the rabbit hole, into another world. A fashionable world of success and excess, a world that swept aside convention, allowing you to paint your Ferrari not the *de rigueur* Italian racing red, but

African violet. Harri suggested we drive around the corner to the Chelsea Arts Club and play a game of snooker.

As he chalked his cue, eyeing the break, I told him of the Rome assignment. "They want me to find out what happened to this Getty boy. I don't have a clue where to begin. These people have to be well insulated."

Harri looked up. "Evidently not well enough."

"There's no sense going to Rome without a lead. It's got to be standing-room only down there."

He took his shot. "A photographer friend of mine, Bob Freeman, was with Paul's girlfriend's sister the night he disappeared. They were in a flat in Rome. I'll ask him for the address."

I lost the game and we left the club.

I called Freeman. He was in New York, photographing a rock concert at Madison Square Garden.

He said, "I spent the week in Rome with Paul before he disappeared. I don't know what happened. Come to my studio when I get back to London and I'll give you an address for the twins. From what I know of Paul," he went on, "I don't think it's a hoax. He didn't seem to have the determination, stamina, or personal organization to pull off a thing like this. I mean, he's a really nice guy, but not terribly together. What's odd is that he was talking casually about wanting to make a film on the perfect kidnapping, with an Italian actor friend. You should get a hold of Roman Polanski. Getty was spending a lot of time at his place while I was there. Maybe Roman knows something."

Polanski was working at 20th Century-Fox in Los Angeles. I telephoned. He recalled, "When I first met Paul in Positano, he was playing the hippie. Later, when I saw him in Rome, he had cut off his long hair and seemed to have changed his outlook. We had a large house in Rome with a garden and a swimming pool, and he often came there to swim and lie in the sun. He seemed like a very nice young boy, well mannered and highly intelligent. I find it very unlikely that he organized his own kidnapping in order to collect a ransom. The boy didn't seem that interested in money. Like most of his peers, he seemed to have rejected it as a curse. He wasn't the adventuresome kind to get involved in something like this. Although that's the first thing people might suspect, I think it's very unlikely. I'd like to know what is really going on."

Polanski had several contacts in Rome. "But I think," he said, "that you should knock on doors gently and expect to get some of them shut in your face."

Freeman had a studio on Fulham Road. Its walls were covered with his photographs. Portraits of the Beatles, famous actors, celebrities of one stripe or another—it was all about success. Slim and tanned, he wore a denim shirt and pants, and a piece of turquoise on a silver necklace. He said he had left Rome the morning of July 9 and had not had contact with anyone there since. He gave me a piece of paper. On it were the names *Martine and Jutta Zacher,* and an address: Via Di San Onofrio, 24.

On the edge of the Campo dei Fiori in the Tiziano Hotel, the desk clerk, a fleshy, smooth-faced young man, left his cage and showed me up the staircase. My room was large with a tall window. For all its white walls and high ceiling, ubiquitous Italian brown predominated. When the clerk had withdrawn, I went to the window and stood looking out across the Via Vittorio Emanuele to the church that backs onto the Piazza Navona. The boy's grandfather had married his fifth wife, Teddy, here in Rome in 1939 after the war broke out. Earlier, at the turn of that century, wishing to return to some simpler life, J. P. Morgan had wandered these streets, mingling anonymously with ordinary citizens. Getty had been more fascinated by the business opportunities that arose in the exodus of wealthy Jews faced with mounting fascism. He spent a lot of time in Berlin in the 1930s.

When I came down, the clerk was sitting in his elegant cage reading a newspaper. I told him why I had come. His eyes brightened; he gave me a conspiratorial look, evidently happy to be taken into my confidence.

I showed him the address on the photographer's notepaper. He pointed to the name "Zacher" and gave me a glum smile. "All Romans are trying to find those women. The paparazzi will pay fifty million for a picture of these. A photograph of the boy will sell for much, much more. Every day there is something in the newspapers. Today there is the mysterious American."

He turned the pages of the newspaper he was reading to show me a photograph of a severe-looking man scowling at the camera, evidently caught off guard. The man was tall with short-cropped gray hair. He wore a raincoat, the collar turned up.

"Who is he?" he asked. "This man was asking many questions about the Golden Hippie to people in the cafés."

"I wonder who he works for," I thought aloud, and then asked him where I could get a taxi.

The taxi took me down across the river and turned up a cobblestone street that climbed the hill on the far bank. I got out into a warm night. Two men passed by me down the hill, engrossed in conversation, the liquid sound of Italian floating in their wake. The girls' names were not on the panel. However, it was the right address, or at least the one the London photographer had written down. One call button was gouged out; an empty brass socket stared like a blind eye. This was the apartment the paparazzi were looking for.

For some time I waited beneath the trees, out of the shadow, so that I would not surprise anyone. No one came and no one went. At last I rose and, treading on uneven cobblestones, made my way to the foot of the hill and took a taxi back to the hotel. The clerk sitting high up in his cage was eager to know what had transpired in the big world beyond the revolving front door. He plainly admired my effort even as, in his great worldliness, he was not surprised to hear about the empty socket.

He looked sternly but not unkindly at me, as if he wanted me to know that in the end we were together in this adventure, he and I. "I tell you, everyone wants them. What can we do?"

"I'll write to them." I was not ungrateful to have a partner in this affair, even if, by and large, a silent one.

In my room I wrote to Martine Zacher on *True* stationery, telling her that I came from New York and Bob Freeman had given me her name and that my magazine would make a deal in exchange for her story. Once more the clerk called for a taxi. As we waited, he told me how much he approved of this strategy. Back at the twins' apartment I slipped the letter through the mail slot and returned to the hotel. As I came in the clerk beckoned and handed me a sheaf of clippings. "I made these for you," he said.

He took me by surprise. "I am most grateful."

"I am here for to help you. I will tell you what they say."

Between the two of us, with me correcting his English, we read the clippings. It was a quiet evening in the hotel and we were scarcely interrupted.

It was immediately clear that the Italian journalists were having a field day with this story. On July 14 *Il Messaggero* asked, WHO IS THE BOY WHO HAS VANISHED?

Who is J. Paul Getty? "He's only 16," cries Martine Zacher, 24, a German girl and last flame of the young Getty, "but already at this age he was thinking like an old man of 69. He has the tormented soul of an old artist. He is a strong character. He likes to live day to day, to make his own money . . ."

The article explained that they were living like many of the other hippies in Trastevere, demonstrating against capitalism, against Vietnam. He had once been arrested at one of these demonstrations for fighting with police. According to another friend, "The only time he ever went to a nightclub was when he managed to sell one of his paintings." Then he'd invite all his friends and treat them and spend all he had. He gave no thought to tomorrow. She said that he refused to take money from his father and grandfather. The article reported that he had lots of women: not one constant companion, until Martine Zacher. She was described as tall with curly hair, very much like the actress Maria Schneider. He had been living with her in Vicolo della Scala 50, in a small apartment on the first floor. In addition the article quoted a crying Martine Zacher saying, "He is a boy with a heart. He has talent. He is intelligent, with a mature vision of life and he scorns the useless things. He's much older than his age. I don't believe that this is a joke."

If these twins were as hard to find as the desk clerk suggested, then they had said what they had to say and gone underground. If they had nothing to hide, why disappear? Probably to avoid the paparazzi. It was odd that the newspaper would say that he was uninterested in the family money and at the same time speculate it was a hoax to extort money from his family.

On July 19 and 20, *Momento Sera* focused on the boy's absent father in an article entitled "Paul Getty II Between Talitha and the Great Old Man." It explained that J. Paul Getty II, heir to probably the largest fortune in the world, grew up at Sutton Place in England, in immense rooms of his father's mansion hung with paintings of the Renaissance masters. It speculated that "the limitations of his father have become his own and are probably the reason why his marriages fail." It reported that he met Talitha Pol in Rome and lived with her in a palazzo in Via Venezia, but she died "in strange circumstances," after which Paul returned to London. Since his son had been kidnapped in Rome, if he returned, he would have to face some very difficult legal questions about Talitha's death.

From what I knew, Paul Junior was raised in San Francisco by his mother, Ann Rork, after a brief marriage to the patriarch had ended in the mid 1930s, but a cold English castle is a more dramatic setting. The beautiful Talitha Pol was one of those legendary characters from London's Swinging Sixties.

And then another article addressed the main issue at last. The headline read: KIDNAPPING: TRUE OR FALSE?

There followed a long list in two columns. The information that most interested me was:

A true kidnapping:

The ransom letter, beyond a doubt, is in the boy's handwriting. As for Gail Getty, a mother would never be in agreement with a son to devise such a trick. She has heard the voice of the kidnapper and is sure that it is no joke. However, is it possible that the mother can have been taken in by a joke played on her by her son?

The police refer to the whole business as a delicate "game of chess." They are therefore taking it seriously.

The kidnappers have asked for 300 million lire [approx. $550,000] in what could be an astute game to keep drama to a minimum. It seems certain that the money has been readied to pay for the boy.

A hoax:

For the first time ever, the authenticity of a kidnapping is in question. Paul Getty has been living a life where all kinds of people do all kinds of odd things. They also find many ways of not doing anything at all. Inventing a kidnapping would be a perfect way to make some money.

Gail Getty's attitude in the first days of the child's disappearance was not that of a woman worried about her son. One must not forget that when Martine Zacher received Paul's letter, she did not find the mother at home. She was at the cinema with the man with whom she is living.

The overly dramatic tone of the letter itself seems false. In it, Paul expresses his fear of being killed but only in very rare cases do kidnappers "kill the goose that lays the golden egg." Above all, he keeps on underlining and trying to convince the mother that this is no joke. No kidnapped person has even thought of not being taken seriously by his family.

And finally, Paul asks more than once that the business should not be taken to the police. However, Martine quickly telephoned the police when she didn't find Gail Getty at home, although she had read Paul's remonstrations. The disappearance of Danielle Devret, described as Paul's girlfriend, and the last person to have seen him, also seems curious.

And why shouldn't Paul's mother have been at the cinema before she was brought the letter? It was all rumor and speculation. With a family this wealthy, nothing was beyond imagining, or the writer's bias. Where was the truth? Where did it leave those of us with deadlines and no time to find out what was really so?

A few days later, the matter seemed to explode, with speculation mingling with fantasy. In an article titled "Explosive Revelations by the Actor Rick Boyd: Paul Will Play Himself in a Film About His Kidnapping," Boyd says in the script there may be a lot or very little of the truth. The leads would be Paul and Danielle Devret. The director, Martine Zacher. Summarizing the script, Paul Getty III goes to a nightclub, Treetops, with a couple of friends and his fiancée. At about two in the morning he quarrels with the girl and he leaves with his friends. They get into a green VW painted with flowers and drive to a village north of Gaeta. They board a motorboat put to sea and head for Capri. Now the friends, who had told Paul it was a joke, change their behavior. The young grandson of the world's richest man becomes a victim, forced to do what his so-called friends tell him. The boat changes course to a remote island. A few phone calls are made, letters are sent demanding money.

The article reported that actor Rick Boyd had made ninety-six films and was often in the newspapers. It ruminated that his story would seem to serve him as a character, but it could be that he did know what he was talking about.

The paper noted that Avvocato Iacovoni had stated that Gail Getty had not moved from the castle in Paoli for three days. "The valiant lawyer does his best in this maze of information. It is not easy for the police, either."

Rick Boyd seemed to me one of those jumping onto the bandwagon to gain a little publicity for themselves. Avvocato Iacovoni, Gail's lawyer, was the man to meet. On the other hand, Boyd might be right. Maybe it was a hoax that had gone wrong.

A few days later, papers wrote that "Gail Getty really is alone," noting that she "is not a mother who ruffles easily. She doesn't tear her hair. She doesn't weep. She doesn't shout. Her desperation is cold. . . ."

Observing that young Paul did not have the compassion of the ordinary people, it reported that despite the vast wealth, there was no help from the family. In fact, it was the grandfather who was the first one to wash his hands of the business. "Gail Getty is alone." No one else could raise the money, nor could she even hope for the "solidarity of other mothers."

The paper wrote that "her son is one of the do-nothings who wander around Piazza Navona from evening to morning always looking for forbidden experiences. . . . When Paul asked if he could go off and taste life on his own, she opened the front door for him, gathering him back every time he needed her, like one does with hungry kittens. This is why a woman like Gail Getty is alone."

The clerk had promised to call me if there was a phone call. I lay on my bed all day, reading Orwell's *Homage to Catalonia*. Orwell had walked the streets of Barcelona, gathering his impressions, a marked contrast to me lying here in a hotel room, waiting for the story to come to me. It's odd the books one reads at times of uncertainty. I waved to the clerk when I went downstairs for dinner. He shrugged, made a long face. I, too, had pretty much lost hope. And then on the third day, in the morning, there was a knock at my door, and there stood the clerk, a delighted smile on his face.

"She is calling," he announced.

I followed him downstairs to the phone box by the revolving door. Martine Zacher's voice sounded a little tense, German, but oddly dolorous. She said, "Mr. Fox, we like your letter. We would like to make some work with you. Can we meet at your hotel?"

They strode through the revolving doors, dark-haired beauties in tight denim pants, jackets turned up at the cuffs and collars, black boots with pointed toes and stacked heels. The desk clerk popped out of his cage. I invited them up to my room. They suggested that we go back to their apartment. Evidently they had wanted to get a look at me before they decided if it was reasonable to take me home.

We took a taxi. I paid. Back to the apartment with the gouged eye socket for a doorbell. Up the stairs into a small, neat apartment with white walls, white sofa, white marble coffee table, white azalea blossoms floating in a silver bowl. A crystal hung on a silver thread in the window. I peered through it, at what I realized were the roofs of the Vatican. Martine offered me a seat on the sofa beside her. Jutta sat opposite.

It was extraordinary to be in the presence of these women, mirror images, dark eyes watching you, amused. The duplication compounded the beauty into fascination. You couldn't take your eyes off them. Until I knew them well enough to look longer, more directly, it was like being watched by a four-eyed creature.

So close in appearance, the difference between them was only in attitude. Martine was soft, with an air of apology. Jutta said little and watched, straight-faced, as though even a smile was some sign of weakness.

"*True* magazine would like to buy your story," I told them. They immediately brightened, glancing at each other.

Martine said, "How much?"

Surely the magazine's budget would never be enough to meet their expectations, elevated by their association with the Getty millions.

I thought of a number the magazine's budget might support and then converted it to lire to make it sound as large as possible. "Half a million lire."

Martine said at once, "Six hundred dollars?"

"Yes."

"Cash?"

"Yes, of course."

She looked at her sister and then back at me. "Okay."

They were broke.

Back at the hotel, the clerk handed me my money from the safe and, struggling to contain himself, watched me count out the bills. I said quietly, "I can't talk now, they're waiting." He grinned and nodded.

"*Capisco.*" From his cage he gave me a wink. "You have a good night."

The twins were waiting. At the sight of the money they brightened, looking to each other, smiling cautiously, shyly. I was about to ask them how they had come to Rome in the first place when Martine, folding her hands across her knees, announced, "We must go and see Marcello Crisi. He's a painter. He's Paul's best friend. He was living with Paul the last days."

When we had finished our tea, we went downstairs together and took a taxi across the river into narrow streets between the ancient city wall and the Tiber. Trastevere. The taxi stopped on Vicolo del Canale outside number 26, a squat, square building, set back from the road, probably a converted machine-gun nest left over from World War II, a pillbox as they were called. A small man in his early thirties came to the door—compact, pale for a Roman, tidy for a painter. He and the twins engaged in a round of kissing cheeks. We went into a large, open room furnished with a plain worktable splattered with paint.

Marcello worked as we spoke. He was drawing, or rather painting, imaginary desert landscapes with a few strokes of his brush— the outline of a hill, cactus plants, a rock here and there, a bird in flight. "I met him in Positano," he began, "a summer place near Naples. He could speak Italian almost perfectly—sometimes he could even speak dialect. He was very intelligent. He could also speak German and French. He's sixteen going on forty.

"In Positano he had long hair. He was playing the hippie, but only for a short time. After, he changed a lot. When he came back to Rome, he was looking for an apartment, a place to be alone. He wanted to get away from the home, to be by himself. He asked me if he could stay here for the time he was looking. The first month there was another boy, Philip, so we were three. The problems of one were the problems of three. It was nice. Paul moved in at the end of the summer in '72—September or October. In the beginning he painted a lot—like, the whole winter.

"He was good. I've seen other painters painting for a long time, using the same techniques as he did. He didn't like figurative painting. He liked compositions of forms and color. I think he had the advantage not to be conventional and follow a straight line. When he wanted to get a certain effect in his paintings he was using spray.

"We made an exhibition. It started like a joke. 'Let's make a show of our paintings.' We divided the room. I had maybe twenty paintings and he had maybe fifteen.

"He surprised me. I thought he wouldn't manage it, because to make a show you have to prepare for months. There's a lot of work, which even for me is hard. You really have to concentrate on it. He did everything—even the physical work. We needed to renew the place—make the walls new. And he really worked and got into it. He even surprised his mother, Gail. She wouldn't believe it until a week before the showing, but as soon as she saw everything was ready, she came here maybe twenty times. She invited a lot of people. I think Paul sent his grandfather an invitation to the showing—not pretending that he would come here for the show but just letting him know. We weren't expecting many people, but we had 350 in this place.

"We sold some pictures. We were completely disorganized. A painter and a curator are completely different. He got drunk and I did too, so did Philip. Since everyone was drunk, nobody was taking care of selling paintings. So you can imagine how it was, and everybody wanted to shake your hand or say something to you. We were very proud. We spent the whole evening just talking. The first day I sold one or two paintings and he sold three or four. We sold more the next day when there was no showing, because the really interested ones came back. I think, if someone was there who could have taken care of selling, we would have sold a lot. But it was a nice experience. We spoke about this—at least he learned that when you do something, people recognize what you have done.

"Paul liked painting, but it was too quiet for his character. He painted a lot, he made sculptures, he was talking about making films, just to see what it looked like."

I asked about money and Marcello answered, "Paul never spoke of his grandfather's money. A couple of times when he saw his grandfather's picture in the paper, he was speaking about him as if he was a very far person, as if he had nothing to do with him. He wasn't proud showing his grandfather like this. Only one time he was really proud. There was a picture of his grandfather because of the museum in California. I think his grandfather got a new painting—I think a Titian. Paul showed us and he was proud. Other than that, nothing.

"Sometimes Paul traded paintings with the people who owned the Botticelli, a restaurant in Trastevere. They made an agreement that he could eat there and pay them with paintings. He was going there practically every day. After dinner they asked, 'Do you want to go dancing?' and so he spent a lot of time with them. They were treating him a little like the young one. They knew he was intelligent. They knew who he was. Often we spoke about this. I told him to be careful, not to go with people he didn't know. The owners of the Botticelli restaurant, they are not *malavita,* they are not criminals. But you never know who they know, who their friends are, and who the friends of the friends are. As long as he was with the owners, nothing would happen. They would even protect him. The safest place in all Rome is Trastevere if you live there. They will never steal your car or from your apartment. If anyone stole the radio from my car, if I had one, I would get it back in one hour. I would give maybe five thousand lire, because the one who stole it needed money.

"Everything was fun for Paul. They'd go to different places and he talked about the people there. He got excited to meet these people and sit at their table, to have eaten with them. He was a little scared. He thought he knew what he was doing, but Paul didn't realize how dangerous it could be.

"He got a bit fed up with them in the end. He met other people more interesting.

Something happened which made him change his mind completely about going out with this crowd. He realized that all these people just pretended to like him, to make him favors because of who he was. He was with a girl one evening and one of them came up to him and said, 'What are we going to do?' Paul said, '*We?* What am *I* going to do? I'm with a girl.' The guy slammed the car door and went away. Since that moment Paul said, 'What stupid people they are.'"

Marcello laid the painting aside. It had taken him no more than ten minutes. "I paint these pictures," he went on, "Paul signs them.

They know his name." He didn't smile. He was beginning another painting. It was, I could see, like printing money.

Marcello was a confusing character. So easily, blithely confessing that the two of them conspired in petty fraud, he seemed too dignified and serious an individual for such things. Perhaps it was Paul's very absence that made him this way. It hung over everyone I met in that small world. The larger world was entertained, but here on the inside, it was very different.

"If he can get to his money, he will be a rich man," Marcello went on. "Very rich. He will do great things for his generation." He shrugged. "That is what I believe."

Marcello shuffled papers on his desk. Evidently, the interview was over. I thanked him. He barely looked up.

The twins and I stepped out of the studio onto cobblestones worn by centuries of passing feet.

The Trastevere was begun by Roman citizens, castoffs, petty thieves, pickpockets, and prostitutes. Ejected from within the ancient walls, they had congregated in the shadow of these same walls for protection against marauders, other bandits, invading armies. So the tradition of petty criminals was an ancient one. *Malavita,* as Marcello had called them, had been here for a long time, and evidently they still were.

The picture Marcello had painted of this young man left large unanswered questions. On the one hand here was a sympathetic youth, apparently uninterested in the family fortune, on the other, all his talk of films, creating a need for money. Above all I found Marcello's words haunting me. *He will do great things for his generation, I believe, if he can reach his money.* I found myself wanting to believe the same, but what did it say about Paul that these two were such good friends? Was Marcello aiding and abetting Paul in a much larger fraud? Paul was somewhere with someone at this moment, but where and with whom?

A chance encounter with a street artist in a seaside town two hours from Rome had led Paul to fall among thieves.

I saw the twins again the following day. Martine did the talking. I asked how they had come to Rome. She backtracked. "Jutta and I left our home in Cassel and went to Berlin. In Berlin we were completely involved in political things. I worked in a factory and was a Communist. After work I was in groups and made posters all the time. I started living with an anarchist, and that made me a black sheep with the Party. I got a job in a film as director's assistant and there I met Rolf, my ex-husband. He had a leading part in the film. I fell completely in love with him. He said, 'I am going to Rome. Do you want to come with me?' And I did. I was already pregnant. The Italian police put Rolf in prison for three days because they found political books in his car. They were looking for members of the Baader-Meinhof Gang. The day the baby was born, Jutta came to the hospital because she had dreamed I needed her and Rolf wasn't there; he didn't care what was going on with the baby. Afterwards he came to me and said, 'That's your trip. Good-bye.' I didn't know what to do. I couldn't take the responsibility. So I phoned my mother and she said, 'I'll take the baby for the time that you can't do it, but see you find a job.' My parents wanted me to stay in Cassel, but I said I couldn't do that. I wanted to go back to Rome. Jutta said we had agents there and we could work there. I just wanted to get out of the situation. I didn't want to see anybody. Out, out, out. I got back to Rome but we had no money. At first we slept in Jutta's VW. Then a little gangster gave us a basement where we could go, but it was cold there and we got very, very sick. We didn't have anything to eat. Some drugs."

Martine broke off and started toward the kitchen. "I'll go and help Jutta with the tea." There, I heard her speak in German with her sister. When they returned and we were drinking our tea, Martine began her story once again but now came something entirely unexpected.

"After we met Paul, we went to live with him and his friend Marcello in Trastevere." She paused. "I never told the story. It's difficult. It was so dangerous to tell it. It doesn't have to do with anybody else. When we moved into Marcello's house, all these people kept coming, and we went to restaurants—the Botticelli, a lot of gangsters, you know, from the south and Milano, they came with coke. I'm sure they had other business too, but I only knew them with big coke business. The men were well dressed. They have big cars. They spend a lot of money on those things. Every day they have new things on. They were young and old. They were quite fucked-up with the coke. It's not like heroin. But they were interesting. I just loved it, going out with them. I like adventure, you know. They behaved nicely. Incredible. Like jewels. Not intelligent, but funny. They made jokes, but I don't think they meant to be funny. There was one who had lots of trouble with the police, and he showed all his marks and all his pistols and I liked to talk with them about having a pistol. There was Ciambellone and another, Walter. He loved us very much. We painted; he bought our pictures. One time we went to a restaurant with them and there were these two whores at the table. We ate with them and the men treated us very, very nicely, making all these compliments. Then one of these whores got really pissed off and she stood up and she screamed that they were never nice to her. She said they would cut our faces. Ciambellone got furious. He stood up and almost pushed over the whole table. And then he threw the two whores out. He was their pimp.

"The gangsters, they never touched us, they respected us completely. It went round that we were twins, completely free, like women they had never met, and we talked with them about our plans about the movie we wanted to do. We wanted to make a film, not about these people, about the little boys—they are called *scippo,* that means to take things away, little thieves—these boys that go up in the street on motorbikes and they take the handbags away. We were looking for a little bit of money to start off to get a camera and some film, half a million lire, less than a thousand dollars.

"I never told this story before.

"One night Paul phoned us and said Ciambellone said he wanted to give us money to produce our film. We took a taxi to the address he gave us in the Trastevere. An old, old house. We came into this one squalid little room with a bathroom and a kitchen. There was a red bed inside and a big carpet, like a bordello. There were all these men. And Paul. I knew them so well and I never had an idea anything could happen. There was a projector and they were showing porno films.

"They sent Paul away. He said he would come back in an hour. He wanted to buy blue jeans or something. We went with Ciambellone and this other man, Roberto, into the kitchen. Ciambellone gave me the money. Half a million lire. I said, 'Now we must go, we have a job we must do, these pictures.' They said, 'No, no, stay a little bit here, now we drink Champagne because you're going to make this film.' 'Okay, but in ten minutes we're going.' Then we drank Champagne and we had a lot of coke. Then they said, 'Now we are seeing porno films.'

"This went on and on, then we had to sit on the bed, and then they took all their clothes off and were sitting in underpants and smoking and playing with themselves. They were quite out of their minds. We tried to get out. I went to the door. They had locked it. They were taking more and more drugs and everything got more and more violent.

"One of them tried to touch me, and I pushed him away and so he slapped me in my face. I appealed to Ciambellone. That started a fight between them; they were shouting and about eight of them split into two groups. There were about four or five others just snorting and watching and laughing. Both groups wanted us.

"Ciambellone wanted Jutta. He wanted her to take off her clothes. The bodyguard and the old man were touching me. The old man was fat, just awful and lecherous, but strong, very strong. You knew there was no joke with him. We tried to fight them, but I was so tired, so heavy. I was really frightened. I got the money from my bag and gave it to Ciambellone, but he put it back in my bag. Ciambellone had taken a lot of speed, maybe fifteen pills and all that snorting. They were losing their minds.

"Then Ciambellone took his knife out and said they must tie us up. So they got their belts and things and tied me and Jutta up on the bed. Our legs and hands . . . Then Ciambellone came with injections and Jutta said, 'No, no.' Ciambellone said he wanted to marry her and he said that he knew he never would get her and the only way is the violent way, and that they are used to getting everything by violence. If they don't get it in another way, they just take what they want.

"Jutta said that she liked him too but in another way, that they could be friends, that he was fucking up their whole relationship. We just tried to speak with them. But the old man said, 'You are a whore, we saw it that he gave you the money so we can fuck you.' Then we said we'd take off our clothes if they didn't give us the injections. So they untied us and let us in the bathroom. We found these gowns that we put on. We talked. Jutta said we must just stay. We had to calm them down because they were completely crazy. I started to cry, my nerves were so finished. But you know it was our fault, too. I don't blame them completely because maybe it was provoking for them somehow.

"Ciambellone phoned Paul, but they spoke in Italian and I didn't understand. They knew that I was with Paul and they were so jealous and thought, How can he get one of them? We are not good enough. Something like that. Then we came out with the gowns on and this older man, the fat man, took me on the bed and Ciambellone pulled Jutta down on the carpet.

"Ciambellone said, 'You are stupid. We could make you the best life. You can have so much money. We can buy you a house and we will only come there once a week.' Then they tied us up again and the old man threw me on the floor and jumped on me and strangled me so hard that I thought, Now it's really over. All the time I was watching my handbag to see if they'd take the money back. I thought, I'm going through hell; at least I want the money to make my film.

"They put us back on the bed and said, 'You must be very hungry.' One of them went out and came back with a big meal, scampi or something, and Champagne. We couldn't eat. Then Ciambellone went out and everything was a little bit quieter and I was lying on the bed completely exhausted. All this time the old man was touching me. So I got the bodyguard, he liked me, to defend me from the old man. For this I had to lie on the bed with him and he held my hand and just talked. He told me how fantastic we could live together, that nothing could happen to us anymore and they would pay for everything.

"Then Ciambellone came back with two suitcases. He offered them. He took out incredible dresses; about ten long dresses from some fancy store. They wanted us to try them on, but we said we didn't want these things, we wanted to go. It went on a whole night and the next day. I didn't know how long, with the coke, I lost all relation to time. We didn't sleep, they didn't sleep. Always speeded, always speeded. Sometimes I thought they would kill us in a fit. They made little games with knives. Knives on the arm and along the breasts and stomach. They said, *'Io sono così'*—'I'm like that.' 'What can I do? We were brought up to be gangsters.'

"I said, 'We are not like that. We don't do it.' I don't know if they would be able to fuck, they were so fucked-up on the cocaine. Ciambellone had a bodyguard and he had pistols. Soon there was shooting outside. Then Ciambellone said to us, 'Now you must stay here because when we let you out, then they will catch you, they are waiting there with guns.' I was more scared of the police because they made so much noise outside that I thought the police would find us and the cocaine and I just thought, We are going to jail for years.

"Then Ciambellone got a little paranoid. He said we must change places. Jutta and I went into the bathroom and we took off the gowns and put on our clothes. We went outside with Ciambellone and the bodyguard. They made this crazy drive around the Trastevere, round and round in circles to confuse us. We passed the restaurant

Botticelli. There were some people in the street. They stopped and they went to talk to them. We got out of the car and they couldn't just run after us because there were a lot of people around. We walked until they couldn't see us and then we took our high-heeled shoes off and we ran.

"We came to Marcello's, beat on the door, and Marcello let us in. He was sleeping. He went back to bed. He didn't realize what had happened to us. Paul did. He was completely white and shaking. We took our suitcase and flung everything in it and I screamed at Paul."

She stopped talking and eyed me, assessing the impact of her story.

She had sung for her supper. It was all different now. The boy had found out about the reality of cocaine, the real thing. We were still watching each other as though we now shared an intimacy. From the kitchen doorway, Jutta was watching the pair of us. She had an inscrutable look. Martine announced, "We have to go now." Thinking about what she said, I gathered up my things, packed the tape recorder back into my briefcase. Naïveté, that's what we all had had in common. Paul had sold these two women. They had been as titillated by the company of gangsters as he had been: These women were filmmakers. Young filmmakers, caught up in the excitement of the chase, tend to forget that they, too, are part of the film.

Paul had been fifteen when he first encountered the *malavita*. At fifteen we may know nothing of cruelty and so be unutterably cruel. Martine had put on a jacket. We went back downstairs and out into the street. It was very good to feel the fresh air, warm as it was, and see the sky open above us.

How much of her hand was she showing me for the money? Had the twins filled the boy's head with their fantasies, compounding his Getty hubris until he had drowned in it? The boy had by chance fallen in with gangsters and, with that supreme confidence of one accustomed to the privileges and protections of wealth, he had toyed with them, using these two women, these ardent and idealistic young

Communists who had fallen in the shadow of the ruthless Baader-Meinhof terrorists . . . or had they used him? They were considerably older than he—eight years, half again his age. He had been fifteen when he left his home and took to the streets. What had driven him out? What were he and his family doing in Rome in the first place? Followed Paul's grandfather was my guess. There was no shortage of information about Old Paul. He had published books on how he'd accumulated his colossal fortune. The death of Talitha and the goings-on in Big Paul's pleasure palace in Morocco were documented too, but not how and why the family had come to Rome.

The long and short of it was that these gangsters had clearly risen up and overwhelmed Paul. That's how it seemed to me. The details weren't all clear, but the thrust of the story was clear to me, and I had a story for the magazine, my immediate concern.

The twins and I said good-bye and a taxi took me back to the hotel. The clerk watched me enter with a look of almost fatherly pride. With his help, we read the daily bulletins on the progress of the kidnapping:

- Gail allegedly says "I give up." Paul's mother has delivered an ultimatum: "Accept our offer or keep the boy. If the kidnappers do not accept this offer, we will be forced to leave Paul to his fate." This ultimatum comes after a long silence from the kidnappers and from her inability to raise this impossibly huge ransom: 10 billion lire [$18 million]. The grandfather has not only refused to pay but to even speak to his daughter-in-law.
- When Gail called the old man to persuade him to change his mind, she reportedly was told: "Mr. Getty is not at the castle."
- Her lawyer, Avvocato Iacovoni, declared, "All attempts at negotiations have failed. Six days from our counter-offer, we have not received any kind of signal, positive or negative. Maybe the kidnappers think that they can break us down with silence, but it is useless. We cannot find these billions."

- As to the people who continue to sell photographs of her son, clothed or naked, dressed in drag, models who take advantage of their casual acquaintance with the boy, and with those who promised to reveal secret details, Gail warned that "they won't get away with impugning the good name of my son for their own publicity."
- In every other kidnapping, the kidnappers allow the kidnapped to give proof of the fact that they are well. Why is Paul silent? Why won't his guards allow him to telephone his mother?

I telephoned Martine. She said she would try to get me a meeting with Gail. Later that afternoon she called. "Gail will see you tomorrow at eleven."

The following morning, Gail Harris Getty called me herself. "Mr. Fox, I think it is better if we do not meet just now." She had a smooth, reasonable tone. "My life is too complicated and I shouldn't talk about what's going on. Why don't you talk to my lawyer? I'll let him know you're coming."

The offices of Giovanni Iacovoni were in Parioli, a wealthy suburb across the Tiber, around the back of a squat office building, on the second floor. The day was getting hot. He was at his desk on the telephone. He was middle-aged, handsome, his curly hair razor-cut and dark as his silk suit. He continued talking, motioning me to sit. When he hung up and we had introduced ourselves, he said, "This morning they found a burned corpse on the beach at Naples. They think it may be the boy's."

"What makes you think it's his?"

"We cannot say."

"Have you talked to the kidnappers?"

"Every day, always the same man. Calabrese. He says to 'call me Fifty.' He never talks long enough that the police can find him. He has a big voice. He calls from Calabria and Naples. Always public phones."

It was strange to be beside the man who talked daily to the kidnappers and still knew so little. A fog hung over everything. The *avvocato* did talk to local reporters, Italians—more specifically, Romans—but he didn't tell them anything of substance. I figured one reason could be that they would keep his name in the newspapers. Perhaps he had political aspirations. I was as close as I was going get to the source of this affair without actually finding the boy in his cave, or wherever he was. It felt like a stalemate.

I took the opportunity to admire the Roman antiquities. At the end of a long day, purely by coincidence, I ran into the twins in a fashionable Roman watering hole. They looked to be as lost as I was.

It was a week before I learned that the burned body on the beach in Naples was not that of the boy, but of a shorter man. Beyond that, there was no movement in the story. There were newspaper articles every day, but they merely stirred the pot. As much as I had become attached to this story, the magazine could not afford to keep me in Rome. The editors assigned me stories elsewhere, promising to send me back the moment there was a break.

It was two months before there was one. I was in London on November 14 when the Italian papers reported that the kidnappers now showed a much greater assurance. They insisted on 2 billion lire [$3.6 million], threatening in a phone call to send a photograph of the boy without his ear. The Sicilian Calabrese voice on the telephone spoke with diabolical calm asking Gail Getty, "How are you?" This ostentatious lack of concern on the part of the man who telephoned her was explainable only because he was secure in his own business.

On November 15, newspapers around the world carried the story EAR IN POST IS GETTY'S:

An ear sent by post to a Rome newspaper almost certainly belonged to the missing grandson of oil millionaire Paul Getty, the boy's mother has told police.

A note with the ear and a lock of hair said they had been sent to impress on the family that 17-year-old Paul Getty III really had been kidnapped and that his captors were in earnest with their ransom demand.

Police are still saying the kidnapping may be a hoax.

Gail Getty is 90% certain that the ear and hair were her son's. Experts are examining the ear to see whether the blood group is the same as Paul's and whether it was cut off while he was alive or dead. His parents have so far offered 700,000 to buy his freedom. But the kidnappers are demanding ten times as much.

I caught a plane to Rome that evening, and the next morning, through Avvocato Iacovoni, found the twins. They were now staying in the center of the city in an ancient bakery converted to a most contemporary apartment.

The "hip girls" were uncertain, subdued, almost apologetic, ghost-like in comparison to how they had been.

I asked, "Now will they let him go?" It was the question everyone was asking.

Martine looked vague, then looked at her sister and said softly, "After so much time he must know their faces. They cannot let him go."

We were drawn together by a mutual concern for this boy, whatever they knew of what he had done or had not. As I was leaving the apartment, Martine, as if to provide the answer to the question no one dared ask, gave me a cassette tape of Dylan singing "Knockin' on Heaven's Door."

Daily thereafter I went to see Avvocato Iacovoni. He remained tight-lipped, admitting only that negotiations were ongoing for the boy's release.

Over the next two weeks the press kept up a steady drumroll, repeatedly asking the same question:

WHY THE WORLD'S RICHEST MAN WON'T PAY
A PENNY RANSOM

A ransom of one million pounds [$2.4 million] has been offered by his father but the mystery remains: is 17-year-old John Paul Getty, grandson of oil billionaire, a kidnap victim?

Police skepticism, four months after the kidnapping, is still strong, despite repeated ransom requests and the grisly delivery this week of an ear and a lock of hair said to belong to the boy.

Meanwhile his grandfather, oil billionaire Paul Getty, 80, continues refuse to part with a penny. . . .

"GIVE ME MY SON" PLEA BY MOTHER

Yesterday, Gail Getty broadcast a dramatic "return him alive" appeal to the kidnappers.

She sobbed repeatedly during the broadcast, which came shortly after a Rome newspaper had published five pictures said to be of the missing boy.

One picture shows a large patch of cotton wool and plaster peeled back to show what appears to be the wound of a severed ear. . . .

IT RAINS LETTERS AND TELEPHONE CALLS,
"OPEN A FUND"

Some have written or telephoned us appealing us to help Paul's mother collect the ransom. Others have actually sent money.

Rosalba C . . . is 16, and telephoned, crying, "Paul is the same age as I am and he may die cut up into small pieces. Do something. Open a fund. . . ."

A mother telephoned, "My son and his friends want to send Paul their savings." A lawyer from Bologna wrote,

"Can't anybody open a fund to raise the ransom demanded by the kidnappers? If we each pay 1000 lire [approx. $2], the amount would be gathered very quickly. I am ready to pledge 10,000 lire [approx. $20]." A Roman doctor called us, "A foreign lady has been seriously offended in Italy and it is right that the Italians give a contribution, even if it is only symbolic. . . .

Finally, around mid-December, when the water in the Bernini fountains in the heart of Piazza Navona was frozen, the souvenir stalls had been decorated for Christmas, and two men in Santa Claus suits shared a cigarette leaning against the church at the northern end, this came:

NEW GETTY PLEA

Mrs. Gail Harris said: "I beg of you . . . I implore you. I am still waiting.

"I want to remind you that on November 30 our family agreed upon all of your conditions for the return of my son and the 1 million dollars raised by his father has been withdrawn in favor of the sum you ask.

"I am waiting . . . I am always waiting for you."

Around the world we were all waiting. As abruptly as it had begun, it ended. On the afternoon of December 15 I went as usual to see Martine and Jutta in their apartment. There was an air of uncertainty about them. They smiled wanly.

"We can't say much," Martine said. "They have Paul. He is in a clinic. I'm going to see him. I cannot talk about it, but we won."

I asked her who was "we." She only smiled.

"I'm going to go home to San Francisco." As I stood in the doorway, half turned, suppressing the urge to ask her to take me along, I said, "I hope he's okay. If he ever wants to tell his story, get in touch with me."

It was a Hail Mary. I didn't honestly expect to ever see any of these people again.

Leonardo da Vinci Airport was choked with Christmas travelers. I got the last seat of the day back to California and the apartment on Telegraph Hill.

Here I set about the writing of the story. In the course of researching background I wrote to my friend D. O. Cozzi, an American writer living in Italy, and asked him to look into the history of kidnapping in his adopted country. I expected to hear of medieval goings-on from the time they made the Spanish Steps in Rome a sanctuary for criminals or the days of Romeo and Juliet, but he wrote:

> Kidnapping
> *"Sequestro di persona a scopo di lucro"*
> At the war's end, there were cases of sheepherders on the island of Sardegna collecting ransom on sheep dogs that had been "lost" and then after a few days "found" thanks to negotiations concerning unfenced land use in the almost empty, sparsely inhabited northern part of Sardegna called "La Barbargia." News of these dognapping episodes didn't get into major newspapers. They were considered unimportant local problems and were not reported to the police or in the newspapers.
>
> In the early sixties the Aga Khan Karim invested in several square miles of then scrub bush, rocks and shoreline in northeastern Sardegna calling it "La costa Smeralda." Khan and his consortium of investors began building luxury summer residences for Europe's moneyed few. They fenced their properties and this was not received well by the indigenous people. Barbed wire and sheep did not mix well.
>
> Then kidnappings began to occur: short duration, penny-ante ransom, no injuries, low-profile crimes. A small payment by that of the family involved, and things were kept very quiet. The police were often only informed after the fact. The victims were

generally not Italian citizens. The actors were locals or at the most Sardi. No one from the "outside" was allowed into the game.

In summer when the Sardi sheepherders transported their sheep to the higher elevations of the Appennines on the mainland, where summer rains keep the edible greenery constantly growing, a criminal element invariably accompanied the flock and this made the shepherds unpopular with the natives, for crime went up when they appeared and down when they left.

In the '70s the number of kidnappings increased in northern Italy. After two or three weeks the victims—random adults, or minors—turned up unharmed, found in some remote area of the Appennines. Then one night a victim was released in the wilds of the Calabria, and everyone was shocked to realize that there was another team on the field.

The Calabresi had been watching and now decided to get into this lucrative, low-risk business. They pushed the Sardis off the mainland by first selling "protection" and then capturing selected victims who refused to pay. Sardis who refused to pay received a shot in the head.

The Calabresi, regarded as a group by many Italians as the most stubborn and violent factions on "Il Continente," vented their hatred for all other citizens by abusing captives. With the Sardis, the victim usually returned, if stressed and in poor physical health. With the Calabresi, some victims never returned even if full ransom had been paid.

Those who survived came back with permanent, incurable psychophysical problems.

I did not write of Martine's abduction. Our Midwestern readers at *True* counted on us not to print sleaze like this. They said that the great thing about *True* was that their fourteen-year-old boy could pick it up in the barber shop and not become contaminated. Gangsters snorting coke, watching porn, and jerking off over captive women would surely contaminate their boys. That's how I justified my decision. I didn't discuss it with my fellow editors. I knew what they would say and I knew how rare it was that we were presented with the opportunity to make some real difference, for I couldn't forget Marcello's words: *If he can get to his money, he will do great things for his generation.* On the strength of these words and my own feelings, I was unwilling to condemn this youth based upon an indiscretion he had made at fifteen—the mark would stay with him forever. I thought of all those who would benefit from Paul's money and I thought that if I could in any way assist him to get to his money, I should. I also thought that there was a distinct possibility that I was just another sycophant, fallen under the spell of the Getty millions. For us it was just another story in another issue of a magazine. So the piece became another "almost-true story," as the editors of the magazine used to say.

There was an account of his kidnapping in *Rolling Stone*. It was superficial, given what I knew, and some of it lifted from my *True* piece. I called the writer and confronted him. I told him, "You used my quotes."

He said, "Don't be ridiculous."

I said, "No one else got those quotes."

Over the next twelve months, I followed the further adventures of Paul and Martine through *People* magazine, the *National Enquirer*, and *Rolling Stone*. They were married. This didn't surprise me, but I wondered how happy it had made Gail. It was, judging by reports in the press, an unorthodox wedding; the Golden Hippie came suddenly back to life. Now he was celebrated, an Odyssean figure, a symbol of revolt, an heir for the sixties, and hordes of delighted hippies showed up. Then they disappeared from the headlines.

When they next showed up, I was surprised. They looked robust and content, as if their misadventure had never happened. They were photographed skiing in Zürs, riding camels in Morocco. Ah, Morocco, the dream that had brought them down.

As Christmas came around once more, I was awakened just before dawn by the doorbell ringing repeatedly. I rose and opened the door to see the face of a man I knew well though we had not met: J. Paul Getty III. He looked gaunt, surprisingly tall; bedraggled auburn hair fell about his thin shoulders. He wore an unusual long, green woolen cloak, its hood thrown back—the cloak was embellished with a pattern of reindeer-shaped symbols in light brown—a dark shirt unbuttoned at the throat, and calf-high boots over Levi's. His right eye blinked sporadically. The face of Martine peeped over his shoulder. For an instant my reality was suspended. As they came in I saw Martine was very pregnant.

We sat around in the living room, he on a beanbag, grasping his long legs, chin on knees, watching me. Martine said in her Germanic English, "We had so much trouble to find you. We came to San Francisco and looked for a long time. Do you remember what you said in Rome?"

Paul interrupted, "Can we get a coffee?"

We walked together down Telegraph Hill to Caffe Trieste, frequented by the remnants of the Beats. An aria was playing on the jukebox. We sat by the window, looking out across upper Grant Street.

Paul leaned forward across the table, scrutinizing me; the air about him seemed to crackle. "I read your story in *True* magazine. I like it. Would you write mine?"

I had long given up on the idea.

I said, "I read the account in *Rolling Stone.*"

He shook his head, "I mean my life, the story of my life. People will never understand the kidnapping unless they know the rest. I promise you. The kidnapping didn't just happen all by itself. It wasn't like I was in a library reading a book and they came in the window, you know?"

"The story of your life."

"Yes."

Martine was watching us.

"The biography of an eighteen-year-old?"

He nodded again. "They want me to go to college. I just want to make my own money, write a good book, and stop people from asking me a lot of questions. It was their money I was kidnapped for. Fucked up my whole life. I was the one that got in trouble for all their shit."

I was being invited into a family feud. They had probably come to me because I'd omitted Martine's account of her own kidnapping from my almost-true story. I'd been sympathetic.

Paul went on. "I need money, I'm sick of having to ask them for money every month."

I heard myself saying, "I'll lend you some." It just came out of my mouth.

"Al Ruddy has offered me ten thousand bucks for my story."

Al Ruddy was the producer of the *Godfather* films. I said, "If Al Ruddy offered you that much, imagine what it's really worth."

He smiled. "I'll introduce you to my mother."

2.

San Francisco, 1956

Baghdad by the Bay was the name Herb Caen used to call San Francisco, referring to its ethnic diversity. It was a modest town of pastel houses built upon the hills around the harbor. Its citizens back then were a slightly self-conscious and provincial crowd. A smattering of "smart" people, business tycoons, lumber and silver barons, they lived on Nob Hill and Pacific Heights, presiding over a union town of longshoremen, Teamsters, and warehouse-men. Prisoners were incarcerated on Alcatraz. This was the home port for the Pacific fleet, and for drag queens and fairies from all over America.

Paul, son of Big Paul and grandson of Old Paul, was born here on November the fourth, 1956. Soon after, a package came in the mail from Old Paul in England. In the package, wrapped in tissue paper was a teething ring in the form of a silver rabbit inscribed to Paul. Oilman J. Paul Getty, America's richest private citizen, disappointed that Roosevelt did not appoint him Secretary of the Navy, had left America after WWII and moved to Europe, ostensibly to better tend his oilfields in the Middle East and his two hundred companies.

Paul's maternal grandfather, U.S. District Court Justice George V. Harris, a shrewd and affable fellow, had seemed certain to be seated on the State Supreme Court, until in 1950 he misruled in the appeal of longshoreman labor leader Harry Bridges against his conviction for being a Communist. This misruling cost him what had seemed a certain future.

The Harrises lived in Pacific Heights near the Gettys—Ann Rork Getty and her two sons, Paul and Gordon. These families were California aristocracy. Theirs was a comfortable life in which can be seen the roots of all the trouble that would come.

Gail's mother, Aileen—a willowy, determined woman—had been inordinately ambitious for her husband. She was bitterly disappointed when he was passed over for the State Supreme Court. These thwarted ambitions she passed on to her only child, Gail.

Ann, daughter of a Hollywood movie mogul, was the third of J. Paul Getty's five wives. He left her in 1936. She drank, worshipped her elder son, and bitterly opposed his marriage to Gail. This effectively drove the young couple away, into J. Paul Getty's business world, a world Big Paul (as Gail called her husband) had no taste for. Big Paul did not inherit his father's business acumen or parsimony. He did, however, inherit his father's youthful good looks and taste for women, and his mother's taste for drink.

Gail was beautiful in a businesslike fashion, with large amber eyes and a strength to the line of her jaw that appeared almost masculine. She was clearly accustomed to authority. A mixture of her father's shrewdness and confidence and her mother's determination and ambition made for a most potent character.

Gail:

I met Paul through a girlfriend. He was going to St. Ignatius High School. He was good-looking, tall and slim, quiet and bright, a lot of fun. When young men fetched the girls after school, they'd come over to my house and sit around and listen to music and talk. Paul Getty; his full brother, Gordon; and his half sister, Donna, lived with their mother, Ann, on Clay Street. It was nothing luxurious, but comfortable. Ann had been beautiful. Her father, Sam Rork, started what is now Warner Bros. He died quite young. It may have been suicide. Ann had been an only child, and spoiled. Hollywood when she was growing up was very exciting. She did a couple of films and then she met Old Paul. She married him whilst he was in Los Angeles, during his playboy period. Paul, her first son, was born in 1932. Gordon was born thirteen months later. When Paul was six and a half, he was sent to a military academy. He's a very gentle person and he was put into this academy. They never saw very much of their mother. They have vague memories of their father, memories of not being able to go into the drawing room because nothing was supposed to be touched. All very severe. The parents were always going out and the children were left with nannies. After the divorce, when the boys wrote to him, he returned their letters with the spelling corrected. Paul also has memories of his grandmother, Sarah Getty, and going to see her. She was sweet to them, but even she was a shock. She was so old, and in a wheelchair. His best memory is their maternal grandmother, who apparently was a marvelous woman. She had moved in with them. She gave any sense of love and family stability that there was. Paul used to go and see her all the time. She died just before we announced our engagement. It was hardly an ordinary existence: no father, very gay mother. She had grown up in this Babylon movie world that had really turned her head, and drinking was a problem. She said, "I go to a party as Beauty and come back as the Beast." She didn't seem to understand her responsibilities to her children. Her answer was to put them in boarding school.

One afternoon Paul, his mother, and I were in the sitting room when a young man came downstairs singing. He wore a dressing gown and scarf. He was Paul's younger brother, Gordon. His mother made fun of him. He went back upstairs. He wasn't part of the group, part of the boys. It was awful. Gordon was very involved in opera. He spent most of his time singing and was looked upon as something of a freak, and this was invariably pointed out by the mother.

The brothers were close. The mother put Gordon down. Paul was the favorite. His mother thought he was fantastic. She took him everywhere. Everyone loved him. He was the pride of Mummy.

Paul started coming over in the afternoons. He had a more sophisticated, freer life than I. People told me, "Paul Getty would really like to take you out." I said, "That's nice, but he drinks too much." It was a big problem with a lot of them.

That summer I went to the Russian River as usual to stay with friends. Paul's mother had a house there and Paul asked me out. I said, "I'd be delighted to go out with you if you don't drink." It was silly, a really horrible sort of thing to say. Paul said, "Fine." We went out and he didn't drink. He couldn't have been sweeter. Then he and his brother left to study French in Paris for six months. He wrote often and sent me sweet little things. When he returned he came over to see me. We resumed going out. He enrolled in the University of San Francisco. He didn't do anything really brilliant with his education. It's too bad, he could have. He was very bright. If you were one of the gay ones or the funny people, you weren't really involved in whether you were learning very much. It was more important to be running around doing nonsense. He was called into the Army. I remember saying good-bye to him and that was that. He arrived in Korea the day the war ended.

I went to university and then to New York. On my return, he asked me to marry him. My parents loved Paul. They still do. I was thrilled.

A couple of nights later we went out and Paul had much too much to drink. I said, "I'm going to break it off unless you stop."

He was upset. He sent a big bunch of roses with promises he would be more considerate. He said, "As long as we're together I'll never again have a drop of hard liquor."

We had a large engagement party. At this party he had his whiskey sour or whatever it was and that was it.

Ann liked me enormously until she realized that I was going to marry her son. Then, she called my father. "I don't want your daughter to marry him. It's going to be a disaster for her." We didn't know what to do. It was violent and horrible.

We did not invite Paul's mother to the wedding. It was a quiet affair in Woodside, a country town down on the Peninsula south of San Francisco.

We had had no communication with Paul's father, except for a telegram when we were married. I think he even sent us a wedding gift—unusual. Ann was left to read about the marriage in the society column of the *Chronicle*.

Ann's never met the children, and I'll never have it. She called me two years ago to wish me a merry Christmas. I can't imagine why. I saw her at Trader Vic's the other day. I walked into the ladies' room and there she was. I ran into the loo. I don't think she recognized me.

Paul decided he would work in the Stock Exchange, because my father could find him a position through an old friend. He got the costume together, the suit and hat, did the whole San Francisco number. He'd come home and laugh, "It's all so silly!" Paul and I spent our time with painters, sculptors, and writers—people who amused us and who liked us. Not businessmen. Paul and business was a contradiction. I said to him, "Why don't you open a little bookshop, serve tea or whatever."

We bought a lovely house on Baker Street. Stanford White had designed it. Then I was pregnant. We were so excited. It was as if nobody else had ever had a child. Paul was beside himself with joy. Little Paul was born on November fourth, 1956.

Old Paul was really excited, Paul was his first grandson.

I then said to Paul, "Why not get in touch with your father about working for Getty Oil?" He wasn't enthusiastic. He liked music; his record collection covered a whole wall, and he liked sailing. Not business. But on the other hand, he now felt a compunction to be a Getty and make money.

He thought he should try, and if it worked, fine. Finally he called his half-brother, George, who was running Getty Oil in Los Angeles. George said he would have to start at the bottom.

We saw a lot of George in those days. As a young man, he was very highly considered and worked very hard. He was the son, a company man. Whether he really wanted to or not, I'll never know, but certainly business was his life: business, business. He therefore had a very serious, almost stuffy demeanor.

Baby Paul went everywhere with us. We had a nanny, Mrs. Taylor, for the first couple of months, and then if we wanted to go out at night, or for a weekend if we wanted to go skiing, she would come and stay. But otherwise we took him with us everywhere.

We decided it would be nice if we lived in the country. So we bought a house on the island of Belvedere and Paul went to work at the Tidewater gas station there, at the crossing where you come off the highway into Tiburon, and there he was, Paul Getty, pumping gas. I have photographs of him in the white uniform with the black hat and tie.

After a while, they moved him to the warehouse operation. We were happy, given a little money every month from Grandfather Getty. It was from a trust, or his good will, I don't know. Then the money just stopped. We found that Paul's mother had telephoned her ex-husband and told him that it was shocking how we were living way above our means, that we had a huge sailboat and we were living a gay life. We had a tiny boat, a sort of dinghy, bought with a friend, Norman Matson, for three hundred and fifty dollars. I urged Paul to talk to his father, find out what was happening. Paul had done everything there was to do for the company in America, other than going to L.A. He'd done the gas-station number, he'd done a factory, he'd done the warehouse (he hadn't gone into the office, he decided he just couldn't do that). He contacted his father, who invited us to Paris. His father said he was going to send us to the desert, the neutral zone between Saudi Arabia and Kuwait, where they have the oil concession. Old Paul had been very ill. It would be their first meeting in a long, time. I stayed in Belvedere with Little Paul. We arranged to sublet the house and the furniture to the Matsons.

In February of '58, Paul left to see his father, whose portrait had just appeared on the cover of *Time*.

He had been born in the right place at the right time. The year was 1892. His father was rich. Oil was starting to become a universal currency. Getty came down from Oxford in 1914 with degrees in economics and political science and began operating as a wildcatter in Oklahoma. He made his first million by the age of twenty-four and retired to become a playboy in Hollywood. In the 1920s he was married three times. His horrified Scots Presbyterian father all but disowned him and then died. With the Wall Street crash in 1929, Getty began gobbling up deflated oil stock, persuading his reluctant mother to lend him two million dollars. She did so on condition that he put up a million of his own and form the Sarah C. Getty Trust. It was this trust that allowed Getty to evade Teddy Roosevelt's antitrust laws, laws that had brought down John D. Rockefeller in his attempt to make Standard Oil the only oil company in the world. In his defense, Rockefeller declared, "Remember, gentlemen, the American Beauty Rose in all its splendor is only created by snipping away all the little buds surrounding it." Getty was the sole trustee of the Sarah C. Getty Trust, and it was this trust that owned the majority interest in his enterprises, so that he effectively controlled them without appearing to do so. By now that three million dollars had turned into three billion. Sarah's great-

grandchildren would divide up the principal when the last of the parents died.

In February of 1958, Time *magazine published a verbal snapshot of a man who lived modestly and worked obsessively:*

In Paris' fashionable George V Hotel, no accommodation is cheaper . . . than the two shabbily genteel, YMCA-sized rooms of Suite 801. 801 was registered only under the name of "Monsieur Paul." [P]apers were scattered over the floor . . . piles of string-tied boxes and suitcases . . . an unmade day bed, the cold remains of a meager meal, a collection of half-filled rum and Coca-Cola bottles. Amid it all sat a tall, heavy-shouldered man whose massive head, topped by long, reddish-brown hair, gave him the appearance of an aging lion. . . . Jean Paul Getty, 65, probably the world's richest private citizen, went calmly about his work.

Getty answered phone calls himself, speaking with importers and shipbuilders. Declining a lunch date, he read and annotated cables and reports, and answered letters, which he'd mail later in the day, not trusting others. "In mid-afternoon Getty received a distinguished visitor: John D. Rockefeller III, 51, scion of an older oil dynasty, who came to ask his financial support for a $75 million art center in Manhattan. Getty expressed interest, made no commitment." Before nightfall he took his "daily two-mile walk through Paris (he carries a pedometer to make sure he goes just the right distance), pondering along his way the problems of the world—his world."

Gail followed her husband to Paris with infant Paul. Postwar Paris was yet a little shabby, down at the heel, but still Paris. Upon meeting them together, Old Paul decided to send them not to the deserts of Saudi Arabia as he had planned, but to Rome. He meant the best but, given his son's taste for hard liquor and distaste for business, and his daughter-in-law's determination to "kick up her heels," it was one of the worst decisions he ever made. While they were in Paris, the Algerian War of Independence spilled over into the streets. The Old Man, grown fearful as his years advanced and his treasure increased, went with them on one last Grand Tour of Europe. He had spent much of his life on the Continent and he was eager to show them what he knew.

Gail:

We flew with little Paul to Los Angeles, and then over the Pole, in one of those old-fashioned planes that have sleeping berths. It was fantastic. Paul loved it. He was seventeen months old, so good, incredible little boy, so cute. He just sat and played with his toys, never cried. He had sacks of things to play with and trays of food and he ate everything and then he got up in this funny double berth we had and we slept.

We landed in Copenhagen. Paul was fascinated with all these people on bicycles. He didn't miss a thing. We went to a hotel for a few hours to give Little Paul breakfast, then we flew on to Paris. Big Paul met us. He was staying in a small hotel two blocks from the George V.

We brought Little Paul over to meet his grandfather. I had never met him before and I didn't know what in God's name to expect, but he was very sweet. He had been terribly ill with shingles. As a young man he was very good-looking, but now he looked old. He was thrilled to meet his grandson, it cheered him up.

We dangled a lot on what Old Paul was going to do. It's the Getty rite. You sit about because you might be going to lunch, but then again you might not.

He really enjoyed being with his son. Paul was interesting and artistic. He didn't know anything about business, he was interested in the arts. It was pleasant for the old man, a common ground for them. Old Paul said, "There's no way I'm going to send you, a young wife, and a little baby to Kuwait." Gordon was in Paris. So he sent brother Gordon to the neutral zone in our place. Poor Gordon got sent out, but he was the bachelor. He didn't last very long.

I don't remember how it happened, but Gordon got himself mixed up in some complication with the Kuwaiti government there. They have their law. I don't remember what it was, but he became indignant about the treatment of someone's wife—a Westerner's wife. As I recall, she had done something that offended the Kuwaitis. They wanted to punish her by stoning her in the local square. Gordon tried to stop them. They told him to leave. You're not supposed to interfere. I don't think he can go back yet.

In Paris in 1959 we met Jack Forrester, Old Paul's best friend and business partner. The two of them were so different, an oilman and an ex-hoofer [a vaudeville song-and-dance man] Jack was in his mid- to late forties then—short, handsome, Irish-looking. He always wore a white jacket. He was with Maurice Chevalier. I think they met in New York or Paris when they were young. Jack was a marvelous dancer. He was with Chevalier for a long time. He's a very gay man, lots of fun. He was horrified that Big Paul wouldn't dance, but Paul was shy.

Jack really became Big Paul's father. That's what really happened. Jack believed tremendously in Big Paul; he felt that with his help, Big Paul could do things. When the Algerian situation flared up in Paris and the streets were filled with soldiers and machine guns, there was panic. Old Paul was terrified. It really upset him. He called and said, "Get ready, it's getting dangerous, we should get out. We'll go to the World's Fair in Brussels." We took the train.

All the old man carried was a funny little suitcase. He'd put a couple of things in it and get on the train. We were in Brussels a month. Once Old Paul settles into a place, that's it. The businessmen flew in.

Old Paul took me to dinner and dancing but Big Paul couldn't come. He didn't have a dark suit. Old Paul said, "Everyone knows you should always bring a dark suit. If you go away for the weekend, you should always bring a dark suit."

In business Paul would sit in on his father's meetings all day long, trying to learn. We'd wheel little Paul about the cobbled streets in his stroller. We spent a lot of time at the fair. Every morning it was "Let's go to the fair!" But Old Paul is like his son and his grandson, he's always late. You'd get everything together, the baby would be ready, but then there'd be stalling and carrying on. Finally we'd go to the Russian Pavilion and eat mountains of caviar. It was divine. The most fantastic caviar I've ever had.

Old Paul loves American things. We'd go to the American Pavilion and stand around incredibly bored—June Castle [the secretary], Big Paul, Little Paul, myself, and Jack—waiting for Old Paul. He was like a child. At the American Pavilion they had a cafeteria counter, with swinging chairs. He'd get up and swivel on the stool at the soda fountain and order ice cream, a soda, a sundae, pancakes. We'd sit there for hours and all we wanted to do was get out.

Then he took us on a grand tour. Old Paul drove a big white Cadillac so slowly it took hours and hours. I couldn't bear it. We were Paul, myself, Little Paul, Big Paul, and Penelope [Old Paul's friend and assistant]. When Old Paul asked us if we wanted to come in the car, I'd say, "Thank you, that's awfully sweet. I won't come in the car, I'll go on the train." We went all 'round Holland, to Amsterdam to see Rembrandt's *The Night Watch*.

In Germany we stayed at Brenners Park-Hotel at the spa in Baden-Baden—beautiful carpets, furniture, and superb food. He hadn't been there since the war, but the owner remembered him. Old Paul was thrilled, he loved Germany. We drank Ohios: Champagne, brandy, and strawberries in huge crystal glasses. A maid would take care of Little Paul while we were drinking, wishing we were some place kicking up our heels, being silly.

From there we went through Switzerland, to Milano. Old Paul was thinking about buying a villa in Ladispoli outside Rome, but we stopped in Milan because he wanted to buy an oil refinery. I like Milan now, but I didn't speak Italian then. We stayed for six months.

While we were there, we noticed Little Paul had a problem with one eye. Doctors said it was a muscle thing and eventually it would straighten out and not to worry about it, so I didn't.

Old Paul had been living in hotels for many years, but we got a big apartment in Milan.

We went to Villa d'Este at Como every weekend with crazy friends. They had a boat. Big Paul would water ski while his father went out of his mind. He was terrified. Little Paul and his grandfather were terribly sweet together. Little Paul is the only grandchild who ever spent much time with the old man.

Old Paul bought the oil refinery. It had offices in Milan. Big Paul went to work there, learning to run it. People came from all over the world for big meetings. Old Paul carried his office with him, boxes of paper, his secretary, us, and whoever else.

In Milan we heard that Timothy, Old Paul's youngest son, had died. He was twelve—sweet and loving. He had brain cancer. I don't think Old Paul ever got over his death. There were a series of personal tragedies leading up to the kidnapping. At the end of the year he decided to move the offices of Getty Oil Italia to Rome. He gave us his old Cadillac and we drove down there. We didn't know anyone.

3.

If Paris was the capital of the twenties, Berlin the thirties,
Hollywood the forties, Rome was that of the fifties. Italy was
emerging from an agricultural to a postindustrial nation. A far
cry from California, Rome was an even further cry from provincial
San Francisco. Whatever their expectations, Big Paul and Gail
could have had no idea of what awaited them. Most Americans
thought of this city then as a kind of Audrey Hepburn Roman
Holiday. *More accurately it was Fellini's* La Dolce Vita—*a*
film that came out the year they arrived. With the advent of
the sixties, naïvete was giving way to something more cynical.
Refugees from Hollywood's blacklist had come to the Cinecittà
studios to make gladiator films—and spaghetti Westerns.

Big Paul and Gail rode in Old Paul's big Cadillac to Rome
in the autumn of 1959. They were a handsome couple in the
bloom of youth with a darling, auburn-haired, two-year-old
son; a country estate; a chauffeured limousine; and a name to
open any door. In the next four years, three more children were
born to them: Mark, Aileen, and Ariadne. Paul did well at
first.

Gail:

In Rome we began meeting young people at last: Ann and George d'Almeida. He was a painter. Jack Zajac, a sculptor, and the Di Robinas, an Italian married to an American, and the writers Phil Murray and Bill Styron. We were a close group, having loads of fun. We used to play "murder" at dinner parties, fall around on the floor, people pinching other people.

Little Paul was good, shy, not anxious to run out to the dance. He made nice friends, brought them home.

In summer we took a huge house down on the coast in a little village, Sabaudia, so everyone could come. Aileen had just been born. Big Paul would work during the week, then take a taxi down on weekends.

Old Paul had made Big Paul the *amministratore delegato* of the Getty Oil Company in Italy—the vice president. The president was a strange man. In the beginning he was very nice, but he seemed to be the kind of person who would do anything, flatter anyone, pretend to be your friend because he wanted to get where he wanted to get. People behave like that with the Gettys. They don't know who's a friend and who's out to get them.

It was a good period for Big Paul. The Getty Oil Company had a contract with the Kuwaitis and the Saudis. The concession is in the neutral zone, controlled by various countries. Big Paul was fantastic at negotiating with the Arabs. He's bright. King Faisal got on tremendously with him. I remember him saying what an extraordinary man Faisal was.

Little Paul has his clear memories of these days too. Somewhere here, in "childhood's darkest hour" as Poe put it, things began to go wrong for him.

Paul:

In Rome our house was on the Appian Way, ten kilometers out, past the Catacombs. Three big houses, one hundred acres of land, pine trees, a long driveway leading to a farmhouse. Built at the time of the Fascists. An outdoor pool and a house for the secretary, Fraser McKno. They grew wheat in the back and grapes. I remember watching the farmers make the pasta. A happy place. We ran around all the time.

Mark, my brother, and my sisters were born then in a hospital in Rome. I'm the only one born in America. We had a nurse to look after us. I didn't see much of my mother until I was ten or so. We had a nursery. "Children are to be seen and not heard." We ate in the nursery. We were close with our servants. Two Austrian nannies did everything. They taught me German. I spoke Italian and was learning French.

For my birthday my father gave me antelopes and gazelles, caught in Africa. He had an old MG car, which he still has, and one day I was in it with my sisters. Someone else was driving, father was riding his bicycle alongside us. Suddenly we saw people running across a meadow with sacks. I thought they were thieves coming to rob him. So I jumped out of the car and tried to stop my father by putting my fingers in the bicycle spokes. I was about five or six.

There was a television in the house but we could only look at it at certain times. I remember the day that Kennedy died, November '63. I was in the children's playroom. They said, "John Kennedy died, so television will be off for the whole day." There was a big love for Kennedy in Italy. Even now in poor people's houses there's still always a little picture of Kennedy and Pope John.

My parents were involved in society, they went to the opera. Very formal. When my father went to the office, all he did was sign letters, sit around looking at models of refineries. When I went, they'd do anything for me. People who work for Getty Oil are completely devoted to the old man. Sad cases, really.

We would spend Christmases with my grandfather. Every year he would have a party for about five hundred kids from an orphanage. He would sit around with this paper hat on and clown with the children. There were magicians and clowns. That's where they got the idea for *The Magic Christian.* My best memory of all is being with Ringo Starr at Sutton Place; the BBC was there, shooting a film on the Beatles. It was New Year's Eve. I went to sleep and they woke me up to see the Beatles on television. I thought the Beatles were little animals.

I slept in Anne Boleyn's room. I get mad when people say they don't believe in ghosts. I've gone to sleep in that room with the closet on the left and woken up with it on the other side. They have to keep it the same way it's been. Each time they move it, it moves right back. My grandfather invites people and has them stay in there and laughs and laughs and laughs.

He's got a big white bedroom, very nice, a bathroom with solid-gold water taps, because he says gold kills bacteria. It's the only sort of ostentatious thing. There is a Chagall above his bed and, in front, a Monet. Otherwise it's all white. Big, big bed, all kinds of buttons and telephones and automatic door locks. He doesn't let anybody in his room. He works till three in the morning. Hard, hard work. He wakes up quite late, eats breakfast in bed. Sometimes I'd go up there at eleven or twelve. I'd just woken up, too. Grandfather played the businessman with me. I know how to play these games, to talk about dividends or selling shares. He would read the *Wall Street Journal* to me.

We went to London a couple of times to screenings. I went to the premiere of the *The Yellow Rolls-Royce* with him. I loved it.

Back in Rome they sent me to St. George's Prep School. It was quite pleasant. Sunley was the headmaster. I got on with him and his wife. They ran an imaginative and free school. I was Mrs. Sunley's pet. We got into theater. We had fun rehearsing. I played Little Chimney Sweep, Puck in *Midsummer's Night Dream . . . Romeo and Juliet,* and *Murder in the Cathedral.* I was a police officer in that. We made our own plays, that I really dug.

It was about that time that my parents began breaking up. I didn't know anything about it. At that time children weren't told anything, especially in a place like Italy. I'm very young, but even I've noticed how children are more respected today.

When I went back to school, a new headmaster came, heavyset, middle-aged, short hair, piggy sort of face, half German and half English. He didn't get along with me. I was too strong.

In Rome they were fine ambassadors for Getty Oil. On the face of it, Big Paul and Gail—he tall and slim, she radiantly beautiful and charming—were a glorious couple, but the shine soon began to wear off. Between the weight of rearing four children, carrying on a lopsided social life—Gail liked to "kick up her heels" and Big Paul listened to Wagner—and keeping up a façade for the business world (a world Gail had known from the start that Big Paul abhorred and yet she insisted he continue), the couple's marriage slowly suffocated. Somewhere in these days is the seed of Paul's unhappiness.

Big Paul withdrew and the family broke up. The children were more and more ignored and the more Paul, now a young boy, was ignored the more he clamored for his father's attention and acted out his unhappiness at not getting it.

Finally, Big Paul acknowledged his dissatisfaction by opening the marriage, ushering him and Gail into the wild world of the all-you-can-eat sixties. A world that would amplify their individual appetites until the family and they themselves were torn apart. Gail was remarkably candid about these days.

Gail:

Big Paul was more and more worried about responsibility, even though he never made an important decision before checking with his father. In the end, the only thing he enjoyed about the oil business was negotiating with the Arabs.

When he came home from the office, he wanted to talk about opera or theater or movies or the children or me or him but not what he had done all day. He had just sat there shuffling papers, sitting in meetings. He wasn't a businessman, that's all. Then slowly, slowly, he found that there was no appreciation for what he was doing and for giving up what he wanted to do. He's a creative person. The office is a stifling atmosphere. One's brain rots if you don't do anything. But he became used to the things that went with the secretary. He adapted. He needed money. He didn't even like to drive a car. The driver picked him up every morning and brought him home. You get used to that kind of thing. He couldn't do anything for himself anymore except just sit and listen to his opera records. I like opera, but it couldn't be my only amusement.

Sometimes he would say, "What kind of music do you want to hear? I'll put on something for you." But I knew he'd be much happier taping an opera that was on than playing anything I wanted. I understand it now. He had so little time for the things that he liked. I liked to go out on Sundays with our friends and the children for a picnic. He didn't want to take the children anywhere—they were shooed away. Of course, it irritated me beyond belief. He just stopped doing the things I wanted.

He had been extraordinarily warm, affectionate, but now he started to lose interest in our marriage. It got very heavy. There was no lightness. I was much gayer. I loved going out, loved to dance. He slowly became a recluse, lost his vitality. I'm not talking about sex, just vitality. After a while in Rome he got old. He had to wear his business suit, and he lost his freedom and, to be very honest, I probably had a lot to do with it, telling him, "Do this because it will make your father happy."

I knew perfectly well that they could never be that close, but it seemed to me that if he made an effort, then maybe his father would be happier. Big Paul wanted to know his father and have his approval and love—an impossible thing to get. It got to the point where I started, in a foolish sort of way, to lose respect for him. I felt he was losing a grip on his character, his personality. It was the suit and the business. He lost his flair.

One day he said to me, "You go on. If you have an affair with anybody, that's okay with me as long as I know. Don't ever do anything unless I know it." It was okay with him, except for this one man, he said, "Anyone but him." He was afraid he would be made a fool of. That was too much for me. He's a very broad-minded man, and I guess I didn't want anyone that broad-minded with me. Right or wrong, there were different morals in those days.

In May of '63 he went to Beirut for business. I must have been very unhappy, because when he was gone I spent my entire time screwing anybody I saw, including the one he had forbidden. It was just insanity.

One night, while he was in Beirut, I went to the Luau. The owner, Jerry Cherchio, had this Maltese friend who had a powerboat he was racing the next day.

Jerry's wife, Ruth, knew that I was alone and said, "If you're not doing anything Sunday, would you like to go? It'll be fun." I said, "I'd love to." She said, "I'll call you in the morning and come and pick you up." Lovely. She called and said, "I hope you don't mind—this man you don't know called Lang Jeffries, who comes into the Luau a lot, doesn't have anything to do and wants to come with us. But he has a little Thunderbird and we can't all fit, so could we use your VW?" I said, "I don't mind at all." She said, "You'd better talk to him and tell him how to get to your house." I talked to him and said, "Do you know where the Appian Way is?" He said, "No." I said, "Do you know where the Catacombs are?" He said, no. So I asked him, "Well, what do you know?"

Finally they arrived. He got in the car and he was so huge, he made me laugh, he just looked so funny in my little car. The races were really fun. It got terribly cold. He was very sweet and polite and gave me his sweater.

A couple of days later I was in the Luau having dinner with Ruth when Lang came in. She said, "Do you mind if he joins us?" I didn't mind at all. I thought he was very attractive. He sat and we started drinking lots of red wine and laughing and talking and then it was getting time for me to go. I got outside and I thought, This is dumb, I don't really want to go home. Why did I leave? I really like him. I had to figure out some way of going back in without looking like a total fool. I made some dumb excuse and sat right back down again and started talking and we had more red wine.

The next thing I knew I woke up in his bed, it was noon, my plane to Beirut was leaving at four, I had a terrible hangover, and I didn't have a car. Lang said, "Promise me, please, please, that you'll call when you come back. I beg you." I said, "Okay!" He got up and got my car for me.

I went to Beirut with a horrible hangover. By the time I arrived, I was in shock. I must have looked pretty awful or marvelous—one or the other. Somehow Paul got out of me that I had slept with the man with whom I wasn't supposed to. We had a huge fight and didn't speak for days.

We came back to Rome. I wasn't back three and a half seconds before I called Lang. Why not? That's how it was from then on. In July we rented a house in Ansedonia, Porto Santo Stefano. [Big] Paul was working in Rome most of the time. He had become friendly with Gordon Scott, a friend of Lang's, so it didn't seem peculiar to him in any way that Lang was always around.

We had a little motor sailor, about twenty-five feet. Neither of us had the first clue how to sail, and it didn't sail very well anyway. People used to wait on the pier to watch us come in and dock and they'd shout, "Here come the Gettys!" Once Paul and I went out in it and the rudder broke and Lang saved us. He was a fantastic sailor. It was an insane summer; we laughed from morning to night, even

[Big] Paul. He wasn't going out with anyone, we were happy. He'd come up from the office on the weekends and sometimes he'd stay a little longer. We'd take the house for a month and then the d'Almeidas would take it for the second month. The house was packed with people. It was insane. I'd get up at six in the morning and cook these incredible meals. We had eight bedrooms and there were people everywhere: Gordon Scott; Brett Halsey; Brett's girlfriend, Amber Tomasini; Lang; Bruce Balaban.

The party never stopped. I don't think I slept the entire summer. We'd dance till five in the morning, go to sleep for a couple of hours, get up at nine, start drinking beer, breakfast, Bloody Marys till lunch, wine through lunch, and then a little tiny rest or lots of swimming and then on into the cocktail hour, then dinner, then up to this funny nightclub in Porto Santo Stefano—the Stega, the witch—with cute little English girls as waitresses. Very popular with the lads and the lads took me everywhere. They knew Lang and I were seeing each other and I got treated like a little puppy dog.

The minute [Big] Paul went back to Rome to work, they'd call, "Come on, Gail," and off we'd go. In August we met a man with a beautiful yacht. I pretended I was living on his boat, but I was really living in the guest cottage with Lang. I'd get up at five in the morning and dash back to the boat and pretend I had slept there. The man with the yacht wanted a crew to sail to St. Tropez and jokingly said, "Why don't you come and cook?"

So I did. There was this man from Texas, an Indian, Lang, a count from England, and myself.

I asked Paul if I could go and he said, "Yes, I guess so. Lang will take good care of you?"

And I said, "Yes, he will, but what about your birthday?"

He said, "I know what we'll do. I'll come up to Genoa and go on part of the way with you for my birthday."

"Wonderful."

It was a fantastic trip. Terrible storms and me cooking standing on my head and translating an Italian script for Lang, we all had fun. We met Big Paul in Genoa and we hadn't left the port for five minutes before he started throwing up everywhere. He was so sick he had to get off in Monte Carlo. We went on. We were supposed to go all the way to Mallorca, but Lang and I got off in St. Tropez. There was just too much going on. We took a taxi from St. Tropez to Nice and flew back to Rome.

Finally one night we went to a dinner party, Big Paul with his French girlfriend, I with Lang. It was too much for me. Things weren't as free then. Nobody really was. I thought, Why are we staying together? Was it fair to the children for me to stay with their father? Do they get enough out of our being together, or is it going to get worse and worse? Are they going to suffer from the tension that had already started? [Big] Paul didn't want to break up the marriage. I was the one who pushed it. I told myself I was doing it for the children. Even before I met Lang, I had left [Big] Paul two or three times. There's no actual reason why I finally left him. I just couldn't be with him anymore.

I left [Big] Paul on the first of February in 1964. As he was leaving for the office, I told him, "I'm sorry but I think we should separate. I'm leaving." He was really upset, destroyed.

I left that day. I had already fixed up a little house, packed things that would fit, like lamps and paintings, into my little red VW and just went back and forth. I broke up with Lang, too.

We moved into a sweet little house I had found in Parioli. It was a safer area for the children and there were trees. I turned the garage into a room. Whilst we were in the process of moving, Little Paul got sick with measles, so he was still in the big house and I used to go back and forth. By now Paul was seven. Everyone said I was out of my mind.

Big Paul was living with his French girlfriend, so the children didn't go to his house. He came to us, or we'd all go out. He often made an appointment and then didn't show up. The children would wait for hours. What does one say? I didn't want to put him down, so I invented some kind of excuse.

Little Paul loved his father, and now his allergies or whatever they were got worse and he blinked a lot.

In '64 he went with his father to England for Christmas.

I felt I owed an explanation to Old Paul, so I went to see him. I'm very forthright with him. I don't think many people are, they just say "yes." I wanted some kind of relationship between the children and their grandfather. He sees all his grandchildren. The only person he doesn't see is Big Paul, and Big Paul's the only one who loves him. The others don't love him at all.

Big Paul met me at the London airport—heavy scene. I went down to Sutton Place to see Old Paul.

He said, "You're so nice to come tell me. You're amazing because you don't want anything from us."

It was all very beautiful at Sutton Place, a superb Tudor mansion, full of art. There's a huge cedar tree on the lawn. He keeps lions and cubs. He visits them every day. He has a head like a lion.

He has ten or fifteen Alsatians to guard the place. Two or three are all right and allowed in the house in the house in the day; the rest are vicious, trained to kill, they're turned loose in the corridors at night. You can't leave your room.

I don't think he knows much about life or people. He gets something in his head and that's it. Not much wisdom there. He's always thinking about his business. That, and the news and politics and things he thinks might possibly affect him eventually.

That Christmas, Big Paul went to a cocktail party given by his close friend Claus von Bülow, and met Talitha. She was engaged to Knighty, the Irish White Knight, but it was love at first sight between Big Paul and Talitha, and the White Knight went off on his charger or drooping mule, very upset. Big Paul went back and forth between London and Rome until Talitha came to Rome.

When I went back after that Christmas, I took up with Lang

again. He was a lot of fun, a good giggle, incredibly good sex life. He had a little Fiat and I had my funny little house. His friends were all nutty and silly and it was just one big laugh.

Paul, still in shock at being separated from his father, suddenly confronted by another man, unrefined and insensitive, didn't share his mother's delight.

Paul:

A couple of months after we moved in, Lang announced he was going to live with us. My mother didn't ask us. This is where the resentment begins. When Lang came, we moved into a two-story duplex across the street.

Lang was an actor playing in gladiator films, Hercules, those kinds of things. Physically he was a big man, a powerful man. He used to be a lumberjack—really dumb. I couldn't get along with him. All of a sudden this new guy comes in. It got to a point of extreme bourgeoisie, like naps. At twelve I still had to sleep two hours. Everybody had to, very rigid. I had to go to sleep at nine-fifteen.

It was heavy with Lang. I was pretty straight then. I didn't like people drinking. It made me furious. People getting drunk, swearing . . . vulgar. We didn't get along at all. That whole life just turned me so off.

He tried to dominate me. That's a thing that no one can do.

The area where we moved to is where all the Fascists live, and the Americans. I just didn't like the American community, the American actors. They thought they were really hot shit, they used to bet on who wouldn't speak a word of Italian. Called them wops. They were vulgar people and I was very modest then.

I'd bring home a report card and it would show I'd been absent. My mother would say, "Don't think your father wouldn't mind." I hardly ever saw my father.

This is when the trouble really began. At the end of the year, I got kerosene in the boiler room and I sprinkled it round in the entrance to the school, the foyer, on the blackboard and the furniture. And then I threw a match on it and went up and said to the boarding master, "Strange, I think I smell burning." They called the fire brigade and then questioned me. My mother came and picked me up right afterwards. She was enraged. The headmaster sent a telegram saying, "Please don't come back." She sent me to my father.

My father picked me up at my mother's house in his Jaguar. He was with his new girlfriend, Talitha. She was very attractive. Her father was Dutch and her mother was from Bali. Rich, dark hair, like Bianca Jagger. Very frail, amusing, gay, light. They were very happy. I liked her, and she liked me. It was a pretty day. We drove forty-five kilometers to my grandfather's castle.

My father felt that he could handle me. He thought my mother and her husband were idiots, that it was because of them my grades were bad, which was right. He wanted me to live with him. We were friends, incredible friends.

The castle, Ladispoli, stood on the sea north of Rome, near Cerveteri, near Lake Bracciano, by the airport. Five feet from the sea, large grounds, a thousand acres. Flat country, tropical. There are palms and gardens. They hunt wild boar and African game—not my father, but the guests. The grounds are surrounded by a big wall. It's where John Huston filmed *The Bible,* the Garden of Eden. There's still this extraordinary Joshua tree with a snake and an apple; Huston painted it pink. My father, Talitha, and I had a picnic under it. We took lots of photographs.

When we came to the house, my grandfather was there. My grandfather didn't like Talitha with my father. He didn't think much of her, which is unfair. He came from London to oversee the rebuilding; it was a ruin, probably two hundred years old, burned out since the twenties. It was a nothing burned-down house.

They found an Etruscan town under it. The town went from in front of the house to all the way out to the sea. You could swim through these ruins, we found tombs.

He put a million pounds into it. Now it looks like the San Simeon of William Randolph Hearst, an enormous house—like, fifty bedrooms, three stories high with elevators.

My grandfather just fascinates me, this paranoid old man. He has this incredible, $100,000 alarm system—guards all the time. All night some guy would have to walk from one [door] to another and if he didn't get to the next one in thirty seconds, the whole thing will go off. He has bars on his windows and motorboats that patrol, and barbed wire all 'round. That fascinated me. We went to Naples with him and drove around with him. I saw this nice house, and I said, "Oh, that's great." He said, "Oh, we should find out about it," and he bought it. A house off Naples, with a guesthouse and an island, which he has never been to again. [Gianni] Agnelli sold it to him—you know, the Fiat guy. It's great, with a helicopter.

He has a lot of art treasures, but he's going to sell them because these fucking Italian authorities clamped down on that sort of thing, so they took almost complete possession of the house. Now it's for sale.

My father bought a house in London, the Rossetti house, and a palace in Marrakesh, and the most beautiful house in Rome on the Piazza Venezia near the Campo d'Olio. I'll draw you a little map. I'll show you. This is the Victor Emmanuel monument. Here's Campo d'Olio. The church, here there's a fountain, here there's a road, here there's a building, here there's a little fountain again. That building on the corner, that's it. It's probably eleven levels—four terraces, top floor enormous, immense, a whole loft sort of thing.

The bathroom was nice. He always had something about bathrooms. It was painted red and there were all these little posters and things, and one was "Fuck Communism"—a big poster in the American flag. It was all marble, a big step to go up to the bathtub, immense, a strange shape. An enormous birdcage with live birds in it. A little stuffed alligator, enormous plants inside and an organ at the window. A huge pipe organ. He really loved his bathrooms.

The room next to where I slept was very modern, with a Jackson Pollock painting.

He had a fantastic Magritte, which was of little trees, then a horse and the horse is split between two trees. I smuggled that into England for him. My father sold that for nothing, for coke.

And there's this painting of Talitha undressing in three stages. Very long, mostly pencil and watercolor. The first one is with black hair, strange Bali look, with a bra. The second one is with half a bra and blond hair, and in the last one she's nude with purple hair.

When my father got together with Talitha, I got much closer to them and away from my mother and my stepfather. They always talked so badly about Talitha and my father. I hadn't seen my father much up until he met Talitha. I got very friendly with her, more friendly with her than with my father, and told her that I wanted to see more of him. She encouraged me.

She was beautiful, with this incredible oriental look. Mild, just mild. A little like Martine and Jutta. Only she was the first. It was just a strange charm. She was the only woman of her kind, with great friends, who did drugs and who was very into sex and relationships with everybody. She was like the first one of her kind. She flipped me out. Beautiful, always beautiful. I was a little bit in love with her. I was the pet, you know. I always liked that.

I wanted to stay with them, to live with them, but they were going off to Bangkok, I think, so I had to go back with my mother.

Gail recalled how it was when Little Paul came home:

Lang had resentments and insecurities and jealousies about who the children were and about my marriage to their father—he couldn't do enough to equal the way I had lived in those days. He was constantly buying gifts for the children and me, anything to outdo the Gettys. He bought me my first Rolls-Royce—for my birthday he gave me a gold candelabra, gold flat[ware] service, jewelry, rings, bracelets, diamonds— spent everything. He was really very nice to the other three children.

Paul saw what was going on and was always needling him about the Getty business. "I'm a Getty"—Paul was full of being Getty, and that used to wear pretty thin.

Big Paul and I were divorced in the spring of 1966. Afterwards, he ordered a whiskey sour, or whatever it was, raised his glass to me, and said, "From now on, I can drink what I like."

Lang and I were married that summer, August 13, 1966, in Rome City Hall, a beautiful Michelangelo building. We didn't go on a honeymoon. We had to go to the Canary Islands, where Lang was doing a film. His films weren't A-films. He knew that perfectly well. But he was successful in the sense that he started from five thousand dollars and ended up doing terribly well. Not as well as the big stars, obviously, but terribly well.

[Paul] blamed me for leaving his father. He didn't want to be put into this other scene. He wanted his father and not a stepfather. It was too bad, because in many ways Lang was really very fond of Paul. He knew what was going on and realized how badly Paul, more than the other three, was hurt by what his father was doing. But instead of being clever and keeping his mouth shut, Lang used to hammer about how unfair their father was being to them and how you just don't do that kind of thing. With Paul's instinctive love of his father, his father's easy way of life looked pretty good to him. There didn't seem to be anything wrong with it. Paul always wanted to be with his father. Lang could have been the pope, Kennedy, anyone, and there would have been something wrong with him. Lang knew this and he took it out on Paul.

A lot of people say Lang was too tough on Paul. I guess, looking back, he was. He believes in a certain amount of discipline. It was fine for the others because they adored him and respected him and if he said don't do something, they wouldn't do it. He never shooed them away. Where he went, they went. But his relationship with Paul was a disaster.

Lang used to punish Paul in the wrong way. Some people shouldn't be punished. I don't mean physically, but intellectually. There were times when he should not have been punished and times when he absolutely should have. Sometimes he really was a devil. He'd take things and go off and lose them. We used to repeat over and over and over again, "Please don't do this!" Paul would do things to irritate me—heavy, psychological things. I'm terribly sensitive. I can't stand a lot of noise. I don't like people arguing, going off in a pout. He did all that kind of thing. He was always causing trouble. He wore on me hard. I continued on and on because I couldn't understand him; he was such a nice boy underneath it all.

If you're trying to live in a house with four children, you have to keep a certain kind of dignity about yourself. Lang believed in that kind of thing. Everyone had to do their little chores, we all helped clean the pool. Lang would ask, "Please help," or "Please help your mother." Sometimes Lang gave him manly things to do that just weren't Paul. Paul was lazy, slovenly.

Lang was a physical fellow, not an intellectual, and Paul had the notion that one had to be an intellectual. Although in those days Paul loved nothing more than to get up and go hiking, boating, swimming. These days he relates to what he is now; he puts [the] Paul [he is] now back then.

Paul resented Lang, thought he wasn't good enough for me. His father felt that way, that's where he got the idea. Or maybe he got it, in his own peculiar way, from my family. But what is that sort of thing? Garbage. Paul was very protective of me, he always has been. He has very mixed-up feelings about me. He used to say, "I want to meet someone I can talk to the way I can sit and talk to you about poetry or painting, and still have some fun. Why can't I meet—why are all the girls so dumb? Why aren't they like you?" He's very caught up in the whole mother thing, Oedipus thing.

4.

—

Talitha Pol, an icon of the Swinging Sixties, the woman with whom Paul had fallen "a little bit in love," would only live for six years beyond this point. Her tragic death would have a stupendous effect on all their lives, particularly Paul's.

Talitha's good friend Lord Christopher Thynne, second son of the sixth Marquess of Bath, remembered her:

We met at a small dinner party. She was very, very pretty, almost beautiful, but slightly heavy in a sort of Dutch way. Her shape was amazing. Very good figure. Rather overmuscular. But just the energy made you forget. She was so energetic, always dancing wildly, incredibly lively and very funny. I was twenty-seven. She was nineteen or twenty. She had some smart friends, but not many. She was rather new to the scene. I thought, Why haven't I seen her before? She gradually appeared in London society and was taken up by quite a lot of people.

She was born in Java in 1940 and interned in a camp by the Japanese, separated from her mother. They were kept in separate camps. She'd talk to her mother every day through the wire.

Immediately after the war, her mother took her back to Holland

and died of tuberculosis contracted in the camp. Talitha adored her mother, although it was a dream because they never really had much of a chance, always separated by a piece of wire.

I think she thought she would make it as an actress, but she never did. She was a show-off and so everyone used to say, "You ought to be an actress." She made one or two little films, small parts, but she wasn't very good. I wouldn't have thought she had social aspirations. She wanted to be rich. But I think everybody wants that, really.

She used to come and stay with me and talk with my father. I could see my father really fancying her. I don't mean he ever made a pass at her, but I see the way he looks at people. He loved her coming down, because he always felt around her he was being attractive and funny. She used to talk to you as if you were the only person in the room. She just made you feel good.

She went out with people like Alastair Londonderry, Desmond FitzGerald, the Knight of Glin, and Lord Lambton. He's one of the most charming men out, rather common knowledge, one of the gossip figures for that set. She got rather involved with them, which probably cheapened her in a way. But in no way was she cheap herself. You could say she was ahead of her time, a very liberated woman, a woman of the sixties. I suppose at the time people might have said—I can only think of pompous words—she was "loose." Whereas now they wouldn't at all. I'm not saying in any way that she was a tart, and I don't mean to knock the tarts by saying that.

Meeting [Big] Paul was fatal for her, and I don't mean that as an obvious remark, but it was totally wrong. She was the leading light at a party, but she wasn't really strong. I think she had that exuberance and when you get involved with that kind of huge set, I think it was just too much for her. It just had to be exuberance, exuberance, exuberance all the way 'round.

I suppose one thinks of her as being very witty, but I'm not certain if she was laughing at other people or whether she actually said anything funny herself. I just remember that you were always laughing when you were with her.

She was absolutely ripe meat for all those Tarzan people who wanted a pretty, amusing girl around to bolster their ego. I thought Paul was another when it started. Except he married her, and from what I'm told he did love her—probably not so much at the end.

He always rather wanted to have sex scenes. I felt it was always there, but I don't know if it was him or her. I always imagined it was him, really.

When they were first living in London sometimes he'd ring me up and I would go out and have dinner with them. There would probably be two other people. But it was basically Talitha who talked. I don't think Paul was ever very amusing. We'd go to a Chinese restaurant and the bill was always split. I was amazed; if you are asked out to dinner, you don't split the bill. He's not all that rich, but certainly he's a hell of a lot richer than I am. One time I paid the whole bill. I said, "No, it's only four pounds for four," or something, I thought I would make a mark. But it didn't work. I think he was always frightened of being taken.

One summer, I remember going 'round to their house with a friend. My friend looked out of the window and said, "God, what a pretty garden." Paul said, "Oh yes, the garden is the only reason we can live in London. It's lovely in the summer and we can sit out there." Talitha said, "Yes, otherwise the house isn't particularly good because it's rather dark. We can always go out in the garden when it's sunny." Paul went on and said, "Oh yes, it's lovely." My friend said, "Could I go out there?" And Paul said, "Oh yes, please, please go out." And my friend said, "What's the way out?" And Paul said, "You go . . . Well, Talitha, how do you get out into the garden?"

Talitha introduced Big Paul to a new circle of friends. They went to Bangkok, Thailand, on their honeymoon and there began smoking opium. When Gail realized that the couple was in trouble with the drug, she introduced them to her Tuscan neighbor Victoria Brooke, whom Gail thought of as an herbalist. Gail told them that Victoria would be a help in their struggle to untangle themselves from opium.

Instead, Victoria, a young, very beautiful English woman, became entangled with the pair of them, something Lord Thynne advised strongly against, saying, "Victoria Brooke is trouble. She's awfully nice and terribly amusing, but she is trouble. God, I like to see her, she's funny and amusing, but never get involved." In due course, Victoria would become "the other woman" in this affair.

Born in England in 1940, she became another of those celebrated beauties in the time of Swinging London. She was the only daughter of a pair of British wartime spies turned "gentleman farmers." She made her debut in London in 1959 and eloped with Lionel Brooke, a nephew of the last White Rajah of Sarawack. When Brooke went "in the loony bin," as Victoria put it, she left him and met Lord Alastair Londonderry on a plane from Paris. Lord Londonderry invited her to stay at his house in Tuscany. That is where she met Big Paul and Talitha.

Victoria:

Paul and Talitha, the great happy, shining couple, were on their way to the Far East.

Talitha was fantastic, a bird of paradise, the most alive, courageous person. She was incredibly tough, physically tough. She'd drink two bottles of vodka the night before, go to bed at three in the morning, and if we had decided to walk up a mountain the next morning, she'd be there. She was like an electric charge; nobody who met her could possibly forget her.

As Paul described it, "At the end of 1966, my father came into a large lump sum of money. A hell of a lot, a frightening amount. He stopped working. He was thirty-five. He lived off the interest."

The late Martin McInnis, longtime family lawyer, recalled how this had come about:

Gordon, the younger brother, sent out to Kuwait in his older brother's place, was thought to be the rebel, eccentric. He's brilliant. In pure intellect he has few equals. He has a frightening IQ, something like 160. When he arrived in Kuwait, the first thing he did was have a grand piano shipped to him. He was in charge of the Getty refinery. There were certain financial arrangements with the local royalty. The emir apparently lived in a mansion which the Getty Company had built for him. And if I remember correctly, the financial gimmick was that the emir paid a token rent for this big establishment, perhaps one hundred dollars a month. But he was behind in his rent. Knowing his father's parsimonious ways, Gordon thought he saw a way to impress his father and sent the emir the equivalent of a three-day notice. The emir's answer was to send a little platoon of soldiers to the office and put Gordon in jail. He was then required to leave the country.

His father then sent him to New York to manage the Hotel Pierre. It was an elegant hotel, but losing money. Gordon's democratic device for cutting down the number of employees was simple: he lined up the entire staff around the walls of the basement. He walked down and tapped every third one on the shoulder and said, "Thank you very much. You are excused." His father considered this an unsound business practice and sent him to Japan to represent the Getty Oil Company, but something happened there, I haven't got it in mind.

After that he came back to San Francisco and, dissatisfied with the amount of money his father was allowing him, he commenced an inquiry into income. I believe his yearly income was ten thousand dollars. The Sarah C. Getty Trust was established in 1931 or 1932. It allowed J. Paul Getty to get the control and usage of a great part of his mother's money, and, through it, control the vast businesses which he knew were going to develop without him seeming to contravene antitrust laws.

Gordon was entitled to receive interest from the Sarah C. Getty Trust. The principal was to be divided among the grandchildren upon the death of the last remainderman. We therefore sued his father for failure to disgorge profits.

I thought J. Paul Getty enjoyed the suit very much and that he wanted badly to win the case just to show Gordon that he was an upstart. Losing the case did not have any terrible consequences for him at all. We had the better case, and he thought he was going to lose. Also we were assigned to Judge Pierry, a judge we thought would be favorable. His opinion in a comparable case the year before had been sustained in a court of appeal. So the lawyers for Getty were very upset when we got Judge Pierry. I thought I argued the case well, but Pierry found against us. I met him in the street a month or so later. He said, "Gee, I'm awfully sorry about ruling against you. I was literally on the fence as to how to rule on both the law and fact. But the more I got to thinking about it, I thought of poor Gordon, who gets all of this money, and I thought that the father had really been pretty good to him." I said, "Judge, the father had nothing to do with this. As you know, this was a device he created to form the springboard for his own power in business." The judge said, "I know, I know, but he has done a wonderful job. He took a trust with $3,500,000, and now you say, based on good figures, that it's worth almost two billion. So, I thought Gordon was not going to suffer, and everybody is going to do all right." So he decided against us with the kindliest of feelings, but they were illogical. However, the trial had the effect of loosening J. Paul's grip on the purse strings and thereafter he began to release increasing amounts of money to his sons every year.

With his newfound wealth, Big Paul bought the three remarkable properties: the landmark London house primarily for Talitha—26

Cheyne Walk, also known as Queen's House or the Rossetti house—the palazzo on the Piazza Venezia in Rome, and a run-down palace in the Mamounia Quarter of Marrakesh, quickly nicknamed "The Pleasure Palace."

In February of 1945, Sir Winston Churchill had invited Joseph Stalin and Franklin D. Roosevelt to meet him at the Mamounia Hotel, which stands in the same quarter, to discuss the reconstruction of postwar Europe. He told them, "This is the most beautiful place on Earth."

When Big Paul bought the palace, it needed considerable restoration. He hired an American, Bill Willis, to do the work and asked him to find a housekeeper. Willis approached a young Englishwoman he knew in Tangier, Nicolette Meers.

Nicolette:

I went out to Morocco in 1961 to visit friends. Bill Burroughs, Allen Ginsberg, and the beatniks were on the road in Tangier. I knew a boy who was staying with Bill. They were all out there that summer. Tangier was utterly rundown, and the Moroccans used to get drunk and say, "Go back to your own country"—they were very possessive about the place.

I stayed in the Spanish Quarter in a tiny hotel, the Hotel l'Amour. There was only a cold bath, but it was the summer so it didn't matter. It had all sorts of odd residents left over from the war. They had been in the French Army, the German, the English, and God knows what else. They'd all drink in the same bars together. A lot of old whores, old con men. It was amusing to go down there at night and sit in the cafés in the little square in the Medina. There was the Parade Bar, run by Lily Whitman and Jay Hazelwood, an American boy who looked just like a very tall Pekinese. Lots of American women whose husbands had long since divorced them, downing drinks and having

Moroccan lovers and raining things on Jay about their emotional entanglements. Jay dropped dead on Christmas Day the second year I was there.

People flooded into Tangier in the wake of Ginsberg, Burroughs, and Kerouac's *On the Road*. They were all shooting speed and smoking then. There were deaths every other day. They took old Arab houses, six or eight together in a house absolutely out of their heads, raving around the streets and getting all geared-up in Arab clothes.

It was outrageous; everybody was swapping girlfriends and wives. The Arabs are very narrow-minded. You couldn't expect them to understand this sort of behavior. The police used to make roundups. They'd go all around the houses and arrest everyone and drag them off to jail for a day or two and escort these people over the border. They really didn't know how to handle it, the beatnik attitude. Then everyone slipped into the psychedelic age and flower power, and things got even weirder because a lot of flower-power people had money. Suddenly, the beatnik with the long hair and the beard was transfigured into something more eccentric, but they paid their way. There were the hippie boys going on their trips around the world, getting their monthly checks. People were very well off in those days. Everyone had so much money. The English had money, the Spanish did, the Moroccans had money, and everyone was spending it like mad. Extraordinary. Where was it all coming from?

I met a Moroccan boy, Amin. We didn't speak each other's language but we didn't need to. In fact, the more we learned the less well we got along. Then my mother came out on a visit with my sister and said, "What are you doing living with this boy? It's lunacy." Actually, I adored him. She said, "Well, either marry him or . . . don't let it drag on, because it will get harder and harder." Then it all happened at once. Bill Willis, the builder, told me, "We must have someone to keep the Getty house in Marrakesh together." I used to see Bill at the Parade Bar all the time and I knew what he was working on. Bill told me, "I suggested to Paul and Talitha that you were the ideal person. So why don't you go down and meet them? They're coming for Easter."

Talitha was pregnant with little Tara when I came down from Tangier to Marrakesh for the interview. They paid my fare.

Talitha came wafting down the grand main ancient marble staircase, very pregnant in an exotic kaftan. She was dark. We were downstairs having drinks with Bill, the builder, when she said, "Come upstairs." So, we girls went up to the boudoir, out came the lines of coke, and that was that. We all just hit it off. She was absolutely enchanting. She was absolutely fascinating, Talitha, really beautiful. It doesn't come out in pictures because she was sort of small and compact, but she was very alive. A most beautiful body apart from a pretty face. She had these funny little hands and funny little feet. I think she must have been Dutch-Japanese or something. She was in a concentration camp, which upset her dreadfully as a child. Then, she went to live with a very strict aunt in Holland. You know what the Dutch are like. In the villages they think that having a television is a sin. Then she was sent to one of those Reichian schools, Steiner, where they do all sorts of strange things. She was a Libra. Truly fascinating.

When we went downstairs, Paul and I haggled over my pay, and he asked me when I would start and I said, "Three months from now." I went back to Tangier, tied up my place, then moved down.

The house was nowhere near complete. Nothing's really that old in Morocco. Everything crumbles after a generation and they rebuild or they build next door. It was madness, really. Electricians and plasterers, little men with baskets of mud and cement tramping through the house day and night. Bill kept finding new things to do. Paul would be freaking out, saying, "Stop that man." And Bill would say, "Look, Paul, we simply have to finish off this end of this courtyard," and, "There's more work required there." Paul was like a patron.

I don't know what Paul paid for the place. It was sold to a false countess from Casablanca who immediately started painting all these sort of things pink, red, blue, and yellow.

There was the kitchen-courtyard with pepper trees and elephant-ear plants with huge leaves growing 'round a fountain. I had a little suite of rooms up behind the trees. You went up a little tiny staircase, and I put up a little tiny notice which said ENTRÉE INTERDITE AUX ÉTRANGERS, and it was as if it led to the powerhouse or something. So I could look out on what was going on and nobody ever knew where I disappeared to. I had my own roof, bedroom, and loo and washbasin, and I had a staircase that went up to Paul and Talitha's bedroom. A tiny little twisted staircase led into my suite and back into their suite, so we could commute while the guests were running in circles wondering where we all were. I had a wonderful view of the mountains, which are almost as high as the Swiss Alps. They go straight up off the desert floor with snow all through the winter and spring.

There was a bathroom and an alcove with banquettes and things, a few big bedrooms. The guest courtyard had a tiny star-shaped fountain in the middle we used to sit in. There's a harem, another suite of guestrooms. The harem was huge. There was an enormous mirror in the harem bathroom. There was another room on top—the *minza,* which I suppose means sun house. It had a huge fireplace with banquettes all around. It was used for lunch and things. The main salon went off. It had a huge fireplace at each end. It was a very long room. The entrance hall was enormous. The very front doors were like enormous sixteen-foot gates you could drive a lorry through, and they were held shut by a great big bolt. You had to bang on the door and shout. The guardian was about eighty. He was called Si Mohammed. He had been a guardian there before for the previous owner, a mad Frenchman. The doors looked down the main courtyard. There was a very big fountain.

Bill tiled all the garden in emerald-green tiles. The jacaranda blossom used to fall, purple flowers on the green tiles. It was ravishing. Of course, when the house was full, the blossoms had to be swept up. Every day the tiles were hosed down. And peacocks. I was given three peacocks. Paul and Talitha didn't really like them because they thought they made nasty fat chickenlike messes on their green tiles. When I was there on my own I let the blossoms fall and the birds and the cat creep back again. A beautiful place to live. I loved it when I was alone there.

The palace was just around the corner from the Mamounia Hotel. The Mamounia is a famous hotel where Churchill and everyone had stayed. It was five stars and run by a Frenchman and it was an absolutely fantastic hotel till independence, when the king took it over. It's still very beautiful.

Marlon Brando rented the house one time. Talitha met him in Hollywood and he said, "I'm filming in Marrakesh," and so Talitha said, "Oh, you must stay at our house." So we had Marlon Brando and his American-Chinese secretary. He was there about three weeks.

He arrived in a pair of stretch jeans and a jersey at the gate with his gray hair tied up in a little elastic band, out of a limousine which was so long it had to drive into the hospital grounds at the other end of the compound to turn around. It couldn't even get into the courtyard. It was hysterical. And nothing else. Just the secretary, who immediately set about buying a toothbrush and toothpaste, a loose robe, and some slippers. He had nothing at all. Then he wanted a map of Morocco, drawing pens, and a magnifying glass, and he strolled around the garden in his white cottons and a shirt to his ankles, playing one of those African things with the metal teeth.

They were filming at night, so he slept most of the day. He was on a diet and so he only wanted filet steaks. It was in the middle of the summer and the steaks all went green in the fridge because fridges never work in hot weather. He said, "Don't leave fruit about. I can't eat fruit."

He bought postcards, which I posted to hundreds of children all over the place: "Daddy wishes you were here to take a look at the mountains with him." About six children.

One night all the lights fused in the main salon, so he said, "Does anyone have a pair of scissors and a little screwdriver?" I produced them and he spent the afternoon happily fixing the lights. He really liked that, cutting off bits of wire. But he's a man that asks continuous questions and doesn't always wait for the answers. It covers up big gaps in knowledge.

The only surprising thing about Brando is that he would pat my behind and say, "You've got a very firm ass." When he left, he gave me a big bottle of Mitsouko and a little card that I have somewhere saying, "For God's sake, carry on painting. Love, Marlon," which was terribly sweet. He was terribly proper. He's an interesting man. I thought he was nice and charming.

Finally, the great day arrived when the house was relatively complete and Paul and Talitha came for the summer with thirty or forty friends. Victoria was one of the first guests. Marianne Faithfull and Mick Jagger came sometimes. He wanted somewhere to write his music. Marianne was really out of it in those days. Paul and Talitha used to come down with the nanny and the baby when it was born, and various houseguests—people from Rome. People would look them up or appear. Two or three times a year, Christmas, Easter, later summer . . . we'd have households with thirty for lunch and thirty for dinner day in and day out. In the evenings I'd do a wee bit of acid, just to keep me going, and then I'd organize everything. Dinner would have to be out on the top roof under the stars, so the boy and the chef had to drag all the carpets and the cushions and tables and the poofs and everything all up there, and heavy brass trays for five or six courses up the stairs and down again. I don't know how they managed it. Of course, I used to let them just sleep for a few months when the house was quiet. They certainly worked hard when the house was full.

Everybody had their breakfast at different times. Everyone wanted fresh orange juice. People, when they are staying with wealthy people, think they can ask for the moon. I used to have to go 'round and say, "Look here, I'm not running a hotel. This is a quiet retreat. Where do you think you are?" Christopher Gibbs wanted his newspapers ironed and the small change in his pocket washed. I said, "Well, you can get someone in England to wash your coins."

Then the Krupps all came down to stay with Paul and Talitha. Arndt Krupp, the armament family. Arndt is the inheritor of it all. He was married to a woman called Princess Hetti or something. She had been a penniless aristocrat looning around the Marbella Club and America and all over the place for years. I met her years ago. Big blond girl. She was one of the entourage of someone called the Marmalade Queen, Robertson's Jam, who had a Syrian-American lover. She had big blue eyes. And Hetti and the Marmalade Queen and Bobby [the Marmalade Queen's Syrian-American lover]. Arndt proposed to her. He was in such a state because some boyfriend he'd had a rendezvous with didn't show up or something, and he said to this girl, "Do you want to get married?" or something. Arndt is fascinating. He's charming and quite mad. He lives in Munich. He always had this joke that it should be Hetti Getty and Talitha and Arndt. Arndt or his father had been presented with some crummy old palace outside the walls of Marrakesh years before, and Arndt decided to look it up and do it up. So they all moved down with his mad Austrian and German friends. So it was the Gettys, the Krupps . . . the St. Laurents were the French contingent. It was really lunacy. Terribly funny. And everyone was smoking, if nothing else. The Krupps gave terribly funny parties. Arndt used to like sniffing poppers—amyl nitrate. There was a lot of good hash down there and a lot of alcohol, too. A lot of cocaine.

Big Paul was very shy and he used to get fed up with the house being full. All these freeloaders. Talitha was really gregarious. She liked lots of people around. So in the end Paul appeared less and less. He'd come down in the evenings and face the salon full of loons wanting to rave and he'd have a drink and put his head in the record cupboard and go for dinner and drift away again. He got into opium on one of their trips to the East, so he brought his opium back with him. He kept it in his bedroom in a jar, in water, with a cloth over it.

When they were away it was my job to keep it moist. I suppose it was too dangerous or difficult or something to take to Rome. In the end nobody ever saw Paul . . . in '67, '68, and '69 people were so into acid, opium, alcohol, coke, anything. It was rave time, and of course after all that raving it was going to lead to tears in the end.

Like that song, "Marrakesh Express." Suddenly all these people appeared, people who had traveled halfway 'round the world to live out some songwriter's concept. It was terribly funny. After San Francisco, it was Marrakesh.

We had to do this whole Moroccan thing. We used to have to go off to these endless Moroccan dos. They would come 'round, too. General [Mohamed] Oufkir, King Hassan's right-hand man, before he was shot. Hassan, who was like a little Frank Sinatra, picked up and spent his whole time making golf courses. Morocco has more golf courses than anywhere in the world. So Oufkir was a professional soldier. He was the Minister of the Interior, the power behind the throne. He kept the whole place going for years. They gave him this Gendarmerie Royale to escort him, and it's very smart. Super-royal policemen on their super motorbikes with grays and reds; they used to flash by.

They used to come over and take over the house. In the winter, the royal entourage was always on the doorstep. They used to take the Mamounia Hotel, which was part of the complex of the quarter we lived in. Paul and Talitha couldn't do much about it. We'd get a message that Oufkir and King Hassan's brother, Prince Moulay Abdellah, were in town and they think it would be very nice to come over for the evening. So we'd have to get dinner together and whiskey. They wanted to come and dance to Elvis Presley and drink whiskey because they couldn't do it in public. King Hassan's brother was very handsome. They were very grand.

The first coup and attempt on the king's life took place at the king's birthday party in 1970. The Belgian ambassador was shot. It was chaos. There were three coups.

After the third coup, the king decided General Oufkir was responsible. I don't think it was him. Why after all these years should he decide he wanted the king out of the way? He had outlived his usefulness, and the king had to find a scapegoat for the public. The king is supposed to have had him shot in the antechamber. Oufkir was invited to see the king. The king retired and Oufkir was left alone in the room with two people and he was supposed to have been shot then and there.

Little Paul came once. He was twelve or so at the time. He was sent to bed and not allowed to stay up but he would sneak down the stairs and feel that all kinds of terrific stuff was going on that he wasn't allowed to see. Big Paul used to take a lot of pictures of Talitha, Maurice, Victoria, and Paul and Christopher and all the people on opium. Talitha and Victoria were having scenes with Paul and the whole thing was getting very complicated. They'd been through so many weird scenes with Dado Ruspoli. They liked to have the grand finale at every one of these raves. I remember once they got an American film star to screw his sister. It was scandalous. Everyone screwing everyone.

Paul and Talitha had a suite at the top with a bathroom tiled like mosaic. Huge. Their double bed was made like a tent. Woven white wool lined with colored embroideries. Mosaic bath and floor. It was absolutely astounding. It had an old-fashioned French jet hose. You could hose someone down in this tiled room and they'd all get stoned and loon off up there.

You know, people lose their minds in other countries. Anything is possible. They live out their fantasies. It was the tenor of the time and it was all totally ridiculous. It was disastrous. You can't play these games. . . .

After you have the beautiful dreams, they become the nightmares.

In the spring of 1968, when Paul was eleven, his father wrote to Gail suggesting that Paul come for Easter. He assured her that

Talitha's stepparents would be there, and his secretary, and he said, "It's all going to be fine."

Paul vividly remembered his visit to Marrakesh. It was brief, but its long-term repercussions would profoundly influence the rest of his life.

Paul:

My father took me to Marrakesh, which was just great. It was incredible. And we started a very, very good friendship. We were hand in hand and we were together with Talitha. We flew down to Casablanca, and then we drove from Casablanca to Marrakesh. On the way, the wheel burst and I fixed the wheel for him. He had the most beautiful house in Marrakesh, when Marrakesh was first starting to be discovered. It had been built by a prince, but it was ruins when he got it. It was very big, had walls around it, almost in the souk. It had three courtyards. Each had its own garden. One had the servants' quarters and the kitchen. They cooked in the courtyard. It was also where Nicolette lived, the caretaker, who is now the cashier at the Casserole, believe it or not.

Then there was the living room and the guest bedrooms around one big—very big—courtyard with palms. And then there was the dining area, beautiful dining room, and then there was the harem, which was incredible, where I slept, with a fountain inside it and all glass. And then on top they had built their area—a bedroom. So it was absolutely immense. It covered several acres. There weren't that many rooms, but they were so immense. Still, it wasn't done like a prince's place. It was nice, servants running around, music and little kids. It had a big gate, parking lot, and a little hut where the guy who opened the gate was, and I became very good friends with him. He's an old, old man and he's still alive. I don't remember his name, Ali something. He always read the Koran and he tried to teach me about it. He lived in a little room for around twenty years with just a mat and a Koran and he sat for the whole day and all he did was open the door when the bell rang.

Really good people were in Marrakesh. Yves St. Laurent was there and the Stones were always there. We had great fun. We used to go around the souk on our bicycles and scream out in French. Everybody spoke French.

There were parties, but it wasn't just parties. People got together, there was a certain community in Marrakesh. Yves St. Laurent, the Saint [Roger Moore], the Stones, the Lovin' Spoonful, Jane Fonda and her brother, Peter.

We went once to a great party, all of us, Yves St. Laurent and the rest. We had these Berbers, from the Berber tribes, organize the party for us in this big house in the mountains. There's Marrakesh, then this desert, and just beyond the desert the Atlas Mountains. The mountains are incredible. They're so steep, all goats and monkeys. An incredible party. There was this big room and all these singers, girls dancing, and incredible mountains of food. Total luxury.

The whole thing was starting to fall into decadence. I remember this episode about a chicken. My father was a vegetarian and had convinced Talitha to become a vegetarian too. I saw her pick up a piece of chicken. I said, "What are you doing, you're a vegetarian?" and she said, "Fuck off," or something like that. It hurt me so much. I think I was always in love with her, you know.

But I remember vividly this party, it was incredible. I had my own area of the house and they let me decorate it. For the first time I was really on my own, like a man, and would run servants and fire gardeners and hire the whole show, and see that everybody was happy, and see that good people got in the house and not bad. The whole show, and I thought that was great. I was there a couple of months. I was going to go to school there, to a French school. I really wanted to stay there and live in Marrakesh, but then it got a little bit dangerous. My father used to be friends with Hassan, the king, and all these other important men in the government. And I remember once we had a big Christmas lunch with the Minister of War, I don't remember his name. It was very nice, he thanked us and said, "See you tomorrow," and the next thing he was on television in front of the firing squad. So things got too heavy and I had to go back to my mother.

I was crying, I wanted to stay there, I didn't want to go to school and tried to convince Talitha to convince my father, but there was no way. And then all of a sudden I had to go back.

Gail corrected her son's memory of this time:

Paul wanted to stay there alone when everybody left and go to school in Marrakesh. Nobody ever had that in mind at all. In fact, his father knew perfectly well that he couldn't possibly take care of any of his children. Of course it wasn't possible, for obvious reasons. Little Paul has this fantasy that he was forced to leave Marrakesh because of political trouble, but it wasn't that. It was just the end of the holiday.

I've heard him talk about a scene where the foreign minister came 'round for dinner and two days later they were watching television and this man was executed. The man did go to dinner and subsequently he was killed. But in reality he was executed much later on.

Paul was flown home. It was Easter time. He was blissfully happy and arrived with all these gifts. He had spent every penny he had on gifts, for the family, and for me. It was the only time he went to Marrakesh.

I suppose he wished I would have come to the airport, but I had the other children. Lang met him at the airport and drove him up to the country. They did a fine number on each other.

5.

Thus Paul was plunged into a different nightmare. The more the conflict raged, the worse the combatants behaved.

Paul:

It was a shock to arrive at the Rome airport expecting to see my mother and finding Lang Jeffries to drive me all the way to Tuscany, because we had a house in Tuscany where my mother lives now. A big house. They had just bought it. A five-hour drive in the car with him. We really hated each other. Real hate. He went through this trip of "now we'll educate you how you should be," and I had to spend entire days building walls. He was trying to dominate me.

That summer they put me to work. Made me work all the time, and incredibly strict. And I tried to run away once. I thought I was going to walk from Siena to Rome. And I started off, but somebody brought me back and Jeffries beat the living shit out of me. It was a whole summer in the country. Can you imagine how closed-in I felt? Three months of absolute hate, of real bullying me around. I wished

I was dead. He beat me till I was bleeding. I think now that he really dug doing those things. The nanny was there, and I remember she fixed me up and cleaned me up and I said to her that I was going to see this guy go down really back. It's got to all happen back to him.

I hated my mother, too, because she was digging it. She probably was worried about it but couldn't get out of it. She loved him so much. He was probably a good ball, I don't know. He was just a bully. In front of his friends he'd lie in the pool on a mattress and order me to get him a drink. I'd have to get in the water and bring it to him, and then he'd tell all his friends, "See what a good servant I have?" I was completely silent, but word got around to him that I told everybody that I hated him.

He probably didn't hate me. It was just the way he is. It was probably that I didn't like him. I just didn't like actors, people that drink, or people that listen to Herb Alpert and the Tijuana Brass. I just didn't like it. The way he treated my mother. Fucked around and really fucked my mother up.

Gail was indeed at her wits' end in knowing how to control her son. She seemed to admit as much when she said that she couldn't remember whose idea it was for Little Paul to board. She thought it might have been his father's. In any case, she was against boarding schools.

As she predicted, Paul didn't like Notre Dame. He started in the autumn of '68 and was there two years, coming home for vacations at Christmas, Easter, and summers. He only saw his father once or twice and Talitha not at all.

Paul:

It was a very tough school, priests, horrible. Oof! Incredible discipline. No imagination, just terrible priests. The big four-thousand-people school, with its boxing matches, was so impersonal after St. George, with its great English humor, nice people, theater, drama, and fencing. They made me box, and of course I'd get the shit beaten out of me. I got beaten there a lot. Used to have this thing called the bo-bo, which was a ruler with holes in it so that it would move quicker through the air.

I hung out with older people in the class and they influenced me badly. I didn't get it then, but they were friendly because I was a Getty. I didn't get along with those kids at Notre Dame. They were stupid. I became introverted. Straight as could be. My mother thought I was smoking dope here, but I never did. I was straight. I belonged to TIP. You know TIP, Turn In a Pusher? I was really straight. They thought I was a pusher, and I spied on people. I tipped in this famous actor's son.

I corresponded heavily with a girl, Bobby. Her father was an opera singer. We'd write at home and give letters to each other every day. I still have the letters. She gave mine back to me. I have the collection, incredible, with little drawings.

It wasn't any good at Notre Dame. I wouldn't do sports. I wouldn't study—my grades went down I began to say I was going there and I wouldn't go. I just wandered around. I would come home with a report card full of bad grades and absences. My mother said, "Don't think your father's going to like this."

He came home between the terms. When his father did come to visit him, it was with Victoria.

Victoria:

Big Paul and I went over to Gail's house in Tuscany and met Lang and the children. Gail was frightfully together, with all the children in their right place. It was Paul's first proper family scene for years. Little

Paul had had such a bad report and I remembered they walked off into the garden. Paul was so upset at Little Paul's report—not angry-upset, just genuinely worried about what was wrong. It was the only time I saw Paul being what I call a proper father—worrying about what he could do for the boy. After this great walk around the garden, Little Paul was sitting out there, crying because he had failed his grades. I never saw Paul be a proper father again except to be proud of his son when it suited him.

At home Lang, too, was in trouble. His drinking had led him into fistfights and his spaghetti James Bond films had been released and had as they said in Hollywood, "gone into the toilet."

Gail:

One afternoon, after he'd been doing all these numbers in school, I heard sobbing. Lang and Little Paul were in the living room. Lang was saying, "Please tell me what it is. If only you would tell me, maybe I could help you. You go 'round corners and you really won't come out and say what it is. Is it your father? Is it me? Do you resent me?"

Lang may have been very unpleasant in some ways, but in others he was extraordinarily patient. He did really want to help Paul and the other children. Paul cried, "I want my father." They both sobbed and held on to each other. It went on for a long time.

Gail suggested Lang return to Hollywood to look for work there and decided to have Paul properly medically examined. She recalled:

Lang had no work. I talked him into moving and giving one more try to California. He said, "I just don't want to leave here. Please, no.

I have a terrible feeling that if we leave here, our marriage will break up. Let's stay."

I said, "Stay for what? Why don't you give it a try? If it doesn't work out, we can always come back." I pushed and pushed and finally he went to Hollywood to visit.

While Lang was gone, Paul developed a serious tic. He started to roll his right eye up into his head. I took him to doctors in Rome. Their answers didn't make any sense to me. I wanted to take him to his old pediatrician in Los Angeles for a full examination.

Lang called from Los Angeles and said, "You stay there, I'm coming back." And I said, "No. no. We're coming; I have to take Paul to his pediatrician." And that was the end of it.

When we got to Los Angeles, the pediatrician said Paul was in excellent health. We went to psychologists and psychoanalysts and took him for all sorts of motor tests, very advanced games. Everything was all right. All these doctors got together and discussed it and then one doctor prepared a lengthy report. I still have it. They said that basically any problems he had stemmed from rejection by his father. It confirmed what I had thought. I don't particularly like assigning blame, but it's just that. Rejection, rejection, rejection. Whether or not he has been, he feels rejected by his father.

Lang and I stayed on in Hollywood, but Lang's reputation had preceded him as a drinker and there was no work. He had no money, nothing. We all tried to live together and it wasn't very successful. That depressed him.

I came back to Rome. Things went downhill from there. In June of 1971, Lang came back to work it out with me. He said, "Let's give it one more try." We lasted about ten days. I said, "Let's forget it."

In June of 1971, Paul was expelled from Notre Dame. Hazily he summed up his academic career.

Paul:

I got kicked out of Notre Dame. My mother came and took me back to Rome. I went, like, four months to high school. What's the last? Eighth grade or tenth grade? Which is twelfth grade—high school? Junior high school is what—seventh, eighth, and ninth? I did half of ninth and half of tenth. I was two years above the other students. The other kids were seventeen. I remember Morocco was '68 and Swinging London was '68 too. So it has been five years. Incredible how time passes.

That summer my mother came to me and just said, "Talitha died." I burst out in tears, but my mother said, "Oh, don't worry. It's okay." It was strange. The night before I had thought a lot about Talitha.

My mother told me not to tell the kids. We went to Rome that day. On the journey down, I was in tears the whole way, and the kids were asking, "What's wrong?" My mother said, "Shut up, Paul."

We went to the beach. It was my sister's birthday. Lang drove up in the Rolls-Royce with another woman, his girlfriend. He took us for a drive—my mother, this woman, and us four kids. As we drove he told the children, like it was nothing, that Talitha had died, right in front of this woman.

The summer after Paul's Easter in Marrakesh Talitha gave birth to a son. They christened him Tara Gabriel Gramophone Galaxy Getty.

After the birth of the boy, Big Paul and Talitha began taking separate paths. According to her, Big Paul got very paranoid and, after a few months, Talitha couldn't take Rome anymore. She said she was going to take their son and move back to London. She assumed that if she did, he would follow, although Big Paul

made it clear that he had no intention of leaving Rome. Every-
thing he wanted was there: Ruspoli, opium, sex scenes . . .

Victoria, the mistress, was there too, waiting in the wings on
the farm in Tuscany, a couple of hours from Rome. She recalled
happier times.

Victoria:

We all went to bed together once. I don't think she or I particularly
wanted to and I think we both did it for Paul. I don't think he wanted
to either. It was one of those things. And he had to leave to get an
airplane or something and she and I were left talking. I don't remember what we talked about, but I felt completely at one with her. We
knew each other so well. As different as we were in every way there
was some kind of contact or joining up. I was devoted to her; that
sounds mad, and Paul never knew or would want to know that. I
really don't think there is another girl like her. A lot of people who
knew her very well hear me laugh and they say, "My God, that was
just like Talitha." We both had the dirtiest laugh.

Lord Thynne was there in London when Talitha returned from
Rome with her baby and moved back into Queen's House on
Cheyne Walk, just around the corner from where he lived on Bat-
tersea Bridge Road. Big Paul sometimes flew in from Rome and
spent time with Talitha and the baby, but as Lord Thynne
remembered:

More and more, Big Paul stayed in Rome. The last time I went
'round, he wasn't even there. She told me she wasn't happy and things
were pointless. She said, "I have to leave him, I really must get out of
it," but it struck me as one of those remarks. I just took her back after
the party. Nothing. I'm showing that she wasn't just a sleep-around. It

wasn't for lack of trying. She began seeing Hiram Keller, an American screen actor, a considerable man about town in those days.

Talitha's liaison with Hiram Keller didn't last. Alone with her infant son in the tall and somber Queen's House, she grew increasingly despondent. Her health faltered, her robustness, her laughter. She was very much aware that in Rome, Victoria was continuing to see Big Paul although she had promised she would not.

Victoria:

I last saw her in March of 1971. She thought I had betrayed her. I wrote her a letter and made her a promise and, not being together enough about it, the promise was broken. It was about going to meet Paul in Rome. He told her and so I went to see her in Cheyne Walk. I had left Paul. I wasn't seeing him anymore. She was in a bad way, very unhappy. She was freaked out about people coming in the house, eating, drinking, and freeloading generally. We had this talk and we made up.

According to people, the last two months she really lost her vivacity. She looked cold and miserable and ill. I think she was doing a lot of mandies [Quaaludes] and vodka. Paul didn't realize, I'm sure, how bad a state she was in. She'd put on a lot of weight and she was having trouble with her thyroid.

She faithfully kept diaries, made novels of her life. The last entry, made two or three days before she left for Rome, says something like, "I hear my baby crying in the next room but I can't even get up to comfort him. If I die I want to be buried under a big oak tree in a country churchyard."

I was in Rome the day Talitha came from London. Big Paul had asked me, "Please stay. Not in the house, but stay around." And I said, "No. This is between you both. I'm going back to the country." I rang on the Saturday and I talked to Talitha. She sounded quite happy and I said, "Why don't you come up to the country next week?"

There are two accounts of Talitha's last days in Rome. They differ, and the differences serve to form a clearer picture of the whole. Paul puts the blame on the mafiosi called in by his father. Jerry Cherchio, owner of the Luau, the tiki bar and restaurant where Gail had met Lang, where the expatriate American movie stars and Dolce Vita crowd mingled with the mafia, gives a much fuller account. He was Big Paul's confidant, it's true, but the detail he goes into makes you wonder if he was someone else's, too.

Cherchio:

When Big Paul didn't come to London, as Talitha thought he would, she decided to go to Rome and make one last attempt at reconciliation. She had filed divorce papers with lawyers in Amsterdam. She flew there from London, told her lawyers to halt the proceedings and not send the papers to Paul, and flew on to Rome to see her husband.

Unknown to Talitha, the lawyers in Amsterdam had sent the divorce papers to Paul anyway. Talitha arrived and Paul told her, "We'll talk about it later." She went off and spent the night somewhere else and she came back the next day two hours after Big Paul had received the papers. He turned on her, shouting. She tried to seduce him. He spurned her. She went into the bedroom and took a massive dose of heroin, and lay on the bed, her back to the door, holding the empty vial. Paul left the apartment for several hours. When he returned, he looked in on her, saw her apparently asleep, poured himself a drink, and remained in the living room for some time before he checked on her again. It was about four-thirty in the morning. She was breathing rapidly, intermittently. He tried to wake her and couldn't. Then he went to the phone and called me, but I was out of town. He called Dado Ruspoli, and Ruspoli came over. Ruspoli said, "Don't worry, my wife has these things all the time." They made a concoction of mustard, salt, and hot water to make her throw up. They forced it down her throat, but it had no effect. They called an American doctor, Dr. Mario Lanza's connection. They had a lot of difficulty reaching him. They didn't get through to the doctor until seven in the morning. He came over and gave the comatose Talitha an injection to bring her around. Nothing. They called an ambulance. She died on the way to the hospital.

Possession of heroin, use or sale in Italy, is seven years automatically. The doctor told Paul he would have to pay the coroner $25,000 to keep heroin from being mentioned on the death certificate. Paul agreed to give the money to Ruspoli to pay the bribe. They put an empty bottle beside the bed and claimed to the police that Talitha had taken an overdose of barbiturates. They said nothing of a doctor having come.

In Paul's account of her death, he once more endeavored to protect his father.

Paul:

For some reason she got on a plane to Rome to tell my father they shouldn't get divorced. She arrived in the morning. He said, "We'll speak about it some other time," and went out. The whole day she was in bed dying. That's why my father is what he is. He's completely guilty of himself. They had both taken too much barbiturates and junk with people at Number One, awful people—they weren't friends. They were around because they had the dope. They were the people involved in the Number One scandal. You know, the disco scandal. Italian dope dealers. Heroin and coke.

Some of these people came back to my father's place that night.

They went in to see her, said, "What's wrong with Talitha? She's still asleep." She was almost gone. My father said, "We've got to call an ambulance." They said no. They held him down and said, "We're going to get in trouble." They convinced him. In the end they did call an ambulance, but she died on the way to the hospital. They could have saved Talitha. They had hours and hours. It's not a flash thing—you can be saved.

They could have brought Talitha to a hospital. But there were all these people holding my father down. He's wanted for murder, you know. He can't go to Italy. Murder charge, which is almost what it is. He knows it too. She did it herself. It wasn't a needle scene. I think it was purely accidental. I remember the amounts she took. She could have been saved. These people thought only of themselves. Fucking Italians.

Talitha's death triggered the nightmares Nicolette had predicted, and spewed chaos that, in Paul's case, marked him for the rest of his days. At first her death seemed to envelop Big Paul in a kind of euphoria. This compounded his inevitable guilt and grief. He fled to Bangkok and there took refuge in opium. He called on Victoria, desperate to have her join and comfort him. She went. For a time it was as if Talitha's death had never been, but soon Victoria found herself become a phantom surrogate for Talitha. Talitha's death was a turning point in all their lives.

Victoria:

I rang on the Sunday all day and there was no reply—not all day, but the morning and most of the afternoon—and about four o'clock Paul stormed through the door and said, "She's dead." That was it.

Before her death I was Paul's mistress. Afterward, I was no longer the mistress. I was nothing. My status was not only unofficial but sub-anything. I'd been playing with something that had suddenly turned bad.

Immediately after Talitha's funeral, I went back to Tuscany. I don't think any of us will ever know what really happened. But I think she was so disordered that she wouldn't even have been positive enough to take an overdose. You'd just take too much of this and too much of that. I think that's the frame of mind one comes to an end in, really.

Paul doesn't realize how much Talitha's death affected the children. I know he doesn't. In '72, when Little Paul was here in London, I confronted his father. I said, "Has it ever occurred to you that Talitha's death not only ruined your life and my life, it absolutely freaked out Little Paul? You have no idea." He said, "You are mad. He hardly knew her."

Little Paul adored Talitha. She was a figurehead of beauty and glamour and everything that is living, and she is dead. Little Paul used to sit with me for hours on the stairs at Cheyne Walk, asking about her.

For his part, Lord Thynne remembered:

Paul could have possibly saved her, but he flapped. Even though I hadn't seen her much, I really was very, very upset. I found myself feeling rather embarrassed about it suddenly, saying, "Christopher, really. You only see her two or three times a year. Why are you making this fuss?" Christopher Logue and Ralph Steadman made this memorial, a poem by Logue and illustrated by Steadman:

Endlessly moving clouds but no sign of you
For three nights running I have dreamt of you
Thank you for coming.

Nicolette Meers was in the desert when she heard the news:

This old friend and I had been planning a camping trip in the Spanish Sahara. We pitched our tents on the beach and we used to drive into a place called Tisnet to pick up some meat and a loaf of bread and we'd cook our meal in the evening. One day I was unwrapping the lamb chops or whatever they were and I read *"La Femme de l'homme le plus riche du monde est morte."* That was how I found out that Talitha had died. It was such a gory way to get the news—on a piece of bloodstained Moroccan newspaper.

[Big] Paul must have been totally out of it. That state where hours pass and you can't get it together. Junkies are utterly ruthless, there's no moral code with them. They don't give a fig for anything. Junk totally dehumanizes you.

Big Paul's immediate reaction to Talitha's death was to bolt, get out of Rome, go back to Bangkok, the place where he and Talitha had spent their honeymoon, where there was opium. Interestingly, now that he was in trouble he turned to his son and invited him to come away. Gail, alarmed, refused to allow Paul to go with his father and instead sent him on a long Mediterranean cruise and then to the country. Big Paul finally persuaded Victoria to join him.

Paul's account of the episode is characteristically vague, but telling nonetheless.

Paul:

My father called for me, so I went. He was on the farm of an Irish poet, Patrick, who is mad, mad. When Patrick's first wife, Lola, put her head in the oven, he had come to my father's house. Now my father went to his. It was strange comedy. My father wanted to take me to Thailand, but my mother said, "No way." He wanted to take Victoria, and she wouldn't go, so he took Jerry Cherchio. They went to Bangkok, where he was supposed to get a cure, but he spent three months in an opium den and never got out. My father didn't talk about Talitha dying. He didn't realize it for a year.

Victoria at first refused Big Paul's entreaties to join him in Bangkok.

Victoria:

I had a dog I was devoted to, an Alsatian called Las, a beautiful dog. I didn't want to leave her and go to the Far East. It wasn't just an excuse. To me it seemed a proper reason why I couldn't go, but then someone poisoned Las the day the astronauts were coming back from the moon. Las took a long time to die. That finished me.

I hadn't really reacted to Talitha's death, but then the dog died. Nothing will ever hurt me again comparatively. First Talitha, then the dog—whack. I sat in a chair for thirty-six hours without moving. I didn't know what was going on.

Paul sent me a final telegram: "If you don't come, I'm going to do something dreadful." I got on a plane to Bangkok.

Jerry met me. He's a funny guy. He was so sweet to me. He was wonderful, so patient with Paul, so good to him. He came over at the drop of a hat if things were too much. God knows he didn't get anything out of it. He was a true friend, a wonderful man. When I arrived in Bangkok, he flew back to Rome.

For Paul, the trouble with his mother's well-intentioned plan to get him out of the way by sending him on a cruise on his girlfriend's father's yacht was that the father refused to allow his daughter to come and so Paul was left alone in the company of the kind of bourgeoisie he so disdained. Upon his return, Gail sent him back into the countryside of Tuscany, and for a while at least the problem of what to do with Paul was solved.

Paul:

Then my father wrote from Bangkok, saying, "Come over. Have your mother organize it." My mother didn't want me to go. She sent me on a cruise on my girlfriend's family's yacht. Her father owns a factory. He's a Fascist, the kind that goes with other women and leaves his wife at home. They wouldn't bring my girlfriend. That brought me completely down. He took friends from the days when my mother was still with my father, and Talitha's supposed friends—painters, sculptors, heads, and freaks from Milano. Everybody was sorry for me, pretending nothing had happened. But they were still cutting down Talitha. It was unbearable.

It was a long sail from Naples to Ischia to Capri, the Aeolians to Sicily, to Calabria. A big yacht, a lot of work. Sometimes it was so rough the boat rocked at a ninety-degree angle. I hated it. Some of it was great—my understanding of nature, the power of it. We saw whales and dolphins. I loved it when they set the spinnaker. They had a wooden thing with flaps that they towed behind. I had a mask and the thing could go down underwater and up. Scuba diving was fun.

But it was heavy, too—I didn't like my mother's friends, straight people. My mother's girlfriend and her husband, the painter, were there. My mother's girlfriend would go out early in the morning on a little motorboat with another woman's husband. It makes me so down, that kind of thing. They're a turn-off, these middle-aged, martini drinking, sex-crazed bourgeoisie. I slept on deck, couldn't sleep below with those people.

We listened to the same tape, "Hey Jude," for three weeks.

When we got back, my mother sent me to John Patrick's farm in Tuscany. I was very down. They were so busy running around trying to figure everything out, they forgot me there. It's a great farm in a county where a lot of English people live. The feminist Germaine

Greer, who showed the world her cunt, all these people. Oxford students come in the summer to help on the farm. He has thousands and thousands of acres of grapes. The farm was beautiful and John Patrick far-out. His son and I fought fires, swam in lakes, and slept out. They were kind. My father was their good friend. A very simple life, drinking wine and playing charades in the evening, no electricity, feeding the pigs. They gave me a goat I called Kate, and two pigs, Messalina and Jane IV. After a while I felt better.

For a brief while in Bangkok, Victoria and Big Paul carried on as if Talitha's death had never happened, but then the depth of Big Paul's opium psychosis broke through and it was then that Victoria realized she had become both a surrogate for a dead wife and, no longer the mistress, the nurse.

Victoria:

Paul was so happy to see me. He met me at the airport and we seemed to latch on to where we had left off before Talitha's death, holding hands, laughing, terribly happy all the way. It wasn't just me. I wouldn't have been like that if he'd been down. I can hardly remember this person as I am talking about him. He's certainly not that way anymore. For about four or five days we were ecstatic—but it seemed like two weeks. Shopping in Bangkok, buying beautiful tribal dresses, a lovely time.

One night in the hotel I woke to sobbing. Paul was in the bathroom. I got up and went in and found him stumbling around, crying, talking to Talitha in his sleep. It stopped me in my tracks. I put him back in bed and calmed him down. He opened his eyes and, looking at me, said, "I'll never forget you." He thought I was Talitha. In that moment I realized that things were absolutely different. I had been euphoric. From then on I was looking after a sick person. He was never the same again. Paul insisted that we go to all the places where he and Talitha had gone on their honeymoon and stay in the same rooms. He told me he was looking for Talitha's ghost. We went to Penang and all sorts of places where they had been together, and finally I took him back to Bangkok.

> *There, Victoria fed Paul opium, reducing his intake, and he went from 140 pounds to 175 pounds and reportedly never looked better. When news came out about Talitha's heroin overdose, Victoria went to London and Big Paul went back to Rome.*
>
> *Why Big Paul returned to Rome when he knew of the coroner's report may be another demonstration of how disconnected he still was from reality.*

Jerry Cherchio:

After two months, the coroner, tired of waiting for the bribe Ruspoli had promised him, published his true findings. He reported that he had found a needle mark, and Talitha had died of a heroin overdose. There was no mention of a doctor present at the time of her death. Ruspoli and the doctor had split and pocketed the $25,000, and didn't pay the coroner.

6.

At the end of his idyllic summer in the Tuscany countryside, Paul, too, returned to Rome, to his mother's house in Parioli. He was fourteen. It was then that he first smoked marijuana and was reunited with his father. It was a realization of Gail's fears, although how much she knew and what she could have done about it are moot questions. What is clear at this point is that she had lost control of her son altogether, thrown up her hands, and handed Paul—for better or worse—over to his father in London, the lion's den as Victoria put it.

So Paul's dream to live with his father came true at last.

Paul:

A man and his old lady I met in the street gave me a ride. All of a sudden he said, "Do you smoke?" and I said yes. I thought he meant cigarettes. He lit a pipe. I didn't know what to do. So I took it in and coughed my arse off. When he dropped me off, he said, "Come and see me." From that day forward I turned on—spaced-out on drugs. I saw the light. I went home and walked up the stairs with this feeling. Better than my first woman. I really felt like hot shit.

When my father just came back from Thailand he wanted to get together with me and we saw a lot of each other. He met my girl-friend, too. I even got him to go and meet her parents. I got close with him. We were giving each other dope and he'd say, "Bring some friends over and we'll watch *Scorpio Rising* and *The Great Dictator*."

I was sitting with my girlfriend and my father getting stoned. We were sitting on the couch by Talitha's bamboo chair. We were talk-ing and laughing our heads off about why Victorians covered the seats, and listening to the test record of *Sticky Fingers* before it came out. It was recorded in Marrakesh and I played the tambourine and my father played drums. They were singing "Wild Horses"—at the end it says "Oh baby." Right at that point, Puddy, Talitha's big Persian cat, jumped up on the record player—a flame came up, *whoosh*, out of Talitha's chair. I can still show you the hole. I'd only smoked a little bit.

My father said he was going to London because Talitha was try-ing to communicate with him. I stayed in Rome. I was at the beach when it came out in the papers about Talitha's death, that she had overdosed on heroin. Nobody really knew why it took so long.

Lang was in L.A. I couldn't stand my mother anymore. She didn't like me because I didn't like her. There was no man in the house. I ran out and came back late. I got into dope and dealing dope with my friend Richard. Him and I were dealing. He was my best friend. He's probably my best friend ever.

We sold dope to Elton John, Charles Bronson, Tony Curtis. A lot of dope—we had money. It was a trip. Nobody else was doing it. We were kids. Full of money, motorcycles; we became independent.

I left my mother's. I just ran away. That day I was in a cab with my girlfriend and we passed a demonstration and we got out, and there were Fascists running around and I said, "I'm really a Fascist. I really dig these people." It's strange the things you think.

Then I went to [stay with] my father's friends, Bob and Sarah. This was Christmas, I remember. Have you been to Piazza Navona at Christmas? All these stalls, and it looks incredible. I stayed two months with Bob and Sarah. They chanted. And that's where I got into Buddhism, to Nisban, Sha Sha . . . They were into it, so I got into it. Now I know it's fascism. They were Nichiren Shoshu, and I chanted every day for three or four hours. The whole time I thought I was free, but at the end I found out my mother sent them money every week. Then one day I became a celebrity. They took a picture of me sprawled out on the floor dressed like a hippie and sold it to a big magazine and then—*whoosh*—I became the "Golden Hippie," a rebel. It was a complete change from the very cool country life in Tuscany.

I became weirder. I saw a girl, Bobby, a lot, tortured her. I wasn't nice to her, and it came back to me.

Then my father got in touch with me and said, "Come to London." He sent me a ticket. Bob and Sarah gave it to me. Later I found out my mother had given it to them. I never saw my mother, never said good-bye, even. I was still turned against her.

I was happy to go to London. I told my Bobby, "I'll probably be gone a long time, so get your rocks off." I went with Mario, the driver for my father, the driver who had driven for Getty Oil for years and who later testified against me.

I hadn't seen my father for a year. Now he was interested in me. He was very into me going to boarding school. The family has this thing about boarding school. It's crazy. They've never gone themselves.

Queen's House is across the river from Battersea Park. Did you ever see the house? It's beautiful, the Rossetti house. Strange vibrations in that house. Rossetti was a strange man. It was a hangout for all those people, Rimbaud, Gabriel Rossetti. Aleister Crowley and all these people were there often. They were doing laudanum, downers made from morphine and opium. Very strong, like heroin. You smoke it. That's what Rossetti died of, an overdose. Have you read "The Burden of Nineveh" and "A Last Confession"? Limbo characters, the strange, beautiful people that die young. Rossetti didn't go out very much. In the house, there's a little painting of him reading poetry to others. He wrote beautiful poetry. They came from Paris and they'd just smoke all day and indulge in prostitutes; they were into black magic. The man who had built the house had married three times, and each of his three wives died in the house. The place has terrible karma. When you're in it, you really feel it. I promise you. Very weird, but fabulous.

I could live in that house. It's just so beautiful. The last time I was there, Talitha had put a parachute in the staircase that went all the way downstairs, curled around, strange colors. I think Talitha and my father lived there in '68, the Swinging London time. Now he doesn't do anything but sit and read about the people who lived in the house. He's completely fascinated by them, he knows all the history. Rossetti had a mistress, she lived with him in the house, he did all these paintings of her. She died there from an overdose. No one knows how it happened. It's like Talitha.

He listens to opera and reads. He has a bookbinding place up-stairs, a big white room. He has machines there to rebind old books, but he never uses them. He has a lot of rare old books, a Gutenberg [Bible], and the Bible Thomas à Becket was holding when they killed him. He watches movies on the television in the study. It has these huge bay windows and it's full of pillows. He sleeps there. Talitha's sitting room, her study, a little room painted yellow, was upstairs. The secretary, who just recently left because she wasn't paid, used to be in it, but now it's locked up.

When Bill Newsom, my godfather, who was my father's best friend, came to London, he slept in my room. My father was down-stairs. Bill'd just come from the airport. He crashed out. He woke in the middle of the night and thought he heard crying. He thought it was because he was so tired, and went back to sleep. He woke up again. Something pressing on his chest, and he kept hearing crying. Something touched him. He couldn't move. He screamed. My father, I'm sure, was there, but he didn't answer. He does this all the time. Bill shouted, "Get out. Leave me alone!" and at this moment it moved away, the pressure. Then he went downstairs, and my father said, "It was Talitha trying to talk to me."

The first day I was in London, I went to Piccadilly Circus to buy drugs. I showed Victoria. I already had a good relationship with Victoria from the summer in Tuscany. She said, "You've been ripped off." They sold me Ampex or something. I told her, "I'd really like to try some coke." So she turned me on to two lines of coke. I'd never done anything like this before. Incredible.

I tried to convince my father to see *Clockwork Orange*. He said, "*No*, I don't want to see it, it's violent." He hasn't been out to see a movie since *Fantasia* on my fourteenth birthday. So Victoria and I did some coke in the bathroom and went to Leicester Square to the premiere. I saw *Clockwork Orange* twenty-three times. I really dug this freak trip, being odd. Anyway, that night her friend came, Fiona Lewis. I think I mentioned her. She's an actress. All these girls around. They would go and tell people that they'd fucked me, and I loved it. I would be terrified if anyone approached me, but I loved the attention. A chip off the old block, they call me.

Fiona was Victoria's best friend. She was beautiful, seemed destructive like Faye Dunaway. I've always been attracted to really destructive women. They always want to fuck everybody else's man. Fiona was staying at the house then. I kept complaining about not having a room to come across in. Victoria got Fiona into it, but when she came on I was too shy.

Victoria, caught somewhere between her fear of hypocrisy and her role as a surrogate mother, defends Fiona and refutes Gail's assertion that she slept with Paul.

Victoria:

Fiona was staying in our house. She asked me, "Do you know what happened this morning? Little Paul came in and said, 'I'm going to get into bed with you.'" He never did, I believe her. Those were things in his mind. When George d'Almeida told me Gail thought *I* had been to bed with him, I thought, My God, I may have done a million things but that wasn't one of them.

I made cardinal errors. I gave him the odd snort of coke. He knew what was going on in the house. He wasn't a bloody fool. But it does sound incredibly irresponsible to give someone a snort at whatever age he was. It is indefensible, I know, but if you've got him in the lion's den you can't lie. You're lying if you don't include him. I made a hopeless mess of it. I couldn't have done worse if I had tried. In the end he felt that I was a traitor to him. His father felt I was a traitor. His mother thinks that not only did I screw him but I turned him on to drugs. It was simply not true. I put my foot in everything, badly, but I've never had any physical contact with Little Paul at all. It would be out of the question.

When I came back to London I found that Talitha's closest friends had a terrifying loathing for Paul and me. It was just an extremely bad time. It was a year after Talitha's death and I was in a rotten way, looking back on it but not realizing I was, but doing my bit—keeping superficial things together, like the house, and remembering to look for a school for Little Paul.

I was playing this impossible role. I was exactly half the age between him and his father. For Paul it was a phenomenal bother to have an adolescent about the house. He thought I'd be more reasonable with his son and I thought I was. I'd say, "Yes, you can go out, but don't be too late." I said, "I expect you are going to smoke dope and stuff but don't overdo it." The first day he was in London I said to him, "If you're going to walk about, do please try not to buy drugs, (a) because we're extremely paranoid here and (b) because you're bound to get ripped off." The first day he came back and said, "I've bought some acid." I made him show it to me. I said, "I bet it's Ampex." It was those little green pills that stop your breath from smelling. He'd bought them for a pound each. I said, "I told you so."

He went through a number of bum purchasing escapades in the Piccadilly Underground.

Disaster struck when "Cockney Pauline," a friend of Victoria's, came to the house with real LSD.

Paul:

My father was sending me to a psychiatrist. Every two days I'd have to take a train down to Winchester to see him. Then I met "Cockney Pauline." She had acid on sugar cubes wrapped in cellophane. I bought a whole bunch from her. I kept it in the fridge, the best place to keep acid. I did some every day.

One night I was on acid watching a late movie with Victoria in the bedroom. At one point I went to my room, up the little staircase. It used to be Tara's nanny's room. It's a dark yellow. It creaks all the time. You know, these old English houses.

I had a strange trip in that room. I had been reading [*The*] *Panic in Needle Park*. Junkies. I had a record player and I had bought *Lexington and the Ants*. I lay down and the whole bed looked like it was full of ants. The whole bed was moving. I screamed. My father came in. I yelled at him: "Hey! Look there. Ants on the bed." Of course, he said, "There's nothing there."

By the bed there was this big chair. I had left my coat and hat on it and somehow they changed into a little hunchbacked monster with no face. All the time he was making fixes with needles and

ODing. People were walking in and out of the room and saying, "It'll be okay." On acid, everything you've been doing the days before is in some way brought back. As in a dream. I called the fire department. At least, that's what Victoria told me. I'm only going by what people told me. Three days this trip went on.

In the garden, in those walls, those little walls, there was a strange paranoia. At the side was bamboo. It turned into the boys they have in *Clockwork Orange.* Paki-bashers with boots with golden toecaps, rockers, throwing stones. I hid behind those horrible big white flowerpots, right under the window, and they were throwing things, and I was throwing things back. Twenty, sometimes thirty whole battles and me screaming to them, "You fuckers!" Details, absolute details, buttons, everything. It's incredible, acid. When I was behind that flowerpot with the little lemon tree, Victoria's head came out of it. Straight out. Then came Lord Lambton's head. I touched them. They spoke. It was weird. I can still feel how it felt, perfectly normal. I was by myself. Only when I looked in the windows, I freaked out. I went to the doors. Everything was locked. My father had locked me out. He invited five or six friends to come and look at me out there freaking out.

They spent the whole day looking through the windows at me. At one point, I picked up all the leaves in the wheelbarrow and there's this little garden house 'round the corner and I went and lay down in there, and then the whole thing started to go *whoosh.*

The day before I had been talking to Victoria about magic, how to be able to do whatever you want to do. I was sure she said something about knowing someone who could teach you how to walk through walls. Some guy that could do it.

I went back to my father's door. I tried to break in then, I tried to walk through the walls. I was completely black and blue. I'd go like this for hours. I got into this whole thing about "Do it again," because slowly, slowly and I could feel the cells, the matter splitting. I really thought that if I could get into it enough, I was sure I could do it. Slow, and slow until you get the right concentration.

Underneath the house, there's a basement. Stairs go up. Here's the garden. Stairs go down to the kitchen there. Stairs go to the study. First I went downstairs. I went crazy. I could see the two workers there. I got this iron bar. I wanted to break the glass. Then I went to the studio; my father's door was closed. I looked through the windows. Tony Lambton, remember? That minister of the RAF was looking out. He wouldn't let me in, so I climbed on the drainpipe to Talitha's room on the second floor. There's a balcony. I really had to get there. That's where the acid was. I was on the drainpipe. For some reason Aron Vejak, a childhood friend, appeared on the second floor. He gave me his arm but I couldn't reach it.

Victoria gave her own account of Paul's trip:

His father woke me at two on Sunday afternoon and said, "There's something unpleasant going on outside. My son is on an acid trip. He's threatened the servants with an ax and he's halfway up the fucking drainpipe."

Well, I got dressed in about two-point-five seconds, took a snort, and rushed downstairs. Big Paul came after me saying, "You will not go out. I have shut him in the garden. You're not to see him."

I went into the garden. Little Paul was halfway up the drainpipe, forty feet off the ground. He came down like a monkey and said, "Dad's trying to kill you." I didn't know whether he was having me on, how much was acting, how much was real horror. I said, "Yes, I know. Let's go out to Richmond Park." So we did. As we drove he tried to get out of the car several times.

We were in the park for hours sitting under a tree. He was beginning to come down, but still spaced out, talking about smack [and a] woman, who was going to get him laid. On the way back we stopped at a hamburger joint. His father never forgave me for interfering, for taking him out. He said, "If he was locked in the garden, he was locked in the garden and there he should bloody well stay!" There was no question of "Have you ever had a bad trip?"

Paul continued the story from this point:

When we came home from the park I crashed out. When I woke up, I had slept for, like, forty hours—an incredible amount—and there was a nurse there, poor nurse. She's my father's nurse, a fantastic lady—big, fat old lady, great, incredibly strong, very protective. She's, you know, for heroin. She comes once a month, stays at the house and they do a cure. She was so nice to me, never said a word, tried to calm me down.

When I woke up, I realized, My God, my father's flipped out. I went downstairs, not realizing what I had done. The neighbor woman came in and said, "You really fucked up my garden."

My father told me to write five hundred lines. In the end I got out of it and we settled for an essay on what I thought drugs would do for me.

The next day he came crying in my face and I was really heavy with him. I wasn't into my father so much; I tortured him. I said the most terrible things to him. Really, I dug torturing him. I think I hated him. I said, "In Rome, the kids at school all say that you're a junkie," and he started crying. I said, "It's all right."

Little sadist. A compulsive liar, saying something like that to my own father. It was terrible to see him cry. What had I done?

The last days he started writing me notes, my father, in the same house. He'd write weird things, strange things. What an act, what a circus it was, using all these incredible words telling me not to swear, not to lie, and not to laugh.

Then one day he just called the driver to take me to my grandfather's. I had a golden ring in my ear and a pair of jeans with green and white stripes with stars, no shoes, and that Leon Russell shirt. My father said, "Are you going like that?" I said yes. I was into these things about [how] "clothes don't make the man."

He gave me a movie camera and said, "Byron [the driver] will be here soon."

It is a measure of just how disconnected Big Paul was from reality that he expected his eighty-year-old father to be able to handle a drug-crazed fourteen-year-old. This was the first real communication the old man and Big Paul had since Talitha's death. Old Paul hadn't seen his once favorite and angelic grandson for several years.

Paul:

My grandfather has an enormous piece of property outside London, about six thousand acres—immense. There are rivers, dams, houses. There's a village in it, very beautiful. Beautiful English lawns—all daffodils. Hedges all clipped, all shapes—birds, elephants, horses. There's a maze. There's a nice church there and a graveyard.

The house is enormous. It looks Russian, with those onion domes on top. The wings come out towards you as you look at it. It goes like this and like that. And there's a statue in front, very nice, very clean. It was all done in Pompeii red clay around the time of Henry VIII. He had it as a country home for Catherine of Aragon and Anne Boleyn and he'd go hunting there. Cardinal Woolsey bought it and after that Cromwell. Very good families. My grandfather paid nothing for it. There are incredible books in there—old. There are some weird medicine books I've looked through. Astrology books.

My grandfather met me at the door. I took a shot of him. He said, "Do you always dress like this?"

They were having a meeting planning the museum in L.A. He said, "You can stay here and we can learn, understand each other." He told me he would look for a school, a day school. He wasn't even going to send me to boarding school. He was fond of me. He was looking for his successor. He wanted a Paul. He didn't believe that my father could do it. He said my father was a hopeless businessman. And he said, "Your father and Talitha disillusioned me and my only heir has died. You can do it. You have the talent."

I said to him, "No. I'll never get into the oil business." I was very heavy into ecology, very heavy to him. Surprised he put up with it. I would say, "You have ruined this planet," and he would laugh.

It was fun, that time. I worked with him on the museum a lot. We had just opened his house to tourists. Lots of people would come. I would show them around. It's open almost every day. There are secret passages, priest holes, and a chapel. An immense room with a throne at the end of it where Henry VIII sat. I have a shot of [my grandfather] walking around with some tourists.

His office looks out onto the gardens, a very simple office. Big white room, very, very big. Two armchairs, a desk. He always sits in the same armchair.

There are two swimming pools—one outside and one inside. He swims every day. An enormous Olympic-size swimming pool. He likes the water hot, hot, hot. The vegetable garden is copied after Washington's in Mt. Vernon.

I'd bring him his mail in the morning and we'd go through the whole thing. The mail that came in there, you wouldn't believe. They're just weird, the letters to my grandfather, treasure maps burned with matches around them, crackpot ideas. He has a printed letter for people who ask for money. That's what I did for a long time—put them in envelopes and sent them off. It's a very funny letter. It says, "You are one of the three thousand people who write me daily asking to contribute to your cause. If I gave you each five pounds I'd go broke in the next twenty-six years (some outrageous figure). I'm sorry I couldn't have helped you." He signs each one and sends them off. Every letter. Some of the things—you die laughing.

He likes Greta Garbo and loves New York and talks about Oklahoma. I think he lost touch when he moved to England in the fifties.

[Francis] Bullimore, the butler, runs the whole show. Parkes is the valet. They're English. They've been with him for twenty years. They travel around with him.

I never got along with Bullimore. He's white with rosy cheeks in this dark house. Hands white and pink, completely clean. White, white. It's impossible to tell his age. He's starting to have white hair.

Bullimore's a faggot. Weird flashes of him. I'd be in the bathroom and he'd knock on the door and say, "Can you manage, sir?" I said that for years after. My English-accent joke was "Can you manage?"

Parkes takes the pictures. My grandfather says, "Parkes, get the camera." There's a whole room next to the office full of photographs. That's mostly all that Parkes does. He polishes the silver and the camera.

Kathy's the cook. She's about forty-five, fifty, enormously fat. She's Irish. She adores me. She made me shortbread cookies. I think there's only one little maid. Nobody remembers her name and nobody remembers what she looks like. She just polishes the silver. That's all.

Derek is the game warden, the animal trainer, and the security guard. He takes care of the dogs and the lion. Great little lion, Nero, incredibly strong. Really sweet. Margaret the Duchess of Argyll gave it to him. I'd play with it every day on the lawn in front of his study window so he could see.

A school chum of mine came. His father owns a famous hotel. We did acid. I opened the study door and asked my grandfather, "You want to meet a friend of mine?" We slid down the fire rope. Not good. We got the golf cart stuck in the mud and a tractor had to come. We drove the tractor into a wall. Secretly that day we hitchhiked to London to see Cockney Pauline to buy more acid. We came back that night and I had a fight with some Paki-bashers and got in quite late.

I never changed. I should have. It got heavy. My grandfather kept on saying, "Why are you dressed like this?" He gave me money to buy clothes and I went out and bought something else outrageous. I fucked it up. The guy really wanted to do something for me but

I fucked it up. There's a point when even when you're not taking, it's just one big acid trip.

He's very generous. He gave me everything I wanted. He was very nice to me, and understanding. Then Victoria wrote me a twenty-page letter in brown ink and it's this whole long thing, saying, "It's okay. You have to understand your father. He's so down about Talitha."

I think of how tolerant [my grandfather] was. How ridiculous I was. How those things that were so important become nothing. Like when a new girlfriend left me, I was going to throw myself off the terrace. And now I think of it and I laugh. That's why it's fun to have brothers and sisters. I just look at them and I laugh.

I really wish I was older. Either I wish I was thirteen again and I could start all over, or I wish I was twenty-four. I wanted to go back, I wanted to see my mother. So I went back to Rome.

Odd that he chose thirteen and twenty-four. He was thirteen when he went to Marrakesh and he would be twenty-four when he ODed. His entire discretionary life lay between these two numbers.

7.

When Gail heard that Paul was leaving his grandfather and returning to Rome, she knew well what she was getting back. She often talked to Old Paul on the telephone and she had followed Paul's progress in London, a period she dismissed dryly as "his King's Road number."

She had done her best to get him out of Rome and she had failed—or, rather, he had. When he bounced back, she didn't make a great effort to contain him. It was beyond her. He was beyond them all. They were reaping the whirlwind.

It would be a relief to Gail in some ways to have him out of the house. The family was horrified when she let him loose. "What is she doing . . . utterly irresponsible," they cried. But by now Gail had no option but to watch him go out into the diaspora with her usual equanimity and optimism and the hope, however pious, that he would be equal to the big world and that it would treat him well.

Gail:

I offered to take Tara after Talitha died. I had to find a house in three days, so I took one on Via Archimedes. It had at least six bedrooms, four drawing rooms, a huge dining room, a library, and it was furnished. The furnishings were so un-me. I'm sure it was all very nice, but it was in that Embassy style. You know, those Roman embassy houses? They all look the same; pale ivory damask on Louis XVI chairs. I was working at my clothes shop at that time so I could pay off my debts. Getting up at seven and coming back late because I was doing the accounts every night. It was an awful time, unfair to the children, which is why I quit. Tara's nanny, a young girl, was looking after them. There were just too many children for her to cope with. There were always twenty for lunch on Saturdays because Mark [Paul's younger brother] would say, "I'm bringing two." Then Paul would say, "I'm bringing Kenlen, plus three," and so on.

Little Paul had a period that was slightly unfortunate. He thought the younger children were interfering when he wanted to be alone with his girlfriend, so he would take her in the living room and lock the door.

Daddy gave the children a blow-up girl—cute, lifelike. They obviously decorated her a bit and they hung a rope around her neck. They waited on the terrace for some nice old lady to walk in and then they'd drop her down from the fourth floor. At a Christmas party, Paul thought it would be a good idea to pull the same stunt, but this time with ketchup all over the doll.

This got old fast and so he went to live with his friend Philip. The children really missed him. But he used to come over a lot and sit around.

The world did not treat him well; he fell among thieves. They were as fascinated by him as he was by them. They quickly got him under their thumb, and the subject of kidnapping came up.

Paul:

That last Christmas I spent with my mother, I snuck out to see *Easy Rider* in English; she didn't want to let me go. I said I was going for a walk and I went and saw the film and it flipped me out. Did you see it? I got so angry when they beat Nicholson up. When you're young, you know, it's just hate for straight people, it became hate. A few weeks after that I rented a motorcycle—Richard [Boyd] already had one—and we went camping. My old girlfriend Bobby was there too, but with Richard, not with me. Five of us went camping—very big motorcycles, lots of dope, Etruscan ruins. There's a big waterfall there. It's beautiful. I smoked so much dope. I took acid and I was so gone, you can't believe it. Those little black ones. You know, steamboats with a toilet roll or something. Then there was that sleeping-bag situation. That was the weirdest hallucination I ever had. The sleeping bag started to go like this and it became a volcano and it became red and brown and rats and snakes and slime and witches and just the shit of the world, the scum of the world. I put my hand on the pole of the tent and the whole tent fell down.

Have you heard *Diamond Dogs?* The cover is by the guy who did *Rock Dreams,* Guy Peelaert. There's a beautiful poem and it goes to music. It goes something like "High on poacher's hill, fleas the size of rats, suck on rats the size of cats, mutant eyes gaze out." Weird thing, very beautiful. You'll have to listen to it.

Then we went to Positano for the first time. In Positano I did exactly what I wanted. I was completely free. No shoes. No family complex. No money, just day to day. I met Marcello then. We went back to Rome after some days. He had a studio in Trastevere and I stayed there with him.

Trastevere is where these *malavita* live. Ciambellone, the big doughnut, was the main coke guy. He lived there and ran the place.

I heard about Martine and Jutta, German twins. They were supposed to be Amazons with these enormous tits. I tracked them down, met them at a restaurant one night. They were stoned on something. Tight curls, lots of makeup, sequined pants with snakes on them, running around in silver high-heeled shoes, Roxy Music, stars in their eyes with ten or fifteen gay guys. They were taking pictures. Really, really, really having fun all the time. I was a bit down on these gays, stern; I was a little bourgeois and straight. But these twins fascinated me.

I got to know Martine. We went to the beach one day. We played around. I was always trying to touch her. In the car she wouldn't sit in the back with me, she would sit in the front with her sister. I was pissed off with her. In the beginning we didn't really like each other very much.

The twins had one of those strange little furnished apartments with just a couple of suitcases. We slept together in one bed and we didn't make love for a month, really. I slept in my underwear. Then they came to live with us and we went to Capri, and Martine and I had our affair there.

When we came back to Rome, living at Marcello's, I met two guys, elegantly dressed, big Fiat 130, always paying cash. They said they worked for Air France. I hung around with them. Ciambellone got a little pissed off.

One night I went out with the Air France guys and they said, "Get us a couple of girls," which I did. We went back to their apartment. They had all these gun magazines, telescopic sights and stuff. I had great fun watching these two old men and these two girls. They wanted coke. We said, "We have coke." We chopped up Vitamin C and gave it to them—that's how we took them—and laughed all night long. These guys said, "Why don't you go to Cannes with us?" I was supposed to spend a week in Cannes in the best hotel and I only had jeans. No suitcase. No brush. Nothing. I asked for money to go shopping. One had no cash on him. I borrowed five thousand lire from the other one for a cab. They said, "Get some proper clothes. See you in a couple of days." We had an appointment to meet at the airport. I hitchhiked there but they never showed. At that point, Marcello's place was crazy. A wild scene, people never slept. Coke, coke, coke. I was selling diamonds. We had machine guns. We were starting to get into big drug deals. Really started to organize a gang. We wanted to eventually have some sort of political thing. In some ways it was even romantic. Then the Air France guys walked in. I always thought of Ciambellone as a big guy, but when these guys came in, he bowed down.

This was just before Martine and Jutta left. Did she tell you about being locked in that room?

Ciambellone tricked me. He woke me at four in the morning and said, "The guy's here with the money for the coke."

"Fantastic," I said. He told me to come to his place. All these guys have little apartments—one-room paranoia places, big locks on the doors. I said, "Where is the guy?" They said, "He's coming." There were maybe fifteen of them and they had been there for a while, so you can imagine the tension.

I was naive. I really thought the film guy was coming. Martine and Jutta wanted to produce a film and I had talked to Ciambellone about this. He said, "Why don't you call them, I'll produce the film." We called them up and he said he was going to give them the money and they had to come immediately. As soon as they came, one of these guys locked the doors. They started showing porno films. I stayed for a while. They wouldn't let us go and I got really a little bit nervous. I told Ciambellone I needed some money for jeans. He gave me the money and I went away. I didn't say anything to Martine. I just went away. I was going to come back but I didn't. I was so fucked-up.

A few days before I was kidnapped I had a fight with my mother. I came home stoned one day and told her, "I am addicted to coke." She began to cry. I said, "I have no problems." I just hated women— because I was with the wrong women, awful whores. I loved only myself. My theory was that if you just love yourself and no one else, then you can't have any problems.

These Air France guys proposed to me, "Why don't we kidnap you?" I was really ready to do it. Just out of economic necessity, political reasons, and wanting to buy weapons and things. I don't want to mention this in the book because it could get me in trouble. I was really mad. When you get into coke you'll do anything to have it. I was even asking for advances. I'd say, "Give me some money now and then later we'll work it out."

After a day I said to Marcello that something was happening and we had to go there. We took his Citroën and went there but they opened the shutters and shot at us. After about three days Martine and Jutta arrived at the door. They had escaped. They were really furious. They thought I had organized the whole thing.

After that it got heavy. It got dangerous. The *malavita* got very jealous of the twins. They talked bad about me. They said that I didn't give a shit about Martine. They had gotten me really under their thumb because I owed them money.

After the twins came back to Marcello's, Jutta left. She didn't speak to me for a long time. Martine stayed a few days longer and I realized how much I liked her, but these gangsters kept coming. She hid in another room. It really destroyed her. She found an apartment and moved out.

I got really jealous when she left. I followed her. I watched her. She and Jutta got an apartment on Via della Scala. I wanted to rent a room from them. They didn't want to rent it to me, so I found an apartment in the same building.

Martine and Jutta were on the first floor and on the ground floor there was Moonie, a painter, very gay, a great guy. Everyone was gay. They had a shop downstairs and Hiram Keller was there all the time. I was seeing a lot of them. You could scream out the windows at the twins, very nice.

After this I completely changed sides. I hung around with fags for a few weeks. I was going to live with Daniel, a gay boy, upstairs. Let's not mention this or tell Martine, but I had an experience with him one night. I went really gay hanging out with Hiram and all these gay people in Trastevere. Morrissey and Warhol. I believe I am gay, but not sexually anymore, it doesn't attract me. But psychologically, I'm pretty feminine.

I was testing Martine. I'd tell her I had fucked six women that night. I was fucked-up.

Martine and Jutta were really getting it together. They were doing pictures, they had a contract with *Playboy*. We even had a little money to buy food and drugs. They got me to do some pictures too.

Things got really great with Martine. We were getting money. I avoided Marcello and that whole scene. We even ran away from Danielle Devret and all those people. Martine and I would stay home all day, then go out in the evening and eat at Piazza Navona. She'd buy me clothes. Nobody had ever done that for me. Everyone had always taken advantage, so I really dug it.

It was a really nice period. We were really happy together, Martine, Jutta, and I. Pretty much in love.

8.

After Paul told the twins that he was going to have himself kidnapped, things began to go well for them. He avoided the gangsters and changed his mind about a kidnapping, but he had set them on his trail and the idea was loose in the air and they were coming for him.

Paul:

I was seeing nice people. Warhol was in Rome and Jagger was in Rome and there was the Andy Warhol scene. Going out to eat one night, we just looked out the window in the bar next door and said, "Oh, they're shooting a movie." We went over and ended up getting a little part in Polanski's film.

Marcello invited me to Gaeta, to Remington [Olmstead]'s place. He said, "Bring down a girl," so I thought I'd bring Danielle. I don't know why I was attracted to her, but I really was. She has connections with all those gangsters, with all the *malavita*. I was very suspicious of her. I still am.

I had been talking to Paul Morrissey, who did *Trash*. In the morning I went out to his house, where Warhol was staying, doing *Frankenstein*. They were cutting it. I went out there with Bob Freeman. There, I met this guy who I had seen with his sister in Trastevere. He went away without speaking to me. I saw his sister that night on the set with Danielle. She said, "Oh, we had this great idea. My brother saw you at Paul Morrissey's." At that time the French were testing their H-bombs in the Pacific. She said, "Why don't we kidnap you and get a boat and sit in the middle of where they are going to throw the bomb. Oh, don't you think it's a good idea."

There was no way I could stop it. It wasn't a joke anymore. People came up to me and made kidnapping proposals. They said, "Oh, why don't we do something together?"

One night I was in a Mercedes with Carlo Shimonova and a car followed us. Very fast—we had to race around town at three in the morning. We even took the license plate of this car, but it was lost. Probably the whole thing would have been solved, but the license plate number was lost.

The next day we did those famous *Cocaine* pictures. We went over to Claudio Abate's apartment. It was only for fun, you know. I had them but Claudio came and took them from our apartment. I don't have a single print anymore.

When Martine and I came back to the apartment one evening, men were waiting by cars in the street under the trees. I stood in the window of the apartment looking down at them. I asked Martine, "What the fuck do they want?" She said, "They've been there for some days." I threw a chair out the window at them. I was really paranoid.

Of the morning of the last day before Paul disappeared, Martine said:

The last morning I was at the house, Paul had been out and he called me around noon time and he took me out to Piazza Navona and told me, "When you get your divorce, I want to marry you." He was excited, I was excited too, he was very sweet. And then he said, "I'll see you later."

What Paul did in the final hours of that afternoon, where he went and whom he saw, are not talked about by either by him or Martine. Paul only picks up his account that evening. It seems clear from Paul's proposal to Martine that he knew something was about to happen and that Danielle, in some fashion, had set him up, but after his row with her in Piazza Navona at three in the morning, we have only Paul's word for what happened next and, in light of Rick Boyd's assertion that Paul had "taken a boat," we have to wonder. Boyd had a reputation as a bad actor, but if Paul is making up the story of his abduction, his details are very convincing. Still, you wonder.

Paul:

Later on I was going to meet Martine. I went to a bar alone and I got a table. Kevin O'Neil, Sue Johnson, and [Roman] Polanski came and sat. Then we all went to another bar and there was Warhol and Jagger and Bianca and Polaroids here and Polaroids there. It got kind of late and I went to the Domiziano and sat down. Warhol, Jagger, and Kevin went off to one section and Kevin left Sue Johnson with me. That's how I ended up with Sue Johnson. Everybody thought I was balling her or something. I wish I'd never seen her. Kevin came running down with Paul Morrissey and said, "Stay here a minute." We stayed for maybe half an hour. He never came back. We went to look for him and never found him. I said, "Why don't we go to the Treetops?" So we went. Later, I wanted to go to Positano. I walked down the hill through the streets to Piazza Navona.

They were starting to close the cafés. I found Danielle Devret with some people. I asked her to take me in her car to Positano and she said no, so I asked her to drive me home. She wouldn't. Why didn't she take me home? She said that I had given her the clap. I freaked out at this woman and I was very drunk and I just said, "Fuck off," right in the middle of the piazza. We shouted at each other. She screamed at me, "You are nothing but a name!"

I had these boots and the heel was broken and I was just wearing my clothes for the disco, tight jeans and T-shirt with glitter. I walked to the Campo dei Fiori. There I bought a newspaper and some cigarettes and I walked on into the street by the French embassy. My head reeled with the argument I had had in Piazza Navona. I didn't want Danielle Devret, only a ride to Positano for the weekend, or home. My head was full of Danielle's scream, *You are nothing but a name!*

At the end of the street there is a fountain, the stone face of a boy, white marble. Water spurted out of his open mouth. It ran over his lip and down his chin, making a dark stain. It was like the boy was leering at me, his mouth half open. I was drunk, hot. My head was swimming and it was difficult to walk on the stones and sometimes I leaned out and touched the wall. All the time I was looking at this stone face of this boy under the light on the wall at the end of the street, he was staring back at me and he smiled. I swear he smiled.

As he did I realized a car was stopping alongside me. These men were coming out of it. They grabbed me and wrestled me to the floor behind the front seats. I can distinctly remember laying like that, bending my feet. There were three guys, two in the front, one in the back. I could feel his heels resting on me. I was just so fucking drunk. The car took off. They drove for an hour in silence. Then the guy in front, the passenger, leaned over the seat and looked down at me. He asked, "Who are you?" I said, "Paul Getty," and instantly realized my mistake.

"Do you have papers?" I said no. That was it. Shortly after we went through the toll gate onto the *autostrada*. If I was smart, I would have screamed at the toll gate or something. I would probably have made it, because they couldn't have escaped from the motor squad, but they could have shot me too or thrown me out going at one hundred miles an hour.

I slept and we drove south for hours. I woke feeling like shit, so thirsty. I said, "Water, water." They would only give me whiskey. I must have drunk a bottle and a half on the trip.

I didn't realize at all what was going on. I remember the drive and voices talking to each other. I thought it was the cops. I would have never dreamed it was real.

When I woke again, the car had stopped. It was getting light. Outside I heard them talking. They blindfolded me. I was carried out. Feet and hands. They made a mistake by carrying me like this because I could see under the blindfold. I saw an Arab-looking guy. Half-beard, like the one Gregg Allman has, and just a brown face. I only saw this part. And a cigar. This was Piccolo, the guy with the bandy legs. They lay me onto the grass. They didn't say anything. Then I said I was hungry and they said, "Okay, now the food comes." The guy who told me this had a thick Arab accent. I thought, "Oh, it must be the Arab guerrillas or something."

I was sure it was political, that they wanted the money, and I thought that's great, I thought that it was Arabs. Then I thought that it was Communists. Or maybe it was Fascists. Or maybe it was Peter Sellers, I didn't know who it was. Then I realized they had nothing, and they were not happy with just a little bit. They wanted it all. They had nothing to do but kidnap people.

Then Piccolo said, "We're not going to talk to you anymore." They devised a system for yes and no answers, the clapping. One clap for yes and two for no.

I just lay there on the grass until they got some food. I think some of them drove off, or another came or something like that. They carried me off for a couple hundred yards, and I lay there for hours.

They brought me beans, those awful things they eat in Mexico, refried beans. In Italy, it's pasta with beans and salad. The cheapest thing, you know. Awful stuff. And wine. Just what I needed.

In the morning, Martine woke early and was instantly alarmed.

Martine:

Every night Paul would come home. He was out late very often, but he always came home. That night he didn't. We had kept missing each other the night before. Marcello and I met and Paul had just gone, then Jutta and I went to the movies, and he had just gone, and so on. Then on this night, the two guys outside our house were gone. In the morning I looked at Jutta and we both said that there was something strange. Very early in the morning, six or seven, we went over to Marcello's house and we woke him up, and he said, "Oh, it's nothing. He's always like this." But we thought that something was wrong.

Martine and Jutta left Marcello's and went to Piazza Navona to try to find someone who had seen him the night before.
Four hundred miles south of Rome, Paul was waiting where they had left him on the ground.

Paul:

They left me there for an interminable amount of time. When the next night came they moved me. They said, "Get up," and took me by the arms. I was still blindfolded. They walked one on either side of me. It was rough ground, it had been plowed, agricultural. They turned me around and around and made me march in circles and then they'd get me in the car and drive me a half mile and then I'd get out again and I'd walk again in circles. We walked all night. It was probably always the same field. Slept for an hour, and then little short drives in a car, a Fiat 600. They didn't say anything. As it was getting light we went to sleep on the ground, on some grass. I woke up with a hell of a headache. They gave me coffee and I had to take a shit, which was as embarrassing as hell. They were all watching me and I was blindfolded. They made me wait till it got dark before we went on walking, we walked the whole night.

I don't think they knew where they wanted to take me. They had caught me and they weren't ready and they were getting things together. We walked again that night, in and out of the car, just like the previous night. I went to sleep again at four in the morning.

It was some time during these two days that Gail got the phone call from the kidnappers' spokesman, the man who liked to be called Fifty. Presumably, Fifty then called either the newspapers or the police themselves, or both, because in the morning of the thirteenth the story appeared on the wires in which she was quoted as saying she thought it must have been a joke. Perhaps these words were squeezed out of her by surprise or her desperate hope or denial. When she called Big Paul, she spoke very differently.

Gail:

I called Big Paul in London. We both just cried our eyes out on the phone. We couldn't talk. Finally I said, "This is kind of silly. We're both crying like babies. Why don't we talk later?" When I called later he was practical, mostly worried about me. There wasn't anything anybody could do at that point. He asked, "Is there any way you think I could help you? Do you think I should try and come down? I'm not supposed to come to Italy, I'll be arrested, but should

I come?" I said, "Of course not. That doesn't make any sense. That wouldn't be the answer." And it was "What should we do, what should we do?"

Gail knew immediately what to do. Paul would have spent the night either at Martine's, Marcello's, or at her place. She called Marcello and asked when the last time was he had seen Paul.

Marcello replied that he hadn't seen him in three days. "We were supposed to meet yesterday in Gaeta for lunch. He didn't show up, but you know how Paul is. It doesn't mean anything."

"Who was he with the last time you saw him?"

"He was with this Sue Johnson in a restaurant in Piazza Navona."

Gail didn't say anything about the caller who claimed Paul was kidnapped.

After the twins appeared at his door, Marcello had gone back to bed but after Gail's call he went out into the street and began looking. In Piazza Navona he found people who had witnessed the row between Paul and Danielle at three a.m. He also came across a man who claimed to have seen Paul still later.

Marcello:

Somebody said they saw him crossing a bridge, there were two people with him. There may have been three, it was too far away. He was sure it was Paul. When you know someone and you see him more than once in the night, you know how he is dressed and Paul is taller than most Italians.

In the evening the police came and they asked me a lot of questions. Then they told me that somebody phoned Gail and said Paul had been kidnapped. However, the words "joke" and "hoax" had been uttered and they would not go away. They lost the boy sympathy, a commodity in short supply for him anyway, and they enraged the kidnappers.

Among those who read the story on the wires were Paul's grandfather in London and, more important, the grandfather's troubleshooter, an ex-CIA man, Fletcher Chace.

Chace was in Calgary at the time. The OPEC (Organization of Petroleum Exporting Countries) Oil Embargo would break out in less than ninety days, sending the price of oil sky-high. Behind the scenes the Western oil companies were wrestling with the issue. Chace wrote in his journal, "On the 9th of July, I was meeting with some Arabs on behalf of the old man in Calgary, Canada. On the 13th I read in the newspapers that Paul had been kidnapped. The old man was sending me to the Middle East anyway. When I called him he told me to come and see him in London on the way so we could talk about it."

Chace caught a night flight from Calgary to London. A kidnapping was the kind of assignment he relished.

His ex-wife Patsy said of him:

He loves adventure. He's not afraid of danger, he's a classic ladies' man. I told him I wouldn't marry him if he went back into the Frogmen. But he married me and went back anyway. He was a Frogman in the Marines, Special Forces, in World War II, and Korea. He did one hundred sixteen missions behind enemy lines and has the DSO [Distinguished Service Order], second highest medal of valor in the British Army, very unusual. He's a karate black belt. His first wife left him to marry his younger brother. His second was a famous model. That didn't last long. He was in the Hall of Fame at Harvard, the greatest stroke in the history of the university rowing team. They called him Spike Chace. They didn't say Harvard won, they said Spike won. I met him in 1950 when I was going out with one of his friends, now president of Coca-Cola. We were married for twenty-three years and I was never bored. I don't think he should know we've talked. He can't be trusted. He'll be very nice and then stab you in the back. He likes to pit one person against another and keep the upper hand. He respects people who stand up to him. Old Man Getty's the same way. There is something in his relationship with Old Man Getty. I think the two of them like to sit around and count their money.

The kidnappers were thrown into a panic when they realized that the kidnapping was not being taken seriously, and strove to stop such talk with a letter to be hand-delivered overnight.

Paul:

Late that night it began to pour. They took me into a hut, a place where you keep tools. One of them dried me off, another gave me some clothes, and another made a fire on the dirt floor. There was no fireplace. They made some pasta. That's when they took the blindfold off for the first time. I had to sit at the other side of the hut, looking at the wall so I couldn't see them.

The man I call Piccolo—"the small one" in Italian—brought me paper and a ballpoint pen. I think he was in the car with me, but I don't know. He dictated a letter to me, low Italian, not my style. It takes a mouse's brain to work that out. It was just a nice letter saying we'll get in touch, I'm okay, they're treating me nice and all that. I addressed the envelope to Marcello and Martine because I didn't want them knowing where my mother lived.

When Chace arrived at London Heathrow in the late morning, he took a taxi to the Westbury Hotel on Bond Street in Mayfair, showered, then rested for precisely two hours and drove down to Old Paul's country mansion, Sutton Place.

Chace:

We discussed our affairs. We didn't know what was involved in Paul's disappearance, if it was a genuine kidnapping. We had no ransom note. The boy had been missing for a couple of days and no one was sure if he'd really been kidnapped.

The old man told me, "Go to Rome on your way to the Middle East and get it straightened out. The boy is missing. Get him back."

I chose the name of Lawrence as a cover name for this assignment. When you pick a false name, you don't pick a name with your own initials.

Martine and Jutta were keeping up their search in Rome.

Martine:

For two days we looked for him. We went to every friend's house and we looked. Someone said Paul was seen on the bridge with two guys, and I thought about the guys that were in the street outside our place. Then it came out in the newspapers that he was missing. Then when I came back in the afternoon there was a letter lying on my bed. I saw at once that it was Paul's handwriting. It was addressed to me, but inside was a note that began *"Cara Mama . . ."* So we took the letter to Gail's apartment, because it said, "Don't call the police," but Gail was not there. The concierge told us she was away, maybe even out of the country, not living in Italy anymore.

We waited outside her building until it got dark, but no one came. We didn't know what to do. On one hand we knew the truth, but we didn't know if it would help if we went to the police, if we said one word too much, boom, the kidnappers must kill him. Finally we decided we had to call the police, we couldn't just leave Paul, we knew something was really wrong. When we were waiting, Jutta and I talked secretly together, and we said they can't know that Paul knew these people. We never told anyone, not even Gail, that Paul was deeply involved with the *malavita*. We'd already had our experience. The police came and picked us up, and they took us to the *questura*. Gail was upset at us because we called the police, but there was no other choice. Jutta and I were taken to different departments and we showed them the letter and they laughed. Nobody took it seriously. The police told us, "Okay, we'll take the letter, thank you very much, you can go now."

They went back to Gail's apartment. This time she was home. Later still that night Gail received another visitor.

Gail:

An Inspector from the *squadra mobile* came to see me. He is a funny little man, very friendly, apparently casual, but then not very forthright, I think. He was very interested in my pictures and furniture. He wanted to know how much they cost, how much the rent was, and why I had not paid the rent this month. He seemed to know everything. I told him I was moving out and had paid the last month's rent when I moved in. He still seemed more interested in how I lived, the way I lived, than in the kidnapping.

He asked me if anyone in the Getty family had ever even alluded to kidnapping. I said, "Do you want me to really tell you the truth? Yes." What do you think, in a family like that? It happens every time someone takes too long coming back from the bathroom. These people have a very different sense of humor than Italians. Jokingly, the children's father has alluded. I don't remember Little Paul mentioning it. Never. But it is the kind of thing in conversation, just being silly, which could have come up.

Martine referred to a conversation, it seems to me, because when she came to see me she was in bad shape. She said, "I don't know what to do. I hope you believe me." We discussed it, but she never ever suggested to me that he had in any way talked about a kidnapping. I think she talked about a joke they had made at some point. She didn't mislead me in the least, but I can see that if somebody got hold of it they could take it out of context.

The Inspector assured Gail that what had passed between them would remain in the strictest confidence.

The following morning news and the content of Paul's letter appeared in Rome's principal newspaper, Il Messaggero.

The letter read:

Dear Mother,

Since Monday after midnight until 3.00 on Tuesday, I have been in the hands of the kidnappers. The telephone call that you received was real. I beg you, do not put my life in danger, have me killed. Please stay away from the police. Do not think that this is a game that I have set up. I beg you, try to put yourself in contact with my kidnappers. Do not tell the Italian police or the foreign police because my life is involved. They will certainly kill me so I wait with trepidation for your interest for my freedom, by paying the money that my kidnappers will ask. I repeat, from the police you will stop the inquiries if you don't want me to be killed and please do not take too long. If you love me, mother, what I have said should be enough. Lots of kisses to everybody.

P.S. If you delay, my kidnappers will cut off a finger and they will send it to you by registered post. I beg you, do not have even the most minimum intervention by the police because otherwise they will kill me. I love you,

Paul

I send my regards to everybody. Communicate with us over the radio, always by radio.

Gail realized, as she said:

The press's reaction was not to Paul's letter, but to the fact that the mother was not home, and the girl could not deliver the letter. Their reaction was how horribly shocking that the mother didn't care, or didn't believe, because the mother wasn't home, she had gone out to a movie. The letter was secondary. It was stupid of Martine. She should have just left when she found I was not there. Instead, she used her own head, and she's hardly a Rhodes Scholar. She got taken down to the police headquarters. The press was on her like, *zing. I* guess she made a comment like, "I don't think it's a hoax," or "Paul said this or that." Who knows what she said, or how scared she was. It must have been her complete lack of Italian, she thinks she speaks Italian, but she doesn't really at all.

9.

On July 15, Chace flew into Rome's Leonardo da Vinci Airport and drove into the city. The man who liked to be in control and couldn't be trusted kept a daily log.

Chace:

I checked into the Eden Hotel. I had a good working relationship with them. The concierge got tipped like any concierge gets tipped. The telephonist got tipped. Paid the switchboard girl to keep quiet and have also taken care of the manager of the Hotel. I didn't pay him anything. He was in on the deal. He put me in a room next to his, on the top floor, overlooking the park, so I had a little security in my room. We used to talk, he and I. He was a very nice fellow. I didn't have to pay everyone, because if you tip a concierge well, the rest of the hotel is under control. I could then live on a few lire and a smile.

Chace's first order of business was to go around to see Gail the following morning:

Met Gail at her apartment with Luigi Della Ratta, the croupier, otherwise known as Lou, super stud. Gail didn't remember meeting me before, although we'd been at the same cocktail party in Rome in 1958. She told me that the kidnappers were calling her and were worried by the idea that it was a hoax. She complained to me that she was being overwhelmed by the press.

Gail said that, despite Lou's presence, Chace made a pass at her, which she rejected. It could not have helped the situation, given that Chace thought himself a ladies' man despite the fact that his first wife had left him to marry his younger brother.

After he left her apartment, he went into the streets and began to investigate Paul's friends and habits. As he put it, "Feeling my way, talking daily with Gail. Lou is always around."

The kidnappers now moved Paul deeper into the mountains. Here, Paul makes it evident that his captors were people with whom he had spoken of his plan to stage a kidnapping to fund a palace in Marrakesh, his "island of eternal happiness." It also becomes clear that his captors had ridden rough-shod over any agreement they may have made with the boy. Once more, we must wonder about Rick Boyd's account of an abduction gone bad and whether the row in Piazza Navona with Danielle Devret wasn't staged to throw people off the scent, or perhaps was she setting him up?

Paul:

We had dinner in the hut: pasta, cheese, and all that. Then they removed my blindfold. They told me to keep my head down too: "Watch out. Don't play no jive games with us." Then we left. We went in the fields, up a mountain and down the other side. All the way up the fucking mountain. It was steep. I was exhausted and they only gave me Sambuca to drink, it's like ouzo, killer stuff. It's made from the sambuca plant, looks like elderberry. Very good to chew. It's sugar, mostly. They swigged at the bottle too. They kept me pretty drunk.

We must have walked about fifteen miles. It was drizzling. We walked through underbrush like poison ivy. It gives you a rash. When we got to the top of the hill, there was a dirt road. They blindfolded me and they put me on the floor of a car. We drove along the top, fast. It became asphalt. I did not try to keep track of what was going on. Then they stopped; it was getting light.

We walked a few yards up a steep rise to a bunker right off the road. It was built like the houses in Laurel Canyon, built into the side, half inside the hill. The sides of the walls were ground-level and stairs were underneath. It was small, very simple. There were bullet holes in the walls and people had fucked in there. Stairs down, two windows, steel door, and the road right underneath. There was writing around the place in German: *"Sieg Heil."* There were slits in the wall where they stuck the guns out, so it must have been as high as a man. Through a slit, there was a view of a mountaintop. It looked over something; I think it was the sea. I never saw because I was lying down all the time. There was no way to get out. I slept on little branches, a blanket under me and a blanket on top.

I bullshitted the kidnappers. They sat on the stairs wearing black nylon stockings and ski masks. I wanted to impress them. I said stupid things, that I had two motorcycles, a Porsche, that I would be worth $850 million. I humored them. I thought they were impressed. Piccolo brought me a radio, a big one, silver and black, with the large antenna and handle, all the dials. They said, "This is for you to see all the things we are trying to do for you. If you and your family don't do as we say, we'll take it away."

They made me write more letters, but I don't think all of them were sent. One day I wrote to my father. They made me leave the ransom amount blank, that's what really frightened me.

Who were "they"? Ciambellone and the malavita *taking revenge for the humiliation of the twins' abduction? The Air France coke dealers? Or was it the "friends of the friends," as Marcello had put it? In these days, Paul began to realize that this business was not going to be quickly resolved and his abductors had absolutely no idea of the nature and extent of his grandfather's fortune, parsimony, or influence.*

Paul:

After a week I heard the amount, on the radio, $17 million. I freaked out. I told them, "There's no way you'll get that much money. I told them much less. I worked out a way to convince them not to do it. I worked out the weight. They wanted the money in five-hundred and one-thousand-lire notes. That amount of lire would weigh three hundred kilos and would be something like three hundred and fifty thousand notes. I knew there was no way that kind of money could be, I don't believe there is that kind of money around.

They said they wanted ten percent of what my grandfather had. Before I was kidnapped, I was a little boy, stupid, dissident, ridiculous. I didn't use my head, that's why they asked for so much money.

Then I realized the whole thing revolves around sex, like Freud said, the whole world revolves around sex. Now I think that wanting more money is wanting to fuck better chicks. I'm serious. The whole world is corrupt. People who have more money have nicer girls. Those kind of Italians, they marry and they're married their whole life to the same woman and children, but they go out at night, snort coke, fuck around, and go home on weekends, you know, 'cause those women take it. All they did it for in the end was to fuck better women. "We'll wait until we have so much money and then we can go with nicer women." That's why there's jealousy between the rich and the poor. I've been with nicer women than they have been with. What it comes down to is, if you're healthy and beautiful, it's okay; otherwise, you're fucked. There's no chance.

Upon hearing the size of the ransom demand, Gail was devastated. She went to a television studio in Rome to tape an appeal to the kidnappers. She was given five minutes of air time, during which she had planned to remind the kidnappers that the grandfather had already refused to pay any ransom for fear of endangering his sixteen other grandchildren, and to point out she couldn't possibly raise this sum herself. However, during the taping she collapsed and nothing was aired.

She had to fight on four fronts: as a mother to her three other children; managing relations with the family whose patriarch, a paranoid eighty-year-old, refused her calls and whose son, Paul's father, was a shuttered recluse addicted to heroin and wracked by guilt and grief over the death of Talitha; the kidnappers, who called her almost daily; and the press, who printed whatever they thought would sell the most newspapers.

Gail:

The press made things up. I was ending the lease on my house, and therefore I had not paid the last two months' rent, as it had come out of my deposit. The headlines read PAUL GETTY'S MOTHER CAN'T PAY HER RENT, SHE'S BEING EVICTED. Garbage, concierge gossip. They were just trying to sell papers, but they were influencing Paul's grandfather, and they were influencing the kidnappers.

Right after Paul disappeared, I moved into a house right near the French embassy and half a block from Piazza Farnese. It was weird, because I had no idea Paul had been kidnapped there. We knew that that girl Danielle refused him a ride home. We knew that he had left Piazza Navona. I assume that he had made his way to Martine's house, or to my house, or to Marcello's house—one of the three.

Fortunately, in the new apartment, all the family photographs and everything were still packed. There was nothing out to hit me over the head. But when I did think about it or saw a photograph, I started becoming emotional.

The Italian press are vultures. They were saying, "Is it some boy's caprice, or did it really happen?" When they found out that Paul and Danielle had a row at Piazza Navona and she disappeared simultaneously, they made a big speculative thing about that. "This must be a hoax, Danielle Devret is missing." She was on holiday in Portugal. They mentioned that "Paul's mother" believed it, but everyone else thought he was going to come home any day. They said maybe he was here, or maybe he was there. It created a basis of doubt. To be fair, they didn't have much to go on. I refused to talk. I had nothing to say. I begged them to leave us alone, to keep the phones free. That's when the press brought up all the old Getty news, Paul's free lifestyle; they raked over all that stuff.

It was damaging because the police were reading the papers, and they were already skeptical. It must have affected Old Paul, those things are translated, and he's a great paper reader, reads everything written about the family. The Getty family is not popular, and the press has used the family over the years, or the family has allowed itself to be used. The Gettys get lousy press, maybe because they never do anything very nice. Getty karma. I'm not a Getty and never was. I married one, but I'm not a Getty, and I resented tremendously the things that were said about me. It must have really upset the kidnappers to have the Italian press saying "This is a joke."

The press refused to leave me alone. They printed everything. They misled the situation. I begged the police to not say anything, because something could happen to Paul. They said, *"Sì, Signora, sì, sì,"* and the next day whatever I had confided was in the papers. There was a leak. We had to keep our own secrets within the family, not tell the police.

The press harassed me ceaselessly. The house was surrounded; they wanted a photograph. I sent my lawyer, Giovanni Iacovoni, out and he said to them, "What's the difference, you have a thousand photographs already." They said, no, we want this and we want that, and we want it now. They rang the doorbell endlessly. They were always standing in the halls.

I couldn't leave from the front. I couldn't go out on the terrace, to look out at the night and get a breath of fresh air because they were always there. I was a prisoner. Vultures. I finally relented, stood outside the front door and they took photographs, had a field day. I was damned. They portrayed me as this ice-cold woman, the mother without emotion. I wasn't going to show them emotion. As far as I'm concerned, I showed them too much emotion. It's none of their damn business. They wanted a weeping mother. How can anyone expect an Italian to understand? It's an extremely unusual family situation.

We tried to use the press to say the right things, to appeal to them to print what the family put out, not their assumptions. We tried to use the press to keep the kidnappers in a positive frame of mind. That was not successful.

Il Tempo saw it in their own way. They wrote an extraordinary letter to Old Paul. The *Il Messaggero* men, Mario Gandolfo and Paolo Graudi, were cooperative. They tried to be responsible. They and *Paese Sera* even came out and said, "Let's leave her alone."

Many had no mercy. They did everything to antagonize me. They told me that my son has been seen in Corsica, and wasn't I happy? I said, "My son is not in Corsica." They say, "Your son is on his grandfather's yacht." Paul's grandfather doesn't have a yacht.

On July 18, Chace noted in his diary:

Letters from Marcello and Martine to the grandfather: "I know I haven't seen you much. He's still young," etc. etc. Five different false leads jump up including a couple from Texas, some South Americans and some Germans from Munich. All claimed to be holding the boy and demanding ransom.

> *On the following day, Chace began his move to take control from Gail. He ordered the kidnappers to only call the office of Iacovoni, Gail's lawyer. He advised Iacovoni that he would need a desk in the office. He didn't introduce himself to Iacovoni by name, just as a "family representative." He would have liked to talk with the kidnappers himself, but he spoke no Italian, just a few words of Spanish mixed in with English.*
>
> *On July 20, he noted in his diary:*

We have made a small amount of money available to the kidnappers to forget the whole thing. Our strategy is to persuade them to take expenses and forget the rest. We aren't going to pay a ransom. Just enough to keep them happy and we will forget the prosecution. Gail wants to raise $200,000. People in Rome are all running around offering to raise various sums of money. The man who calls himself Fifty is getting worried. He called Iacovoni and assured him, "It is we who have the boy. He may be killed. Pay the ransom." Paul II [the boy's father] is showing great interest wondering what he can do to help. At this point someone telephones an offer of $500,000. May be a false lead.

> *On that same day, Fifty introduced himself to Iacovoni and for the first time, after two weeks of waiting, the kidnappers revealed their ransom demand.*

Iacovoni:

I get a call at nine forty-five in the morning in my studio. The voice was Calabrian-Sicilian; he called himself "Fifty." He told me to prepare a white automobile and to put an advertisement for Cynar on the radiator. Only Gail and I were supposed to go. I ask if we can be accompanied by a friend of the lady's, that is Lou, but the Calabrese is adamant and denies me this. He tells me that we will have other instructions for the payment and during the morning somebody will arrive. I ask who this somebody is, but the Calabrese hangs up. At one o'clock the postman arrived and brought an express letter with the request for ten billion lire [approx. $18 million].

There was also a letter from Paul:

ROME, JULY 23.

If you don't do as they say, dear Mother, it will mean that you want me dead. They have made all the arrangements. If one of them is taken, the others have orders to kill me without requesting the money. Take the road indicated with two people in a white Mercedes. Drive normally. Take it from Rome to Ban. Turn back. Take the *autostrada* to Palermo—stay on the *autostrada*. Leave in the morning. The evening before you leave, give an interview on television at 8.30 P.M. Say these words: 'Please show up. The family will pay.' The money should be in sacks. The signal is two pieces of gravel will strike your windshield. Stop at once, leave the money on the road and go. Study this letter and what I say in it. The car must be unaccompanied. Nobody else in the car, no radios. If you don't follow these instructions it will mean my life.

Paul

In Rome, after a week of his investigation, asking questions of the police and people on the street, Chace revealed his true position. He did not do so to anyone but his boss, Old Man Getty, or in his own diary.

Chace:

I heard from someone that Paul was forging travelers' checks, was involved in the use and distribution of drugs and an extraordinary number of sexual vices. I contacted the police. The vice president of the *squadra mobile* homicidal kidnap division is convinced the whole thing is a trick by Paul. He doesn't buy it. He thinks that the case is possibly a family affair. He says that there are certain discrepancies. The boy, he says, was leading a very costly life, had lots of girlfriends, went out a great deal, he was a pseudo-artist, and that there is a considerable difference between his mother and his father, so they don't get along. Paul made fun of the police. If you make fun of the police, they won't like you. Not only that, but his mother is hard up and is going around with a very shady character. There is nothing official on it, but he is definitely shady. They go to the Luau Club, a mafia place. The boy has connections with the underworld. Ciambellone and Mammoliti, he says, may be involved. But somebody is behind them. Theoretically, it could be the boy's mother. If she is involved at all, she was probably involved not initially, but informed of the plan later on. She is a strong woman, a very strong woman.

I talked to Old Paul on the phone. I spent the day talking to him about business affairs in the world and the Middle East, the Getty case, how he was feeling. He feels all right and he feels about the kidnapping just like I do. He keeps an open mind and he listens and he deduces. He doesn't say a great deal but when he does, he's specific. He listens carefully before he says something. He asks very good questions when you're talking to him. If you didn't know him, you might wonder if he's paying attention because he goes for a long time without saying anything.

He told me he had issued a statement to the press to the effect that he had fifteen grandchildren, and if he paid a ransom for one, it would put the rest in jeopardy. Therefore he would not pay Paul's ransom. He told me he'd contacted the boy's father, Big Paul, in private, and agreed to advance him the amount of a ransom to be deducted from his future inheritance. He said he was awaiting a reply.

10.

Big Paul, a recluse in the Rossetti house on Cheyne Walk, no longer spoke directly to his father. Old Paul had come around occasionally, despite the fact that he much preferred Gail to Talitha. He stopped visiting after his grandson Tara was born and he discovered that his son and Talitha had christened the boy Gabriel Galaxy Gramophone Getty. The last time he did visit, he sat down on a poof in the living room and couldn't get up.

If Big Paul didn't reply to his father, he did reveal his opinion of the matter in a phone call he took from Victoria.

Victoria:

I was in Mexico when the drama began, engaged to a Dutch banker. I got desperately ill and was admitted to the ABC Hospital in Mexico City.

Someone called me from London and said, "Old Paul has died." Two hours later they called again and said, "No, it was George." He had committed suicide. God, I thought, Big Paul must be devastated.

Then someone called me and said Little Paul had been kidnapped. When I rang his father, Big Paul, from my hospital bed, he said, "I don't think it's true." I remember relaxing.

Occasionally after that I'd ring Paul up. He didn't want to talk about the kidnapping. He made allusions. He said, "I'll tell you later," as if he had a whole lot of things he wanted to say, but it has never come up. I always thought it was strange that Jerry Cherchio didn't come forward. He always used to come forward in trouble. So I was in my hospital bed in Mexico City, figuring out what the situation was . . . Where was Jerry?

Eventually my mother flew out and I came back to London on a stretcher. I was moved to a hospital in England and then to the London Clinic to convalesce.

When I talked to George d'Almeida about it, he told me that after I left for Mexico he had gone to London to tell Paul that the kidnapping was real and that he absolutely had to do something. He's a very special person, George. He really is rather extraordinary and a very serious human being and this was beyond his comprehension.

He said [Big] Paul was in the most frightful state, taking a lot of things. There was chaos in the house. He said the first night that he was there [Big] Paul was quite friendly and nice. The next day George laid it on the line. He said, "As long as there is one chance in a million that it is so, then the ransom has to be paid. There's no such thing as playing for time. You are playing with someone's life." Paul was quite unreceptive. He said, "Do you realize that if I have to pay the ransom, I would have to sell my entire library, for that useless son?" In the morning, George left without saying good-bye, vowing never to darken his doors again.

Gail presumably heard the news of the note from Chace. She knew as well as anyone what was happening with Big Paul.

Gail:

I never saw it, but I heard that Old Paul had written to [Big] Paul telling him that all he had to do was sign it and the funds would be there for the ransom. The money was there, waiting to be released. I don't know if Old Paul asked for interest. We went into a time warp when this piece of paper from his father came to him. [Big] Paul came up with every possible reason not to. Bill Newsom went back to London to ask [Big] Paul to sign the note and pay the money. People went there day and night, but Big Paul wouldn't sign.

In July, Gail had been at the center of negotiations with both kidnappers and press, but Chace tightened his control.

Gail:

Chace wanted to get me out of touch for a few days so that the press would leave the telephone alone. If they stopped calling, then the kidnappers could get through. We couldn't think of how; if I just disappeared, there wouldn't be any sympathy. Chace said to me, "Do you think you can fake a collapse? Can you fall down, cry, scream, whatever?" If I was sick and unreachable, the papers would sympathize.

I said, "Well, I'll try." No one knew, except Lou, Chace, and myself. It was lovely for them because they didn't have to do the act.

Gail planned to stage her false collapse before the group of paparazzi camped outside her front door day and night:

We waited until everyone was out of the house. Lou asked me how much time I would need to do my spell. He needed to know so he could get someone to drive us to the hospital. Obviously, he couldn't drive me by myself, because then we wouldn't have a witness. I fell on the floor and I started crying, crying, crying. I really got myself going. It was a tremendous relief. I had held it all in. I had tried never to cry, because I knew if I started, I'd fall apart. I was in a real state.

At a certain point you get tired of crying, and no one was there. Lou had to run down and get the car. I walked very feebly down; it was all an act. At the hospital, they put me in a wheelchair. I told the press, "I've known this doctor for a long time." I was carrying on. They fell for it. They gave me all kinds of medication, tranquilizers. By the time I had gotten through with it, I believed it. Really, I absolutely believed it because it was actually there.

Apparently, it was quite believable, because Chace asked Old Paul if I could stay at Ladispoli. When I arrived there, I was really out of it from the drugs. Mario's wife sent me to bed. I stayed in bed for a few days, because people would visit me and I had to maintain the act.

Chace then asked me to get out of Italy altogether. I was suspicious of why they wanted me away. I had lost control. It's in the hands of Chace and Old Paul and Fraser McKno, and who knows who else. My idea was to go to London for a few days and come right back.

The kidnappers were clearly rattled. How could a family hesitate to pay for one of its own? Such a thing would never happen in Italy. These Americans were barbarians. Their response to the delay was to move Paul to a hole-in-the-wall hideout higher up the mountains, sealed at one end. There was only one way in and only one way out of this hole in the wall. The gang was digging in, preparing for a siege.

Paul:

We moved at dawn. Left the bunker. We walked on the road, up the hill three-quarters of a mile, and then turned off onto a path that went down into a valley so steep it took three or four hours to get down to the bottom of the gorge. They carried the radio. They had cut a path with machetes. It must have been cut the day before, because it was still fresh. They didn't say anything.

The area, Aspromonte, if you see it on a map, is all mountains, very few inhabitants, like, one person per square mile—just goats and sheep. The bottom of the gorge under the trees is swampy, unbelievably quiet. The soil is lightly packed, rich, and dark, with lots of wood in it, covered with leaves, great for planting—blackberries, chestnuts, pines. At the bottom of the gorge there was a stream. It was crazy; I don't think a man had ever been to that spot before.

That afternoon, Fifty called Iacovoni's office in Rome. His cousin answered and told him to call back in half an hour. Fifty did so and Iacovoni's secretary answered the phone and asked whom she was talking to. He threatened her and told her to call him Fifty. She fetched Iacovoni:

Fifty: Avvocato, listen, has the family come to some decision?

I: The family has already told you. They cannot pay that sum.

Fifty: Tell me how much they can pay.

I: Tell me what you want. Why don't we meet one day?

Fifty: No. You tell me if the family has intentions of paying.

I: The family has intentions of paying. The mother is obviously worried for the life of her son. But the economic possibilities of the mother are extremely limited. You know that better than I do because Paul has already told you.

Fifty: Well, at least tell me what they want to pay.

I: Around two hundred to three hundred million lire [$360,000 to $540,000].

Fifty: What?

I: Three hundred million.

Fifty: Rubbish.

I: What?

Fifty: Rubbish.

I: Why can't we meet? You could be safe. We could meet in
Rome.

Fifty: No. Tell them that two hundred to three hundred million have already been spent. Did you understand?

I: I understand, but tell me how much you want. Make a request.

Fifty: It's you who has to say—I don't know. I can't tell you.

I: I have to consult the family now and then you will have to
call me back.

Fifty: I will call you.

I: You talk with your friends and then give me an answer and
above all, tell me this, is the boy well?

Fifty: Yes, well.

I: Are you sure?

Fifty: He's well. He's being well treated but he suffers at the
same time.

I: Hello?

*As Iacovoni was reassuring the kidnappers that a ransom would
be paid, Old Paul was issuing the opposite directions. Chace
noted:*

Old Paul says there's 400 million lire to work with [approx. $730,000].
Settle it quietly. Pay it off. Get Paul out of the country. Pay expenses,
not ransom. Kidnap ransom is deductible under U.S. law, but that's
not the grandfather's concern. He's told them he won't pay a penny
ransom so now he doesn't want to pay ransom but he will pay expenses. Strategy at this point is to try and get the kidnappers to see me
and talk to me. Try and splinter them. Offer them $600 because they
can accept $600 under Italian law and it doesn't constitute grand ex-
tortion. Try to break them apart, separate one of them from the game.

Chace didn't speak of his plans with Iacovoni. Iacovoni was Gail's lawyer, and if Gail was involved, then Chace figured the lawyer might be too. Chace firmly believed in keeping his powder dry. Gail and Iacovoni, struggling to cover the delay, decided to demand proof that Paul was alive.

Iacovoni had been juggling calls from a number of parties claiming to have the boy. On August 8, Iacovoni recorded the following conversation:

Man: Avvocato Iacovoni, did you receive the telephone call yesterday?

I: I had left a few minutes before that. Listen, from now on, call me between ten and noon.

Man: I'm only a spokesman. If there's another sum, I can't tell you anything.

I: How is the boy?

Man: Well.

I: Be careful. The grandfather will not pay a penny for the boy, but if something happens to the boy, he is capable of spending more money than you can imagine to take revenge.

Man: You be careful or I'll hang up and we'll lose another week of time like last time.

I: Listen, we need to know if the boy is alive.

Man: The boy is well.

I: Yes, but we want proof.

Man: We can give you proof. If you want we can bring him there.

I: No, no, don't bring him here.

Man: We are immigrants.

I: I see. You could send us a photograph of him holding a newspaper.

Man: We can't send it. How can we develop a photograph? We don't have a photographic laboratory.

I: Yes, but don't you have a Polaroid?

Man: No, we don't have anything.

I: Well, at least you could send us a letter.

Man: Let me finish talking. Prepare one million marks—
that's around three hundred million [lire].

I: Yes.

Man: One million marks and tomorrow morning I will be
able to tell—

I: Wait a minute. Before fixing the sum we want proof that
the boy is alive.

Man: The proof is this, my dear *avvocato*.

I: What is that?

Man: The proof is this. Once you are here with one million
marks in notes of a hundred that have not been marked,
once we have counted the money, after half an hour the
boy will be free.

I: Yes, but before I give you three hundred million lire [ap-
prox. $550,000], which I believe is a million marks, Mrs.
Harris must have the authorization of her husband in London because I've already told you how much money is available in Italy. Anyway, I will make your proposal. Send me a
letter written in Paul's handwriting in which he should tell
us the name that he had at school and the name of his
Yugoslav friend of about three years ago. So, if you send me
this letter by express, written in Paul's handwriting, with
these two details and the surname of the dog—can you
hear me?

Man: Yes.

I: When we have this proof and we are sure that Paul is alive,
then we can face the problem of the money and the way of
delivering it. When will you call me back?

Man: I must meet with the others.

The caller never identified himself and suddenly began demanding marks. Iacovoni didn't indicate surprise at the demand for marks.

The following day, Chace received a letter from Düsseldorf that read: "Bring the money in a couple of red suitcases to the train station and we'll give you Paul."
    Chace (notes):

Because of the accuracy of the information they had, I figured out that [Marcello] Crisi's ex-wife is in Germany. Either Crisi's German wife or two girls Paul shacked up with. I don't mean the twins. One of the girls had a Spanish name, moved to Cologne, Frankfurt or Düsseldorf. There are similarities between this letter we received from Düsseldorf and the other letters. In my own mind, I believe that those people up there are trying their hand at getting some money too. Whether or not they are in it with Paul or trying their hand at a little extortion, I don't know.

11.

Paul waited beside the stream at the bottom of the gorge. His constant and mostly sole guard was the man he called the Chipmunk.

Paul:

I built a hut from four trees, a plastic roof with branches on it so that helicopters couldn't see it. I had this whole trip, I really dug it; each time I'd see an airplane I'd run in and duck inside.

I was chained near the stream. It was an incredibly long chain. For a while I didn't mind the stream, getting out of the city, all the stress and everything. I mean, it was totally different, just being in nature and quiet. There was a little beach of sand where I drew pictures with sticks. They gave me a knife and I carved these wood things shaped like little knives and I would throw them at a target I drew on the other side of the stream. There was a shallow place where you could cross. I made friends with this little bird. I left crumbs and it came every day. I thought it was dependent on me, and I liked that. I liked that I could do something for someone. I had to play these games with myself to keep from thinking about the same thing over and over. I watched my fingers. I put them in the water, played with the water, and I would watch the water for hours. I studied my toes, really looked at them, or at a rock. I thought about how I should be with the kidnappers at certain times, what I should say to them at certain times.

They started to give me freedom. In many ways this was the saddest and the best time. At least I was allowed to be in nature and I had some freedom. I could walk two hundred meters, but they told me there were people all around. I wouldn't run away, because where would I go? If I went to the police station, I'm sure they'd just bring me back.

The kidnappers gave me paints and paper. I painted rocks and wrote a diary. A log, what I did, what I ate, what was on the radio, what I thought was happening. It was their idea; they thought I was intelligent, they thought I could work it out. It was difficult; I was not allowed to write in English. I wrote a whole pad.

The Chipmunk was always with me. Because I wasn't allowed to look at them, I had to keep my eyes down. Sometimes I thought he was Piccolo. I was confused.

I hid some things, painted stones and pages. I have a lot of things hidden there, because I was there for the longest time, the whole summer. Some of my things I've left behind in various places. I have a whole collection of painted rocks. They'd be worth a fortune. I have their fingerprints. I had them touch a glass and then I hid the glass. They were smoking some really weird Swiss cigarettes. I buried them, with their fingerprints on them. I think I could make the perfect crime, 'cause I would never do something like that. Can you imagine giving a cigarette pack with your prints on it?

It's right next to the stream. I have a Louis V belt, which I was wearing, which I hid there. I had Martine's house keys. I just wanted them to be buried.

I didn't have anything else to do, so I made these incredible escape plans. By the stream, I had this whole thing with diagrams in a book, with an elastic band, a pencil and a match and a matchbox, and a cigar tube. I'd built a space where I put this cigar tube and I had thrown hay right outside this. And on the cigar tube I had two little nails and an elastic band, and a pencil sharp like an arrow. And inside the cigar tube, matches, and there was a match on top of the pencil. I tried it out, too, and it worked; if I had released the elastic band, it would have—*whoosh.* If I'd lit the match, it would have landed in the hay, but I didn't want to do it. It was so hot and dry there it would have started a giant fire, and there was no way out of the canyon. And I wasn't going to try to escape unless I was ninety-nine percent sure I wasn't going to be shot.

When Gail left Old Paul's Italian villa, she flew to London.

Gail:

My idea was to go to London for a few days, talk to the children's father, and come right back. I didn't really have the time to talk to him on the phone. Undoubtedly he was upset and probably going more and more into his scene, which meant I wouldn't be able to reason with him. Whatever was going on was very heavy.

I met with Chace in a park, all very secretive, everybody looking twice. Chace felt I should stay out of Italy. Chace, Old Paul, and whoever else was deciding all of this, felt that Iacovoni, my lawyer, the man I had asked to handle the kidnappers' phone calls, was no longer necessary; he had performed his services. If I wished to carry on with him, he would be my responsibility and I would have to pay him. Chace wanted to pay him off, thank you very much, and that was that. I wrote to Iacovoni, thanking him. It seems to me they paid him and sent him off. They continued using his secretary and his office while he was gone, so they would "have a connection, a phone contact with the kidnappers while Gail's not here." I felt, and I could be absolutely wrong, this could be a terrible judgment on my part, that they really believed I was involved. I finally got terribly irritated and got on the plane with a pair of jeans, a bag.

I stopped giving the press the chance to print anything. No news. The press got really unpleasant, like I had just run away and could not care less; that I had gone on a holiday.

In Rome, Chace was also taking control from Gail's lawyer.
Chace (notes):

I told Iacovoni to go to Greece and take a vacation. He wanted all eleven million lire [approx. $20,000] for payment. I said no. He's very upset and wants a letter of thanks for all he has done and all the money he has asked for. On the evening of August 10, Gail went to London alone. She met Lou and they went out that night. She was in London with Lou on August 11th.

When Gail arrived in London, the first thing she did was telephone Old Paul.

Gail:

He was sweet. He said, "I hope you're all right. I just can't see you. I hope you understand." I did understand. He was terrified. He's just an old man and no old man's capable of contending with this kind of thing. If he saw me, it would create a storm of emotion, tears. He's just not capable. I didn't want to test his emotions. I didn't see him during the whole kidnapping.

I got to the house to talk to Big Paul. We had a very difficult time. We couldn't sit down, the minute I walked in and talked about what I'd come to talk about. We talked about eight thousand other things. I hadn't been there long, and Victoria arrived. Ping, "You poor dear"—all that crap. From the second she arrived, she was nasty to me.

She and I went upstairs and talked.

My sister-in-law was there, Donna, Paul's sister. At some point Victoria said, "We're expecting some guests. Would you mind going out for the evening?" I remember opening the door for the guests and then I guess I left. I don't know where I went. I didn't know anyone. I was alone, walking, in my own head. I didn't know where I was or who I was. I don't think I came back to the house that night. I was really wild. I'm sure if you went to Paul and asked, "Did this actually happen?" He would say, "You poor dear. No." I don't think he really knows. This is what's so awful—that other world he's dealing with. It was as though he didn't even know who I was or what was going on. I blamed it on Victoria.

While I was in London I received a call from Chace. He said in a very cynical voice, "Your son is just fine." I said to him, "I know my son is not just fine, so don't tell me that he is." He went on to say, "Someone very close to the family, someone who's known him for many years, told me."

Whenever I did go back to Big Paul's, I was there two or three days before we finally got 'round to it. Paul said, "Bring the children." I was concerned about them. They should be with me. They were really upset. So they came, the two girls, with Lou. Mark was in San Francisco with my parents.

I rented a little flat in Kingston. We were there two or three weeks, just sort of staying there in limbo, stalling for time.

Chace came to London and we had meetings.

Every day I called Paul's house from Kingston and said to the secretary or the butler, Derek, "Should I bring the children over? What should happen? Is he ready to see them?" The answer was always "We don't know."

Finally, Lou drove us over to the house. I told him, "This is a touchy situation. Wait in the drawing room. I'll take the children in to see their father." I walked in Big Paul's study with the two girls and he flipped out: "You didn't make an appointment." I said, "I didn't know your children had to have an appointment."

"How dare you bring uninvited people?"

There was a horrible scene, really an awful scene. I was really wild. I could have taken him and hung him upside down. I couldn't have cared less. Who turned him, what happened, I don't know. Why he became so bitter, what had I done, I don't know. Whether it was years of resentment and he finally exploded, I just don't know. I knew there was no way I was going to have any sort of relationship with him as far as the kidnapping was concerned. I knew then— forget him; it's out of the question. I said to the children, "Come on, here we go." We walked out of the study, out of the house.

We went to a movie, went to dinner, and then went back to Kingston.

Chace was uncharacteristically patient in getting to the bottom of this business. His dilemma was that his lack of Italian meant that he needed Iacovoni, whichever side the lawyer was on. He therefore did what he could.

Chace:

I put Iacovoni on my payroll to control him. He was very unhappy and left town with his wife. I heard that Gail was planning a visit to Malta. I had that house under surveillance for months because I thought Paul was part of the deal and Cherchio was in on it. I always suspected him, so I had the Malta place under surveillance for a long time. Cherchio has an apartment in Malta and I thought Paul might pop up there. And then when Gail said she was going to Malta, I really increased the surveillance. I was beginning to get the feel of the situation at this point.

Tension was arising on all sides as this thing dragged on. Nowhere more so than among the members of the gang who were holding Paul. The family's resistance had not been anticipated; its resources and logistics were being tested. It was one thing to move Paul to a more remote spot, another to keep changing the guard and supplying food and replacements. The more activity there was, the more likely they were to draw attention to themselves and, if there was one thing they all knew, it was that there were other players on the field besides the police. Paul himself began to see what he dared hope was a fracture within the gang, the very thing that Chace was aiming for.

Paul:

One guard liked to walk miles upstream, over the rocks and water, through enormous waterfalls. He'd walk in front. He always had a gun at his back. He said, "You know they call me the Chipmunk." He could jump up and down the rocks, climb trees. A little, little guy, so strong, he'd get things out of the way for me. He'd pick up enormous logs and throw them in the stream. A monster, a creep, he'd set me down and show me his pistol. It was terrifying, from the war, a German pistol. He was so proud of it. He said he would never sell it; he'd had it almost all his life. I asked him why he was like this now, he said, "I've always wanted to be a bandit, to rob the rich and give to the poor." His father bought him comics about bandits. Since he was five he read about cowboys and bandits; he loved the adventure. He's a quite learned man, more than the others. He went to university, had lived in Rome, had been to New York. He was the smartest one. He had read a lot and could speak a little French.

He questioned me on how much they could get. I think he was trying to do it on his own, do a separate deal. He was, like, working with me on it. I told him probably $300 million, if they sold the houses, sold everything, every piece of jewelry, but probably $200 million, because my father would never sell his house for anybody, no way. The Chipmunk said, "Don't tell the others what we talked about."

He was with me all the time. Sometimes he was nice, but sometimes he was hell.

The level of tension was clear from a letter received by Iacovoni in Rome on the sixteenth and in two subsequent phone calls to him:

> Dear Mother and Father,
> I have been with my kidnappers a month. The waiting is terrible. Will my family pay or will I be killed? Mama and Papa, see that they don't kill me. I am so young. I'm not even 17 and never, I say never, as in these terrible days have I dreamt to live for the rest of my life even in misery. If you think of me, if you love me as I hope, take me out of this hell. The amount is not 10 billion [approx. $18 million], what they are asking now for is what they really want: 3 billion [$5.5 million]. You have 20 days to prepare the money. It is useless to tell the press that you don't have the money. If you don't deliver it to my kidnappers according to the same instructions, that is, announce on television you are ready to pay . . .
> Paul
> PS: After the 20th day has passed, it will be difficult for you to see me alive.

The day following the arrival of this letter, the spokesman for the kidnapper—Fifty and—Iacovoni spoke:

I: So now tell me.
Fifty: Did that person come?
I: No.

Fifty: What do you mean no?

I: Nothing has come. Nobody has arrived. Only a letter dated sixth August—it's rather old—delivered today. It's an express in which there is talk of three billion [$5.5 million].

Fifty: Ah yes, that one, that's it.

I: Anyway, listen, the news is the following: the father is disinterested in the business, the mother cannot do anything. The grandfather has sent an American. He has arrived. You still have to send me proof that the boy is alive.

Fifty: This you'll have.

I: Well then, send it to us. Now, listen. An emissary from some of the American relations has arrived. This man will be here for ten days, after which he goes. Be very careful. He has with him about $100,000.

Fifty: I understand.

I: This is all we can offer you. Or you could kill the boy and turn yourself into assassins. . . .

Fifty: I didn't understand, I didn't understand.

I: This is necessary. You have to decide within ten days, because after ten days this man will go away.

Fifty: Ah—and the three hundred million from before, what then?

I: Nothing, no.

Fifty: Nothing?!

I: We don't have it. Look, let us know. The father doesn't want to know anything at all. The mother even went to London.

Fifty: Oh yes?

I: There is no money. The grandfather will not pay. This man from America has come and has with him one hundred thousand dollars roughly. Give us a precise answer, and rather quickly.

Fifty: Look, if it's for that amount of money . . . There is nothing to be done because too little—too little. . . .

I: Listen. The father is disinterested in the question. The mother doesn't have a lira. The grandfather will not pay even one lira. Therefore, this emissary of the American relations has come.

Fifty: Look, I'm talking seriously. Don't let's play games [*sound of cars honking*]. You said that there were three hundred million and now . . .

I: We can't make miracles, unfortunately. You understand? Hello?

Fifty: Yes?

I: You understand me?

Fifty: Yes. This man has come.

I: I'm telling you. I repeat—he has come specially from America.

Fifty: Yes, I understand. I understand.

I: We have only this amount of money.

Fifty: OK.

I: When will you call me?

Fifty: I don't know.

I: Hello?

The following day came a second phone call in the course of which the tension within the gang became very evident, as did Iacovoni's effort to on the one hand stall the kidnappers and on the other keep them, as Gail put it, "In a positive frame of mind."

Fifty: Hello. Avvocato Iacovoni?

I: Yes, speaking.

Fifty: Well, have you decided?

I: Yes.

Fifty: Can you hear me?

I: Yes. Tell me.

Fifty: You asked me for the names of certain particulars. The name of the Yugoslav friend.

I: OK, go ahead.

Fifty: B-R-A-T-I-S-L-A-W.

I: Bratislaw?

Fifty: Now I will tell you the name of some dog he wrote for me.

I: Tell me properly.

Fifty: Ussi, Snoopy, Pick, Ping-Pong. Then I'll give you another one, dictated letter by letter. P-A-U-T-O-G-O-L-O. Then something else, Tava. I don't know if this is male or female. One year ago he lost a lot of blood—always from the nose.

I: Who are you talking about? Who lost blood from his nose?

Fifty: Tava. I don't know. Tava, as it is written, used to lose blood from his nose.

I: Is that all?

Fifty: Yes. Now, wait a moment. Wait a moment.

I: Yes, yes. I'm waiting.

(different voice comes on the phone)

Voice: Are you looking after the interests of the Getty family?

I: Yes.

V: In that case, listen. What is this story?

I: What story? What story of what?

V: Be careful. Be careful, you and all the Getty family. You understand?

I: Yes.

V: Listen.

I: Yes. Hello. But you have to send this to me in writing— these . . .

V: I'm not going to send you a thing. I'll send you his body.

I: Well, in that case you don't want the money?

V: Listen; send it immediately.

I: But how?

V: Stop all this. Listen very carefully.

I: Yes, but the money—how?

V: Were these names sufficient, yes or no?

I: Yes, but the money. You have to tell us where we have to take the money. Show us that the boy is alive.

V: The boy is alive and if you want him dead, you can have him dead.

I: But we don't want him dead.

V: Together with him, the entire Getty family will be exterminated with this false and lying bullshit. With all the others, and you too—*avvocato*, my balls . . .

I: Yes, I understand.

V: You've got to stop with the press.

I: But the press invent everything. We can't stop the press. Anyway, you want the money—this fifty-three million . . .

V: Shove it up your ass, you and the whole of the Getty family.

I: All right. I understand. But what do you want?

V: Three billion. Three billion. Three billion. Three billion. Not a penny less, otherwise you will have his body and you will be the ones to kill him. Bastards, and I swear to you, and this is not idle anymore. I hope I have made myself clear.

I: I understand. How do you want the money? Where?

V: Exactly as it was explained in the letter. It's always been made clear in the letter. What do you want, an arm or a leg? If you want Paul dead, you can have him dead. It is you who will be killing him.

I: But after we bring you the money, when will you give us Paul?

V: Tell the mother she will be responsible for the death of her son.

I: Hello?

Five days after this phone call to the Inspector, a letter came to the lawyer's office and it was intercepted by Chace. It reiterated the substance of the phone call in still more violent terms.

The letter basically said:

With the two telephone calls to the lawyer you have had proof of the existence of Paul. Your son is in danger of death if you do not hurry and publicly go on television to state your intentions to pay the money, not fifty-six million, which was offered by that bastard of a lawyer or whoever did it through him. If you don't pay the three billion we have asked, you will not see your son alive again. We will send you a finger if you do not quickly make a decision whether or not you want to pay. If you don't want to pay, you will then receive an arm and a lock of hair and if you still don't want to pay it is finished forever. This interview in the press should affirm your intentions to pay the money—the amount of three billion. Make the interview whether you intend to pay or not. If you don't pay the money requested, you will be decreeing the death of Paul, because if you don't have remorse for your son, it could incite us to kill him. It's up to you whether you want him alive or dead.

To reinforce this letter to Gail, Paul was made to write a letter that was published in Il Messaggero *two days later, making the whole matter public:*

To *Il Messaggero:* I appeal to the press so that this letter can be published.

Dear Mother and Father, I beg you to pay to not have me killed. I have a great desire to live. I would never have believed that you don't care about me. I am also sick and have fever. I've had fever for ten days. I beg you again to get me out. I want to live. I beg you, I beg you, I beg you. My grandfather—please pay the money. You asked for the names of the dogs. Here they are. The details of the family that were requested on the telephone by the lawyer. I pray you once more—let me come out alive. Much love, Paul. The dogs are: Kamarad, Ping and Pong, Partogolo,

Brey, Stella, Gus. I heard that the lawyer said you don't care anything about me. I hope this is not true. I want to live.

Paul

Chace was working closely with the squadra mobile *detective and through him received information that only confirmed his suspicion of Paul and Gail.*

Chace (notes):

The Roman Squadra Mobile follows the tracks of Paul's contacts with the low-life of Rome. The boy was often seen in a restaurant frequented by Sergio Maccarelli, where he had even shown his paintings. There is talk, which isn't clarified, of contacts with an unidentified man from Marseille. The Getty family has launched an ultimatum. Either the kidnappers accept 250 million lire by the end of August, or they will do nothing at all.

Once more there was silence from the other side.

12.

Gail, still in London, had now had a second breakdown. This time it was unrehearsed and clearly shows the strain on her. It was the end of August, six weeks since Paul had disappeared, and there was no sign that they were any closer to a solution.

Gail:

Lou went back to Rome. Then a very dear friend of mine loaned me a great big house in Kensington. He ran an oil company for Armand Hammer, my friend. He went on holiday with his family. He said, "Take the house and do what you want."

I'm not sure exactly how it happened. I think Big Paul had one of his lucid moments and suddenly said, "Oh my goodness, of course the children can stay." It was probably something like, "It isn't a very good time for you, dear, but the children are more than welcome." So I sent the girls back to their father. His fifty-first birthday was coming up.

I didn't have any money. I couldn't get any money out of Italy. I didn't have anything, no money. I was alone. Lou, when he went back, sent me some money.

I went out to dinner with Donna, my sister-in-law, George d'Almeida, and some friends of theirs. It was an Italian restaurant at Kensington Gate or somewhere around there. I had a blue jean shirt on that I wore for good luck. It had been Little Paul's and I thought some kind of vibrations might rub off. I wore it all the time. Someone at the dinner said to me, "What a nice-looking shirt," and I burst into tears. I got up from the table, went into the loo. I went on for twenty or thirty minutes, sobbing hysterically. They finally got me out and I came back to the table and sat down. I got through a little bit more spaghetti with corn or whatever and then it happened again. George took me back to their house. Everybody was sitting round talking and it happened a third time. I went to bed. I shouldn't have been out, socially anyway.

I thought, This is crazy. What am I achieving here? I'm being crucified. I'm alone. My parents couldn't do anything. I was supposed to be here because they were trying to cool down the press. The whole plan just blew up in everybody's face.

Paul's friend Philip came up from Bath. He felt there should be a man in the house with me because I was absolutely, totally alone. Lou had gone back to Rome once we left the house in Kingston. The children were at their father's house. Donna was supposedly staying at her brother's but she would come over because nobody thought I should be alone.

Big Paul's birthday was September 7. The plan was to give him a really extensive party.

But then my parents called me and said that Fraser McKno had called them and told them that Paul was planning to take the children from me. If I had to go back to Rome, I shouldn't leave them with him. He wanted to take them from me. Chace may have been in on it too, because he called and said, "Be careful. I have a feeling Paul wants to take the children from you." So when I knew I really had to go back to Rome, I called Lou and I said, "I don't have a penny. Please do me a favor and send me some tickets." And he did. The children were with me. I had gotten them out. I called Paul from the house in Kensington and said I was leaving and taking the children with me. He said, "You can't do that. It's my birthday and I've been planning and they're so excited about staying. You promised me they could stay for my birthday." I said, "I'm taking them back." He said, "You can't do this, I'm their father too." I said, "I think it's better if I take them back with me." I didn't say then that I had heard that he wanted to take them but I should have. Today, Paul says that he absolutely never wanted to. What would he have done with them? So who told Fraser to call my parents and say he wanted the children? Apparently there was definitely something going on that Paul didn't know about.

He was terribly upset. I guess he couldn't figure out in God's name what I was doing. Why was I keeping his children from him? I wouldn't let them go over to the house anymore. But when you have two people telling you, and my mother and father panicking, my father saying, "Gail, Fraser says you have to be disloyal to Paul. He is up to something," what do you do?

Anyway, I said, "We're just going to go." And he said, "I'll show you who I am. They're my children too. You wait and see what I do."

By the stream in the mountains, things exploded in Paul's face. The tension that had been brewing within the gang burst out. It's not exactly clear what happened, whether the gang had grown suspicious of the Chipmunk or had been taken over by a different group altogether.

Paul:

Once, when he was crossing the stream, the Chipmunk thought I saw his face. He came up and said, "You saw me." But I hadn't. He said, "You bastard, you looked at me. I'm gonna tell the others. I'll have to leave you." He left. When he came back, he gave me a magazine article saying that my mother and Martine thought the whole thing was a hoax. He pleaded with me to tell the others that I did not see him, because otherwise they were going to kill him.

When the others came back they were very heavy and dark. One by one they came to me, they sat me out on a rock in the middle of the stream, with my back to them. I didn't know what was going on, I thought they were going to shoot me. "Did you see his face or didn't you? You have to tell us the truth." I did tell the truth, I didn't see him. I guess they had a big conference and they took the Chipmunk away. They told me that evening that they killed him. They said, "We're like cannibals, we kill ourselves so we can let you go."

I heard on the radio the next day that they found the burnt body of a man on the beach in Naples. He had been mutilated.

After Chipmunk was killed, everyone got paranoid. I got the feeling the chief was around. They started being mean to me. They were scared of one another. That's how I got the idea that they were recruited, because none of them got along. It was fine to be with one alone, but as soon as it was two, they'd show off who could be the meanest. They said to me, "Oh, you know when you were sitting out there, the chief wanted to blow your brains out and throw you in the water." Things that were really heavy.

After that I really didn't care. I tried to irritate them, turn up the radio when they were talking, that sort of thing. I didn't care anymore.

On the outside there was a collective gasp when the mutilated, half-burned corpse was found on the beach in Naples. Such finds can't be that unusual in a city so large and notoriously violent as Naples. But so involved in the day-to-day drama of the Getty kidnapping was Italy—and the world, for that matter—that it was immediately assumed that the body was Paul's, the "Golden Hippie," the "Oil Prince." Chace stepped in at once and, to Gail's relief, took over.

Chace (notes):

Well-roasted corpse found on the beach in Naples. Thought to be Paul's. Called police in Naples, requested measurements, determined instantly not Paul. Burned bodies shrivel, but corpse still too short. Paul is a very tall lad. This was a short man.

> *A short man. The Chipmunk was a short man. Perhaps that's something of a reach, but whatever the case Chace made a considerable concession at this point and as summer's heat loosened its grip on Rome and the mountains, the nights were cold.*
> *Chace (notes):*

Rome September 2nd, I've dropped the idea of trying to break them up and told them, "Okay. We'll pay the money: it must be a simultaneous exchange." We have moved away from the idea of no ransom at all. We have failed on the thrust of only paying expenses, trying to get the boy out, but now we will not pay the money unless it is a simultaneous exchange. I am working on devising plans and presenting them over the phone, looking at it from their point of view, how they could exchange the boy for money with complete protection against any ambush. One of them was obvious, they have lookouts along the road and then show me the boy at 100 yards. Someone along the road certifies I have the money then there is a car exchange. Variations of that.

> *From the start Gail tried desperately to persuade Chace this was a terrible idea. Whatever had happened in the mountains was reverberating in Rome. The kidnappers were getting worn down by Chace, and it would be Paul who paid the price.*

Gail:

Chace talked of simultaneous exchange. I pleaded with him to do it the Italian way. Do it their way. They have him. They have what we want. He said, "We have what they want." I tried to make him understand that what the kidnappers had was much more important than what we had.

Chace kept making battle plans, crossing bridges, passing behind cars: "You shoot him on a rock over this mountain and we'll shoot the money in the air." Have a meeting on a bridge, the boy brought out onto the middle of the bridge and bring the money on the other side of the bridge, then do the exchange and then shoot the kidnappers. Maybe it would have worked in some other world, some other country, or some other time.

When the body was found on the beach in Naples, the press were back at my door. They wanted to know, "Do you think that's your son, the young man who's just been killed in Naples?"

After I came back from London I talked to the kidnappers almost every day; they didn't trust Chace. Fifty said he preferred to talk to me, but we didn't seem to get anywhere.

I tried to explain to Fifty and the kidnappers that Big Paul had a lot of problems, health problems, emotional problems. His wife had died. But that, with all the goodwill in the world, he had changed his mind about paying. I tried to tell them not to believe things he had printed in the newspapers, because he was at the end of his rope too. Fifty said to me, "Why haven't you told me things about the family before?" I said, "Possibly because I think families are pretty private things. If we didn't have to go into any of our particular relationships, wouldn't it be better?" He said, "It would have been better if we'd understood." But who has the time to explain all that kind of thing?

I used to wonder if Paul had tried to explain it to them. I said, "Hasn't Paul told you anything?" And Fifty said, "Some things, but we should hear these things from you."

I continued to talk with Fifty even after Iacovoni was given as the contact. He would call Iacovoni sometimes, and sometimes he would call me. He and I had long conversations. "We want to talk to you.

We don't want Fletcher Chace. We don't trust him. We trust you. You're the boy's mother, you have his interest at heart."

I would have liked to meet Fifty. Sometimes he felt so sorry for us, so at a loss. Sometimes he was terribly human, he called and said they had a meeting and they had a vote—most everybody wanted to kill Paul and there were a few who said no, but if things don't improve, even the ones who were saving him were going to go. He was really upset, really sad. Sometimes we used to yell and scream at each other. But no one could have anticipated the amount of time it was taking, the amount of suffering. I'm sure Fifty suffered personally— their lives were all messed-up.

At this point, our kidnappers—Fifty and the group—were coinciding with this other group in Germany. We had letters, and we couldn't decide if the letters were from the Munich group or not. At this point, we thought Paul was being held by them. They were very consistent. They had come in right at the beginning and they kept calling and writing. They wanted me to bring the money to Munich in two red suitcases. We were very tempted.

Fifty was beside himself, he figured the money was going to go to Munich. He yelled, "No. It's us. We're the real kidnappers. You've got to believe me."

A few days after the kidnappers first called and after it was in all the papers, an operator called and asked me if I would like to arrange a conference call between, what's her name? Joey Heatherton, a well-known Hollywood actress who was married to the Texan football player Lance Rentzel, who had exposed himself to a ten-year-old girl, and a third party. I said, "I've heard of this actress, but I don't know her or the girl. Why do they want to talk to me?" The operator said, "Will you accept a conference call?" I didn't know what a conference call was. The operator tried to explain it to me but it all fell apart.

Then I had a collect call from the girl, the girl in Texas, half saccharine, half threatening. She said she knew where Paul was. She wanted me to fly her sister in from Texas, hinting it would be very nice if I was clever enough to give this lovely young girl a home for about a year, because if I did, she might tell me some very interesting things. It was weird. I don't think the phone was tapped at that time, so I had to try to remember everything she said. I said, "I've got enough problems right now without some girls in Texas trying to use me for money and plane tickets. If you have something to say, tell me. If I think there's something in it, I'll bring you here, but I'm not going to bring you here on some nonsense—I don't have that kind of money." She said, "It is very interesting information, we think possibly we could help let you know where Paul is, or at least who has him. We know it's a serious kidnapping. Do you know that?" I said, "Yes, I know that. Do you know that?"

I put it over to the FBI. Then the girl called me again. I didn't know whether or not to accept the call, but her message was intriguing. She was afraid. All she could say was she had been present at a meeting where they discussed plans to kidnap Paul. She was afraid she knew too much and of what was going to happen. That was the last time I heard from her. The FBI looked into it and decided it was just a pair of nuts. I don't know. I had a lot of phone calls, and it really sounded like they knew where he was. They may somehow have been involved in an early discussion with some gangster who had the idea. They didn't arrest anybody. Joey Heatherton's name never came into it again. I don't know what that was.

Then came a letter from Paraguay all in Spanish. They said, "We have your son," and how much money they wanted, how to take care of the delivery. Then came a fine nut from Canada, who had apparently been released from an institution a few weeks before. There were lots of phone calls from him.

Then a boy who had suffered an amnesia attack was found in an American church in Paris. The people who ran the church had seen photographs; this boy didn't know who he was. Maybe it was Paul. That was a huge hope, although really I knew perfectly well Paul was somewhere in Italy.

A few days later Margarita, Iacovoni's secretary, took a telephone call from a man who wanted to set up a meeting with Mario, the Getty chauffeur, at Ladispoli, Old Paul's villa:

Man: Tell Mario he is to meet me at the end of the Alessandro Farnese in his car.

Margarita: What car?

Man: In his car. I know his car and I'll know him. He's to meet me there on the corner between Corrienzo and Alessandro Farnese. If something happens and we don't make contact, he should go back to the office and I'll contact him by phone.

The supposed kidnapper told Margarita that they were going to show Paul to Mario and everything was supposed to go through Mario. Margarita told the caller she had been instructed that the family wanted prior assurance that these people were real and gave the caller the list of detailed questions that Iacovoni had previously asked Fifty, questions that only the boy could answer. They warned Margarita that it would take time and said they would call back.
Immediately afterward, Fifty called:

Fifty: I would like to speak to Avvocato Iacovoni.

M: Avvocato Iacovoni is not here. Is it about those particular questions?

Fifty: Yes.

M: Well, you'd better call Mario.

Fifty: What Mario. Who is Mario?

M: You know, Mario. We gave you the number.

Fifty: No, no, I don't know anything about him. I want to talk to Avvocato Iacovoni. Where is he?

M: Just a minute. The door's ringing. Maybe he's coming up the stairs.

Margarita ran and got Iacovoni's cousin, who was next door, and brought him to the phone. The cousin had no idea it was the real kidnappers and was extremely rude to Fifty, who was getting madder by the minute.

Cousin: Avvocato Iacovoni is not here! You've already spoken.
      You already have the number.
Fifty: What number? I don't have any number.
C: Yes, you do—Mario's number.
Fifty: I don't have Mario's number. I don't know who Mario
      is. I want to speak to Avvocato Iacovoni.
C: If it's about a personal matter, you're just going to have to
   wait.
Fifty: It *is* a personal matter. I would like to speak to him.
C: You're just going to have to wait two or three days or call
   that number we gave you.
Fifty: But I don't have any other number.

They went back and forth at each other and finally the cousin said, "You'll have to wait two or three days," and hung up.

Two weeks later, on September 17, the kidnappers had finally changed their tune and agreed to meet with Chace.

Chace:

One of the Calabresi wanted me to meet with him on his turf, under his control, and I was ready to go. He wanted me to bring a priest. I went to see the archbishop from Chicago, who was visiting Rome, a friend of Ed Daley's. He refused. He sent me to another priest; this one wanted to be a hero and go with me. A lot of people wanted to be heroes in those days, volunteering themselves as hostages, intermediaries, to be a warm body. We even had a girl begging to take

Paul's place. I went to call on this priest myself. He lived in a very nice house, but when I said, "We're all set to go," he got cold feet and changed his mind. He didn't want to be a hero. I offered to go alone, but the Calabresi refused.

In the mountains the nights were becoming intolerably cold and the kidnappers were growing tired of having their supply lines so stretched. It wasn't clear what had happened by the stream, but a new and different cadre appeared, and Paul's treatment grew worse as the kidnappers, or at least their soldiers, built up more and more resentment.

Paul:

After the thing with the Chipmunk, that was the end, and they started getting cold and they said we would have to go farther down. We left the stream in the morning.

We climbed out of the gorge and we walked down, and then up the ridge the whole day to this cave. We arrived in the night. It must be a six-kilometer-long ridge with all these little caves. There's a path this size, and then down, I happened to see the drop once—it must have been three hundred or four hundred feet. They found a cave. It was so small that I couldn't lie on my back except on one side, because the other guy had to sleep next to me. We had to sleep side by side on our sides.

During the day they were outside. I think they were out having fun and I could have just walked out of there. They told me they would shoot me if I did, but I think they trusted me so much that they'd just leave, because they'd leave the cave early in the morning. They had very straight hours, leave in the morning, back in the evening. I'd listen to American radio, and do my own food; not cook, but I had things I could mix together—tuna fish and tomato. Every other day they would bring me hot food, like spaghetti, which was a real treat, you know it's really incredible the way nothing excites you anymore, but I got into this whole trip, a ritual of just eating pasta. You really appreciate the little things in life. I would spend hours and hours on spaghetti, save some for later.

All the caves were man-made. I must have stayed in ten different ones, mostly a clay sort of thing. There's a flap down there, mountains on the other side where I came across from. Down is the swamp and the river at the bottom, and it goes up here. The first cave was terrifying. I'm not joking: it was only this high, and as long as me. That was the smallest one. They said, "This is going to be your final resting place. Isn't this great? All we have to do if you do something is bury you right here." You can't believe what it is to be in a thing this high, the paranoia that it put me in. I couldn't turn around. You're facing inwards, so they can just shoot you. They covered the hole with leaves and things. They said that this was at the top of the cliff and there was a guy on top and a guy at the bottom who would shoot me if I tried to get out.

There was friction between all the guys. They had come to really hate and despise me. They took my radio away. Piccolo said to me, "Please try to escape. We can use that as an excuse to kill you, you fucking little rich smut."

The next afternoon I heard ladies singing on the road right down the hill from the cave. Piccolo tore in and said, "You bastard." He dragged me out and stayed like this against me until the women passed because one can tell the songs and the accent exactly; each little town has their accent. She passed. He was furious with me because I had pretended not to hear, I was crying and I said, "Please, change the place." That was when they started stuffing wax in my ears, but really with such hate, pushing it in with a pencil. I guess I did convince them to move me because the day after they took me to a cave right nearby.

This cave was a large one, very long, different passages with the

1945 Army jeep inside it. They told me it was where they had kept artillery and cannons during the war. That's how I worked out the idea with Marcello about where this was. We figured out it must be a defense place, a strategic point, and it's quite obvious it must have been a place resisting the allied invasion. I don't want you to write this down, but I think it was the town of Madonna Dell Etna or something like that.

I was quite free in this cave, I had my own room and bed at the back of it and they were down on the other side. One night they had a very big dinner. Things seemed to be okay then; they ate little birds, turkey, the best Chianti, '66 wine, pasta, candles, tablecloth—the whole thing. They were all there that night—all the guards, like, seven of them, drinking and dancing till the early hours. They had a tape player. I went off to sleep and they told me we were going to move the next day, but we didn't. We must have stayed there quite a while.

Piccolo left to see his family. I don't know why, but one day soon after they said, "We're scared you're going to run away, so a mean guy is going to come." This mean guy must have stayed five nights with no break the whole time. He was trying to scare me psychologically. He walked up and down. It echoed. The echo in this cave was strange. He spent the day loading and reloading his pistol, cleaning it, making noises to scare me. He only fed me every other day, hard bread. He only gave me a little water. He hit me and pushed me around. He must have hated me. He didn't speak a word for days. Then he said, "I'm going to get your mother. Do you want to see your mother?" He talked like a drug freak. The only other time I heard his voice was when the guys would come down to ask what supplies he needed. That's the only thing I heard him say, *"Porta un po di vino."* Except he said "bino," like a South American—he talka like dis, you know? That's why I call him VB1. He made all the telephone calls. In the end, I got that guy who was mean in trouble. I said, "Hey, people, it's ridiculous this guy trying to scare me so much psychologically." They said, "Don't worry. I'll protect you." And he never came again.

Then the other South American–sounding guy who I made the connection with came, VB2. I'm sure I had met one of these VB guys at Marcello's. South Americans run the whole coke scene in Rome. He showed off by pulling all this money out of his pocket. He tried to freak me out. I went to my room, but he was making so much noise I couldn't sleep, so I went back in and told him, "Get out." We had a fight. I don't know if they ever caught him, I don't think so. It shows how fucked-up the police are. They had his voice from the phone calls, but they never recorded and printed them. I have so much proof, like that VB2 snores. They could go outside his cell at night and see if he snores, but they don't want to.

I didn't know anything at that time, no information. I still didn't have my radio, so what I'd do is say, "I had a dream," and I would say what I thought was happening. He told me his dreams. We did this every day, just VB2 and me comparing dreams. I would make up wild fantasy dreams and he'd make up sexual dreams. I liked him until the day he said, "I had a dream I fucked a woman and my cock was as big as a *manganello*." A *manganello* is a policeman's nightstick; it was an expression the Fascists used. If you think about a cock as weapon it relates to violence and ignorance. So I said, "I don't want to hear." We never spoke again.

Then Piccolo came back. He was nicer to me. I said, "Let's try to get it together as we were." It's strange, but really I could say anything to him. It was the kind of relationship where we could say, "I know it's not your fault." He told me everything about his family and his children. The guy had spent three months in the mountains with me and hadn't seen his children. That must have frustrated him. I knew everything about these guys' families. It would be interesting to do a chapter about them.

One day Piccolo said, "Paolo, I think I'm going to let you go." He said, "I want to get out of this. It's going to take too long." I was sure, as well, that it was never going to end. So I said, "I'll pay you something." He said he would take me away, do it separately from the others for fifty million. I would have done everything with him.

Then he said, "I'm just going to let you go. I want to get back to my family." He said, "Do you know how much I'm getting for this? Two million. To spend months with you in the mountains is not worth it." So he said, "We'll wait until the guys come down and I'll take them around the corner. I'll make some kind of sign and you run. I'll have to do it when they're around or they'll think I let you go." I was sure he would do it, but he never did. If he had trusted me, I would have trusted him.

At this point in the kidnapping several elements, real or imagined, seemed to collide.

Chace (notes):

September 17th: The man Mario calls Bruno, who claims to be a disaffected gang member, met us in Campo Di Fiore [*sic*] at 12:15. He's a tough little guy, dark, like he worked outdoors, Sicilian maybe. I don't think his name is really Bruno. I gave him a little money yesterday and I gave him the balance when I met him today, $600.

I told him, "Look, if you're pulling my leg, it's a game, don't waste my time. Disappear any time. Now go make your first phone call and go out the back door of the bar and take off for all I care. I don't want to spend a whole day playing games with you. Here's your money. If you're playing games, conning me. If you're not playing games let's try and do it right."

I didn't want to waste an afternoon. He told me we had to go to Monte Casino [*sic*]. Brought Mario as driver and interpreter. I notified the police in the car, I went down the *autostrada*. The police could have stopped me at the gate but they didn't identify me. We drove down to Monte Casino. I sat in the back seat and Mario drove with

Bruno in the front. He was friendly. He said that when he was a young man he was involved in a personal vendetta and killed somebody, so it had always been a life of crime. He was forced into it, that was the way it was where he came from. He told me he had been in jail and he showed me his parole report—his pink book from the police showing he had been in jail. He said that two or three times he had gotten jobs as an earth moving equipment operator. We passed a yard with earth moving equipment stored out there and I asked him, "What's the name of that piece of equipment and how do you use it?" Based on my own knowledge I think Bruno was telling the truth when he said he was a heavy equipment operator. He asked me if I could give him a job. He would like to leave Italy and work for an American company. Several times during the day he called into where Paul was being held. At one point driving high in the mountains in the Monte Casino area he said that Paul was in one of the houses up there. We stopped in Monte Casino and he phoned his contact. Mario monitored his calls. He talked to a man he said was called Franco who was with Paul and somebody else on watch. He said that he and Franco had been the ones who left Rome with Paul, he described the car correctly. Bruno said that when the other man left in the evening, Franco would bring Paul down to meet me at the bar. He said I should give Franco $600 too. Bruno left convinced it was all set and he said he was going to leave and he did. I wished him lots of luck in his future life and he said he was sure Paul would be down because the other guy was going to go and get some groceries and Franco would be alone with the boy. I waited in the street watching the bar until it got dark and then drove back to Rome. I thought I had Paul but I didn't. Nothing came of it. Paul never appeared. That was the end of that one.

Chace didn't appear to flinch. He simply fell back to the idea of simultaneous exchange and came up with a plan he considered a masterpiece:

On September twenty-third I propose a new plan to Fifty. One man should come across a footbridge over a chasm with Paul. I come out from the other end with the money and exchange it for the boy. They would have the better side as far as getting away from the area, and I'd be on the footbridge with the boy and couldn't be following with my people.

They took all the plans that I made and processed them through their councils. They came back and reported on them; it took time to develop these things, argue them out, and finally they'd reject them—reject them for flaws, not outright. They were considering simultaneous exchange. They didn't like the idea of simultaneous exchange, and when they took my proposals back, they picked them apart. This was the steady grind of the negotiations as they went on.

Chace's uncharacteristic patience in these negotiations seems to reflect his determination not to be bested by these brigands and to demonstrate to Old Paul that the two of them were indeed peas in a pod when it came to parsimony. Chace had given up on Gail at this point and found himself a girlfriend, a Roman socialite whose apartment was not far from the Eden Hotel.

However, the kidnappers had no such patience, as they made clear in a letter to Il Messaggero *published in the newspaper October 5:*

We beg you to publish our ultimatum. The Getty family has fifteen days to find the money for Paul's release. The fifteen days will begin from the day on which this ultimatum will be published in *Il Messaggero*. At the end of this period maybe it will be you yourself who will open the letter containing an ear with a lock of hair from Paul. After which if they don't hurry up and bring the money, Paul will be killed. His family has offered a sum which is unacceptable, as though they were one of the poorest families in the world. Therefore we are now decided to end it in one way or another. After the fact that they have not kept their appointment, we will now pass to hard facts. Now, if they want Paul they have to say so seriously. In order to not lose any more time they will have to accept our conditions:

To do an interview and publicly accept the offer on our terms, not theirs. We, in our turn, will let them know the way and the place for the delivery of the money. When this has taken place Paul will be released after three or four days. We have committed a crime with great risk and we know what to expect and one crime is worth another. Therefore, either the offer is accepted immediately or else as above said just as well—first we will kill and we won't think twice about it. The crime will come of its own without the right amount of money.

P.S. We have always used Paul's handwriting in order to run less risk.

Paul heard this ultimatum over the radio and the kidnappers moved him from the caves down the hill to a house in preparation for mayhem. There was running water in the house and apparently a telephone.

Paul:

Then we moved to the house. I'll make a little diagram. The area was an olive-growing area, and this is where they kept the tools, right? Not very old, light-colored; from the outside it looked very modern, but still fucked-up with the cement not painted. Inside, it looked like a castle—the walls were this thick. People must have slept there sometimes because there was a bed. On the other side of the bed was a wooden chopping block, where I ate every day. I would eat on that side of the bed and the door was there. The door was tall, and on the other side was a corridor.

The walls were cement. The chopping block I sat down on was where they killed pigs, too. There were spots of blood and shit all over. The floor was dirt. There was a window with shutters. They were closed, so it was dim. Very high ceiling, about twelve feet. Large. Completely empty, a lot of flypaper. There was a little Madonna picture over the bed, Mother Protector, with the name of the town, Sallopaco, written. The room was dark; they never saw it.

They spent the day in the next room, probably a garage. Here was the entrance. The entrance itself must have been half the size of the room. It was more like a large corridor. They had done it up. They were like ladies, these people. It was like a real little house with shelves with pasta and all kinds of food on them and white wine. They cooked there each day—big soups. They were excellent cooks. We even had chickens. The chickens stayed in the room with me. I had battles with them. I never ate so much chicken.

They must have been so bored. They organized this whole thing where I was to tell a story. I had my back to, like, ten people, and one of them was the boss. They told me that the story better be good, because they had told him that it was *sooo* good, and I thought, Oh my God.

13.

The kidnappers were clearly not enthusiastic over the idea of mutilating their captive. When there was some confusion over the dog Tava, which Paul had reported as "bleeding from the mouth," the kidnappers seemed to pick up on the idea and, working on evident concern that the boy was unwell, reported as much to Gail. She then agreed to meet with them. Chace saw this as an opportunity to get rough with the kidnappers. Once more he was oblivious to the fact that Paul was in the middle, whatever he had done.

Gail:

A note came to Iacovoni's office saying "Paul is bleeding from the mouth." Apparently he was hemorrhaging—coughing up blood. They were referring to his being ill at that point.

I wanted to go and see him, with someone if possible, but I wouldn't want to go to try and capture them. Chace was still trying to convince me: "If we could get one or two of them, we could break them down." I didn't want to know about that. I wasn't interested.

Once again the kidnappers prepared to meet with the family. They clearly expected to be ambushed and made plans accordingly. Paul's words make clear at that point how strong had become the Stockholm syndrome, as the interdependency between captive and captor is known, and how much Paul's freedom depended on the kidnappers' success.

Paul:

They were nice to me the day they moved me down to the house. That night we had a discussion. There were lots of people involved but only Piccolo asked me the questions. And the next day they made me write another letter. "This is the last thing we can do to help you," they told me. So I wrote a letter to Iacovoni with a copy to my mother. All letters were addressed to Iacovoni. One to the lawyer and one to my mother. I think I had written about twenty or thirty letters in all. I said, "I can't understand. How can you do this? I wish I had been the son of an *operaio,* a workman, instead. You've been cruel to me. I'm not going to ask you for help again. I just want an answer yes or no." When the bandits called, they said no letter had arrived. They didn't respond at all.

But then they said they had made an appointment with my mother. I helped them arrange it, I told them what kind of car my mother drove, the license plate, what kind of tricks to watch out for if Chace was coming. I really believed it would work. She was to drive south on the *autostrada.* They organized it all with my mother, and they were going to meet miles away. The day Iacovoni and my mother were going to meet the kidnappers they moved me down to the swamp, near the house. All of them went off to the meeting with my mother, I think—maybe they left one guy with me. There was very weird vegetation in that area, and strange rocks with moss that haven't been moved in years, damp, flat, and tall—tall bamboo. It was cold, freezing, but then you stick your hand above the bamboo and it was hot.

But my mother didn't come. So then they said, "Okay tomorrow." They really didn't want to do it, but my mother didn't come the next day. We were all disillusioned. Once, okay, but twice? Then they phoned her and she said to them, "Why should I believe you, I can't trust you." That's what really pissed me off, you know. You can mess with them, but you can't insult them, you have to treat them right.

So now they said, "Okay, we'll have to do it." And I said, "When?" And they said, "We don't exactly know. We have to get some medical things together." They said, "About a week." So I waited. They kept saying, "Tomorrow, tomorrow." And then they finally said "Okay." They said, "We can wait more if you want," but I said, "Let's do it." I said I thought it was the only way. I'd still be there if they hadn't done it. So they said, "Okay, okay, okay."

That Gail agreed to drive for hours in the middle of the night to meet with the kidnappers was surely a measure of her desperation.

Gail:

We arranged for me to meet the kidnappers because we felt we weren't getting anywhere. They felt it and I felt it. They were terribly concerned about minute details. I had to bring my car. I had an Opel station wagon—it was beat up, the tires weren't so good, and I didn't have the proper licensing. They told me to put a Cynar sign on the front bumper so they could recognize the car, and leave at eight in the morning. I was told to take the *autostrada* south towards Naples, drive a certain way, never to exceed a certain speed, eighty kilometers.

They wouldn't let me see Paul. I begged them. I said, "Please let me see him. Please bring him." They refused. I said, "My car isn't in very good condition and I'm not lying to you. It really isn't." We argued back and forth. They said rent one and tell us what kind of car it is. I said, "Fine with me. We will talk before I leave." I was prepared to leave in the middle of the night. I didn't care, although, at this point I honestly didn't think I was capable of driving a car and I was afraid I'd find myself halfway there on the floor of the car. We had established that I was coming, but I wasn't really very pleased with various aspects of the meeting.

They also insisted I come alone. I wanted to meet them. I wanted to go but they wouldn't allow anyone to come with me. I agreed to go by myself, but Chace wouldn't let me. He said it was the biggest trap I could possibly walk into. He said no. They were to call me back first or we were supposed to speak again, but we never did.

It was Iacovoni who suggested a solution to the disappointment at the failure of this meeting. These people, the kidnappers, the Calabrese, might not be God-fearing, but they came from a Catholic region and undoubtedly respected the sanctity of the confessional, even if for them they were outside Italy. On October 15, the lawyer recorded from his office in Rome:

The Calabrese telephoned. I had a long conversation with him and I tried to convince him to go to a priest in any large city of his own choice. The priest could then go to another priest, or directly to us. I explained to the Calabrese that the priest has to keep the secret of the confessional and that never ever in history has this secret been betrayed. The Calabrese refused, but not categorically. I therefore proposed that I organize a meeting between him and a priest of the Getty family, a Mexican, a certain Don Pedro that Paul knew well. The Calabrese agreed. I therefore invited him to telephone directly to the house of Signora Gail and I told Gail that they would call around four-thirty P.M.

A second meeting was arranged. In the course of doing so, the kidnappers again threatened mayhem, but neither Gail nor Chace believed them.

Gail:

I was to meet them within the boundaries of the city of Rome. A monsignor was going to go with me if they accepted, because they refused Chace. They didn't want to know him, see him. They didn't trust him. I talked to this monsignor friend and asked him, "Would you need special permission to come with me or to talk to these people for me?" He said it really depended on what he had to do, but he would like to. He spoke on the phone to the kidnappers, and told me they were asking much too much. That they wanted everything their way, and that it was a very dangerous situation. He concluded that if they'd meet him or me in a place where we felt safe, then okay. The meeting was only to finally establish a price. He said they told him that if we didn't pay, they were going to cut Paul's ear off and mail it to us.

I thought it was part of their whole bullshit thing. I just didn't believe that they'd cut somebody's ear off. If this had been the first time they'd threatened mutilation, perhaps I would have. But they had been crying wolf, ranting and raving. "Hey, we're going to get Iacovoni." They were going to get his child. They were going to get everybody, the whole family, total hysteria. Chace agreed with me. So again the whole thing collapsed.

They were wrong.

Paul:

About a week passed. I was trying, I was, to be tough. I would imagine the pain and try to think of a way to make it easier for them to do it. They were going to do it with scissors; that would have been just agony. I think three days before they did it, they said, "We're going to do it tonight," but they didn't. The next day they washed me and disinfected me. That's why my hair, you can see my hair is a little bit shorter here. And they shaved it right around there and cleaned it. They put me in bed and I knew it was happening because they brought me the radio back.

They had taken the radio away for a long time and they brought it back that morning, so I knew. You know, they really liked to make me happy. It was a different one. It was a red one—bright red. The first one, the guy broke. So that day, I was really, really happy. They brought me newspapers and I felt really good with these guys. They opened the windows while I was writing a letter. Piccolo promised me, "Three days after the ear is cut off, we swear to release you." I listened to the radio for the whole day—it seemed like ages. I projected myself to the day after.

They told me it would happen at seven o'clock, and it didn't. I waited. Nothing happened.

October 21 . . .

Paul:

About four in the morning they cooked me four steaks. They said, "This is to help you." I ate them all. They didn't eat. They said, "We just can't. We feel so upset about this." At about seven o'clock in the morning, three hours after I had eaten, I heard them come in and I heard all these sounds. They said, "Okay. It's now." They said to me, "Do you want to hold off for a couple of days?" And I said, "No. Get on with it." They said, "Get up."

They said, "Paul, blindfold yourself." I could have put it on so I could see them, but I didn't. They said, "Blindfold yourself and sit on this thing."

So I put it on and sat down on the chopping block. I was quite petrified and all I said was, *Paul, think tomorrow—what it will be like tomorrow.* I was sure that the day after—I was sure that I would feel great. Piccolo said, "Do you want anything?"

Some people came in the room and I knew what was going on. There must have been about seven people in the room. I heard the clink of the surgical things and the plastic. Piccolo was sadistic. I would have been too, the way the whole thing was. He started to hate everybody. Piccolo was the only one who talked. They had a candle. I could tell by the flicker of light. Piccolo told someone, "Prepare the cotton and that red stuff"—iodine. I said, "Can I have a handkerchief?" I rolled it up and put it in my mouth like a gag. I said, "Is it going to hurt?" and Piccolo said, "Of course it's going to hurt." Another man, I'd never heard his voice before, told Piccolo, "Don't be like that to him." I said, *"Io capisco."* I told him I understand, and they all laughed. I said, "You can do it," so they pulled back my shirt.

He moved my blindfold out of the way, just like this. I put my head up and I said, "Do it. Quickly." He rested the razor on my ear. He played around and held it there. There was a sound like ripping paper. It was done in two strokes. The noise was the worst thing.

There's a limit to pain. If you prepare yourself, you can withstand it. Because of this there was no pain. I said, "Are you finished?"

He said, "Yes, we have already finished." There wasn't much blood. Then I could hear them bringing in all this stuff, and they put alcohol on it, and, oh Jesus, that just flipped me out and everybody was saying, "Ah, you're so brave, so brave." Then they bandaged me up, big whole thing like in those Polaroid pictures you've seen—a whole construction. Then they said, "Lie on your side on the bed." So I lay on the bed, and they gave me an anti-tetanus shot and a penicillin shot, and now I felt exactly like I knew I was going to feel. I lay down on the bed and in about half and hour I began to bleed. I bled so much and I felt worse than I ever felt. Then in two hours I got scared. It was coming out normally, but after about five hours of continuous bleeding, it came out in, like, jelly. I had to lie down, I couldn't move. They started to get scared. They gave me about six shots an hour of penicillin. I only found out after that I'm completely allergic to it. I can die from penicillin. I got really flipped out from the smell.

I asked, "Can you take this off?" and they took the blindfold off and they were right there and I could have raised my eyes like that, but I didn't want to look. The smell, I can still smell the smell. So much blood and gooeyness, it was in my hair, all over my body, down my back, the whole thing. It couldn't cure itself, because if I just touched it like that, it started bleeding again. There was blood all over the room. They started giving me another kind of shot, a coagulant. I told them, "I have to shit." Normally I was only allowed to shit at night, so they brought in this big pail and carried me to it, and I shit and I felt sick and I vomited. I fell down on the floor and they carried me back onto the bed and by that time I had been bleeding for seventeen hours straight. I had to go to the bathroom again. I got up and everything just went—I promise you, acid is nothing—blood on the walls. For a long time after I could see the blood on the walls. I freaked out. They told me I would be all right. But I had almost no feeling left. Everything was just vomiting, vomiting and screaming, screaming. I was absolutely mad from loss of blood. I was so weak, just so weak, incredibly weak and the vomiting was all over the place. I couldn't eat. But it stopped after about a day and a half, the bleeding and the vomiting.

They never changed the bandage again. They probably would

have, but if they took it off, the scab would have come off and it would have started again.

The kidnappers called Gail and told her what they had done. She didn't believe them.

Gail:

They kept calling, panic-stricken. They told me they've cut off his ear, and he's bleeding and he's hemorrhaging. I thought they were putting me on. They always talked about mutilation. They had threatened so many times—not only Mr. Fifty, but another man. They had from the very beginning threatened every kind of possible mutilation. Now they say he was dying, but how did one know? I said, "Let me come and see him. Let me come and take care of him." But they refused.

In the mountains Paul's nightmare grew worse.

Paul:

The day after, my head felt like a box. The bandage, my body, the bed, everything, everything was completely red. And always the smell. The smell, rats; rats came in and ate the jelly blood off the floor. They were on my bandages.

By the third day I was sure I was going to die. However, on that day I started to eat, but I couldn't open my mouth. They'd bandaged me so I couldn't open it. I could only eat with a straw. I had very good food at that time, little warm soups that I drank through the straw, and fruit juices and milk. Finally they came and they said, "We spoke to them. We've come to an agreement."

Then they moved me to another house. They carried me over some very weird no-man's-land, covered in ash.

What happened next remains obscure. The kidnappers may have had reason to fear they had been in one place too long or were concerned that word might have leaked out in some other way, but in either case, they were now pinpointed by the man who had called himself Bruno. On October 29, Iacovoni received a letter. The handwriting was crude, the Italian very poor:

I, the undersigned, declare that I have nothing to do with the kidnapping of Paul Getty and I have never taken part because I don't want any trouble with the forces of justice. However, I knew about the kidnapping and up till now I have been quiet. Instead now I want to talk because I'm fed up of the whole business and now I want to tell you where you can find Paul and that Paul is well. The place that he is to be found is in the province of Caserta. He is to be found precisely in the village that is called Sallopaco near the old windmill—that is in an abandoned house. Also the owner of the house is an accomplice. He is thirty-three years old. But now, however, you have to be careful because he is dangerous and they are all armed with pistols and sawn-off shotguns and they won't stop at anything. I can say no more than this. Now I can't remember anything else and I am ready to be on the part of the law and I hope that my name is never mentioned because otherwise certainly I am a dead man. With thanks.

Iacovoni handed this letter over to Chace. In his dry, xenophobic fashion, Chace's notes recorded his speculation about what he imagined happened next.
  Chace (notes):

Informed Carabinieri Captain Martino Elisco of the contents of this letter. He has located house, so he says, outside Sallapaco [sic]. Small town in mountains. Captain Elisco says he took his people there arriving approx. 4:30 A.M., but then sent for coffee, fearing confusion if they approached in dark. It was daylight before they had coffee, according to the captain. It was agreed approaching house in daylight was too dangerous, better to wait 'til after lunch when the occupiers would be sleeping off wine and food. Elisco and his men ate a large lunch, then didn't feel ready for an attack. They finally advanced at dusk, and found the house empty. No wonder Italians made such terrible Nazis.

Upon Paul's seventeenth birthday, November 4, no ear had arrived, and the kidnappers were beside themselves with rage. Chace was still talking about a simultaneous exchange and the police were still trying to trace Fifty's phone calls, so Gail took matters into her own hands and forced the pace.

Gail:

Fifty kept calling. "Have you received the ear?" I kept saying to him, "Honestly we haven't. Why would I lie to you? How could we hide it from you anyway?" They thought the family had bought *Il Messaggero*.

They kept saying, "You're lying to us. You have it. You don't want to admit it. You're doing it for reasons that we don't understand." Everyone figured that if they had done it, then it would arrive, but it hadn't arrived, and they had cried wolf for so long. Deep, deep down I really knew it was going to come. Every day I'd waken with the fear that it was going to arrive today. I really didn't know what to do. Chace was pushing me heavily, saying, "They keep saying they've cut the ear off, nothing has arrived, but something has happened, the situation has changed drastically."

Chace said, "If this is true, and maybe it is, should we not be prepared?" I got together all the photos of Paul I could, and we looked at them. We checked the shape of the top, looked at how the lobe was attached, how long it was, how the two ears differed, how they were in connection to the head.

I really longed for an ear to arrive because I felt that if there wasn't some kind of shock, what was going to happen? How many years was Paul going to sit there? If something didn't happen to jolt "the family" into action, we were just going to go on and on and he was going to be there suffering.

The kidnappers were angry. There was no understanding or warmth. They thought we were lying, that we had received the ear, but we really hadn't. The kidnapper V said to me, "I know you have it, I put it in the post box."

When I heard that, I just went wild. "You horrible beasts, animals, you put an ear in a post box?"

Finally, in desperation I told Fifty we had the money. I told him we'd pay the three million dollars. They believed me, I even told them where it was and I told Fifty we had to work out the details of the drop. Anything to stall for time. Now we had to find the money and find it fast. Fifty said Paul had really wanted to be out by his birthday. I told him, "We all did."

The police were still trying to trace Fifty. They set up another phone with a recorder or something and I had to get him to call me back on that other number. He was calling at random times, so I had to stay in the apartment all the time. I couldn't leave. So I told them, "I have to take my other children to school at such-and-such a time and I have to fetch them at another time. So please don't call me then or, if you have to, let me know, I'll work out something else." I had to keep Fifty on this other phone for ten minutes. So I'd say, "Excuse me, I haven't understood. How are we going to do this?" Anything, repeating things over and over again, telling him how much each sack weighed, telling him not to be worried, everything was going to go all right, the money was going to be delivered, there were no police involved, that it would all be fine. Once the police did trace Fifty—he was calling from a phone box in Naples, but he got nervous and broke off.

I called my father. "What do you think? Please help. Please tell me if I've lost my mind." He had a conference with the FBI director, who said, "Hold Chace off."

Gail's father, Judge Harris, turned to his attorney, Martin McInnis, and asked him to explore every possibility, because the money was there in abundance. McInnis in his dry legal language recounted:

I wrote to Fletcher Chace telling him that we intended to use the Sarah C. Getty Trust to get the ransom money for J. Paul Getty III. We pointed out to J. Paul Getty that if he was disposed to paying the ransom, he could take it out of the trust rather than paying it himself. It would be a tax deduction because the trust, like other trusts, contains a provision for invasion of corpus in the event of an emergency. So the payment of funds from that source would not represent income to anybody. The letter was sent to Chace, who replied that there was no wish to take this course of action. I sent a copy of this letter to J. Paul Getty, but I didn't receive a reply.

Finally, the thing Gail both feared and hoped for occurred.

Gail:

On the night of the tenth, a week after Paul's birthday, a man from *Il Messaggero* called me: A package had arrived, would I come down? I didn't trust these people, the press, and anyway I don't think I believed it or didn't want to because I said, "If the police call me and say they have my son's ear or whatever is in the package, then I will go. But because *you* tell me, I won't accept that." I hung up and called Masone, the *squadra mobile* detective, and asked him if it was true that something had arrived. We almost had a fight, we were so tense. He finally said, "Yes, a package has arrived. Are you capable of coming down and looking?" "Yes, I am."

Iacovoni and Chace were in the police car that came to get me. They walked me out. There was an even bigger crowd of paparazzi than usual outside my door. They took us to the *questura*. It was dark. When we walked into the office, the police seemed more nervous than I was. They didn't know how to approach it, how to show me, what to do, whether I was going to fall apart, faint. There were a lot of policemen all standing around this desk with a big bright light over it. They were shaking and nervous. They warned me the ear had been under tons of mail and was a little squashed. They told me that it had been held up by a long mail strike down in the south. We hadn't been aware of it in Rome because mail was still arriving from other places.

They took out this little plastic bag with the ear in it. We looked at it. The formaldehyde had removed some of the color—it was really a weird-looking thing—there were still little marks, pigmentations. One can't even say they were freckles.

I picked it up—*phew*—but it's my son's. I turned it over and I looked at it and I looked at the shape and the structure. Even though it had been lightly flattened, this part of it was very much Paul's and the lobe—there was little question.

I wasn't absolutely, hundred-percent sure it was his right off. How can you be when you're looking at something that's been in the mail for a month? It was amazing. It was really very well preserved. But the hair was the thing that really blew my mind. There was no question about whose hair it was. Chace was more positive than I. The police asked us how either of us could be so sure. Chace's answer was very simple, clinical: "I know an ear when I see one."

I was able to touch it because if you've ever had anyone in your family die—I had my aunt die in my arms—somehow because there's something awful happening, it doesn't mean you can't touch something that belonged to a person you love.

But so as not to seem like the emotional mother, I told them I wasn't one hundred percent sure. I said, "As far as I'm concerned, yes, it's my son's ear, but would you like it in percentages? I am seventy-five, eighty percent sure."

They said, "We have to find out if the ear came off someone dead or alive."

Chace's notes of the same occasion are characteristically full of bravado:

The ear arrived. It took twenty-eight days in the mail for the ear to travel from Naples to Rome. The Italian mail's not very good. The ear was mailed on the twenty-second October to *Il Messaggero*. Got the call in the hotel at seven P.M. Ear and hair has arrived. The police picked me up and then we picked up Gail. Nobody's going to be calm if the police tell you an ear has arrived in the mail. The newspaper instantly gave it to the cops to take pictures. Swarms outside the police station. It's a big attraction. Everyone gets in on it to get their picture taken. They argued about it. It was all a big drama. The Italians love drama. They get excited easily. There's nothing dignified about excitement. If they get a murder everyone sticks their finger to the wind. Iacovoni turned pale and blasted off in the corner and I wondered if he was going to keep his cookies. The thing was lying flat on the table and someone said, "Maybe it's not a human ear," and I decided to pull it out. I picked it up and plunked it out and I said, "It looks like one to me." It was rather traumatic to see a red ear and a bunch of hair and for someone to ask Gail, "Is this your boy's? Can you identify it?" I could identify it of course. Gail was calm and very much under control. She handled herself very well.

I went back to the station after they'd all gone and spent some time communing with the ear, matching up the freckles. It is the boy's ear.

Like her son, Gail assumed that now that the deed was done and the ear at last had arrived, that would be the end of it. The log-jam would release and the money would flow. She was wrong.

Gail:

Every day I called and asked if they had the test results. "Was the ear from a dead body?" It all came back to the same old filthy thing, money. Would they pay if he was dead?

We were afraid because Fifty had said that Little Paul was bleed-ing and there was hemorrhaging. Had he really survived this thing? Maybe he wasn't all right. Maybe he was dead. I didn't think so, but I also wanted to find out if they had him doped up on medicine, or if he was lucid.

To determine Paul's state, I asked Fifty to ask him a lot of really difficult questions. I asked for the floor plan of a house we'd had in Rome. He described a portrait on the wall; he was able to remember the name of the painter. I knew that not only was he alive, but he was lucid. There was no question.

When the report came from the scientific department of the po-lice, it went into unnerving detail. They had it figured out how many cuts there were and where the cuts were made.

Then I heard from someone that when Big Paul heard I had iden-tified Little Paul's ear his answer was, "She wouldn't know the differ-ence between an ear and a piece of prosciutto."

I was really, really angry. Nothing was going to stop me, my back was against the wall. Chace was terribly good. He really knew how to make me fight. When he saw me sink he'd say something he knew was going to pull me up again, challenge me.

I wanted them to see every horrible detail in England. Maybe they don't print these kinds of things there, but in Italy the front page of every paper had a blow up of the plastic bag with the ear in it, and it's pretty disgusting. It makes your stomach turn. I had blow-ups made. Very large poster-size photographs from different angles. I sent them to Old Paul and Big Paul. I wanted them to really hurt.

Fifty told me that if we didn't start to cooperate, then they were going to have to do it again. I promised him the money had arrived, no problem. We told them two days. I said, "Look, please, I believe you. Let's stop fighting each other. Please give me time. I'm fighting an empire."

14.

It became apparent that Big Paul was still the problem. He would not sign his father's note. Chace scoffed at the family infighting and boasted that he'd had the power to pay the ransom all along.

November 14.

Chace (notes):

Gail was having a fine old time with Big Paul, but I wasn't involved with him at all then. I said, "Fine. Bully for you. I hope you get Big Paul to give you x million dollars. Go to it kid." I didn't give a damn about Gail's relations with her ex-husband. It was family business, dirty laundry. I'm not going to get involved. There was a big argument about whether Big Paul was going to give us the money or Old Paul was going to pay the whole thing. It was on and off, on and off. I didn't have the money from Old Paul yet. I didn't talk to anybody about whether or not I could get it. The whole thing was whether Big Paul was going to come through with something. It was back and forth. He kept changing his mind.

I wasn't concerned because I had confidence in the Old Man that whatever money we had to pay we could pay. I didn't say anything about it but I wasn't ready to get away from simultaneous exchange. I was aware of all the family feuds going on but I didn't get involved or give a damn because I wasn't really concerned. From the beginning I was the person who was going to pay the money, obviously. I knew when I needed x amount of dollars, I would get x amount of dollars, I knew that all the time. I didn't have to worry about the money I was paying to my informants and other expenses. I knew I had strong financial backing because Old Paul told me, but I wanted to handle it all properly. I didn't need to pin him down to dollars and cents. He's never questioned one of my expense accounts yet. He trusts my judgment on millions of dollars. I spent sixty million dollars of his money in Japan. He trusts me with it. And I didn't have to pin him down on two million or $750 million. I was single-minded and I was trying to get something worked-out. I couldn't get involved in all this family haggling and I didn't care, I knew there was money when I needed it.

As time passed, pressure continued to build on Gail, the kidnappers kept threatening, and in London the family quarrel dragged on.

Gail:

I had to keep thinking; maybe a new idea would come to us on how to get the money. It was like bashing your head against the wall. What do I do? How do I convince them it happens to be their grandson, their son, *my* son. It was absolutely day in and day out. I was so desperate I wanted to scream, "I can't take one more second." I just couldn't do it. I used to run into the bathroom and cry till I thought I'd die but then I had to come out because the press were there, or the police, or Fletcher, or I had to call my father, or the kidnappers were going to call.

My mother asked me, "How do you empty out your mind, not exactly turning off, but what is it that you do?" Well, you learn it—I don't know how, you just do. There are times when you aren't dealing with it anymore, when it's time to go to bed. Then what do you do? You really empty your mind out. You don't allow yourself to think about what's happening. Obviously, I did it some of the time, but had I done it all the time, I would never have been able to talk to anybody. We didn't know what we were dealing with. We had no idea.

Everyone used to say, "Oh, you poor thing" and "How you must be suffering." I'd say, no. Yes, I'm suffering emotionally and I'm hurting because this is happening to one of my children whom I love very dearly, but he's the one who's suffering. I'm not. I'm locked in a house. I have a nice home and I have people around me and I'm comfortable and everybody is trying to see that I'm comfortable. And where is he? What does he have? It was really Paul's guts that got me through. Because, somehow, I knew he was going to make it and they didn't understand that. "Oh, you poor thing." Me? Me, the poor thing? Here I am, surrounded more or less by everything that I know, except I'm forced to fight. What does he have? I have a bed to sleep in. Nobody is hurting me. Nobody cut my ear off.

Two days later at five o'clock in the morning the doorbell rang. It was a reporter from *Intento* saying they had some photographs that I must see. I was in bed, Lou went down to answer the door and told the caller over the intercom I would look at them at noon because I didn't get very much sleep and to not torture me in the middle of the night when it was dark and I was scared.

The man said, "She should see them. It's important that she sees them."

Lou said, "The answer is no. What difference does it make anyway? The photographs won't change."

After a half hour they gave up and left the photos there. I couldn't look. I finally did, at least I tried. These photographs were the saddest thing I've ever seen in my life. It's one thing to look at an ear in a plastic bag and it's another thing to see Paul's face just like that. I hid the photographs under my mattress.

Chace arrived at noon. He shook his head. He just didn't believe it. He didn't know what to do. He said that Big Paul was demanding custody of the children and until he had it wouldn't sign the note. He would pay a ransom of one million dollars if the children were on the next plane to London.

I blew up. "I don't want to give up my children, but if it means that he'll pay Paul's ransom, I'll take five million, and the children will be on the next plane." Chace went to telephone. When he came back he told me that Big Paul was still saying, "No. One million and the children."

I said, "No way, no way."

Chace said he'd tell Iacovoni to offer one million dollars anyway.

A week later the kidnappers rejected Big Paul's offer. Big Paul said publicly he wouldn't pay more. The old man was waiting for his son to do his duty. The son didn't know what his duty was or didn't want to accept it, or still didn't believe, or couldn't face reality.

The kidnappers told me they were going to cut off the other ear. They'd cut off one, it would be much easier to do the second. They were going to get off on mutilation. I didn't know what to do. I spent a lot of time on the phone with my family, trying to figure it out. Chace said he was trying to figure it out.

Then, at three o'clock in the morning I was talking with Lou and this idea came up. I'd appeal directly to Nixon. Old Paul was one of his big supporters. Why not? It was absurd, ludicrous, silly, but why not try? The worst that could happen was I would look like a fool, but what did I care? I picked up the telephone and called ANSA, the Italian news service, asked them how I would go about it. They suggested that I call either AP or UPI. I did; then I dictated a telegram to President Nixon in the White House.

"I'm appealing to you as a citizen of the United States. I have no more options. As a citizen, one is supposed to be able to appeal to their president. As a friend of my father-in-law, and as a human being, please help. I don't know what else to do."

Two days later I opened a newspaper and saw in the headlines that the family had agreed to pay the money. I called Iacovoni. He was sheepish. He said yes, he had received a telephone call from London saying that they would pay the full three million. I didn't believe it. I said, "Why didn't you tell me?" He told me that a second of the grandfather's men had arrived and was using his office. This man had told Iacovoni, "Now that it's coming down to real money and the arrangements of the drop, we don't want Gail talking to the kidnappers. Chace has to do all the talking. He's setting up a phone in an empty apartment and having it monitored by the police and recorded. He's told the kidnappers to only call at certain times because otherwise no one will be there. Then he can go down to the police station and re-listen to the conversations."

All of a sudden the money was there, I wasn't about to ask any questions or make any waves. I just wanted to get on with it as quickly as possible. I assumed that the boy's father had signed his father's note.

Chace told Old Paul's other man, "Okay. I'll handle it from here." He started taking the kidnappers' calls and they got pissed off. They didn't understand a word he said. An interpreter wasn't allowed. Fifty told me that Chace would shout at them in Spanish mixed with one Italian word, four English words, and two half-Spanish words. It made me sick to my stomach. The kidnappers were silent for days. We thought maybe they were cutting Paul up again.

December came in as they waited. The cold was bitter. There was an extraordinary tension in the air.

Gail:

To get three million dollars [1.6 billion lire] together in small used notes is an incredible logistical exercise. There were a lot of people working on it. All of a sudden there was an awful lot of fuss going on in the bank; there are various clerks involved in preparing a large amount of money. They had to find a special machine to photograph all the notes because, obviously, the kidnappers were concerned about whether the money was going to be marked. It was the first thing they thought of. I assured them it wasn't marked, and it wasn't.

The fact that the ransom money was being prepared was, like everything else, in the papers every day. We tried to persuade the kidnappers that the handlers of the money should be armed. Maybe someone would follow the money out of the bank. They said, "No way." I said, "Okay. It's your risk. It's your money, and if something happens . . ." They said, "How could anything happen?" I said, "If you lose the money, we lose." They said, "If we lose the money, you lose your son." I said, "You're the ones causing this. Please let them be armed, they're not going to use their guns on you."

There was very little discussion about the details of the drop. Fifty didn't want to go into it with me. He told me they wanted me to make the same run I had been instructed to make in July. That was their pattern. They had a reason for everything I was to do. They gave me the same instructions except that in July, they had wanted a Cynar sign, but now didn't. Now they wanted a car with a luggage rack with either two white suitcases on top or a plastic water container—one of those big, plastic, square things. Fifty told me, "You tell us what kind of a car, do the same thing. Leave at eight o'clock in the morning, proceed down the *autostrada,* eighty kilometers an hour, don't go over eighty, don't go under eighty." If had I to stop, where and how to do it? Pull in a certain way? Obviously, the car would be watched all the time. Which is probably why they said we didn't need to be armed, because they would be following me anyway. Who was going to be in the car? They didn't want Chace. They didn't trust him. They wanted me. They kept saying, "Please have faith in us. Please trust us, it's our honor," all that kind of thing. But Chace wouldn't hear of it. The family didn't want me around the money. The kidnappers realized in the end they didn't have any choice. Either he dropped it or there was no money.

> *Five months almost to the day since it was begun, Chace took sole and undisputed control of the proceedings. He rode into power showing no sign of annoyance at all about his carefully laid plans for splintering the gang or simultaneous exchange being peremptorily swept aside. What remained was a perfect mission for the man who loved danger, though the kidnappers seemed in fact to have him under their thumb throughout. Now, too, at the last, his complicated relationship with Gail came close to exploding.*
>
> *Chace (notes):*

I rented a big car, the Fiat version of a Mercedes, a 132, a big, fancy, heavy car. I just changed cars for the hell of it. I didn't care what the kidnappers had told Gail. When they called Iacovoni for the last time, he would tell them. The money was in the *Banca Commerciale*. I counted it forever in the boardroom. The bank's cashier was there and their director. We had stuff all over the table, money all over the place in bundles. It was all there. We counted and sacked it. I had the money in three sacks in the trunk; it weighed about sixty-seven pounds a sack. It took two hands to swing a sack. I had Frazer [sic] with me, a personal gunman in case tourists stopped us and beat us over the head with their wristwatches. A shotgun man because I was carrying three million dollars. We both had guns. He wasn't Italian or American.

I left Rome on the morning of December seventh. My instructions were to go through the *autostrada* gate at exactly nine A.M. I only told Iovinella [of the Rome police] I was leaving and not to let the police anywhere near me. I didn't want it spread around because I didn't trust the police not to have some cousin in the Mafia hijack me. If they could keep a close eye on the operation, fine. The police never spotted me going through the *autostrada* gate. I went with a mysterious person. The kidnappers told us to continue on the road to Reggio Calabria. We would be given a signal; they would throw gravel on the windshield. I drove 460 kilometers south, beyond Lagonegro. I had to drive slowly due to the instructions, the hills, snow, horrible weather. Nobody threw the gravel. We were finally stopped by the fog, snow, and ice. We came back with difficulty because of all the gasoline stations being closed due to the oil embargo. There was a curfew and the police had refused to give me a pass. No one was supposed to be on the road at all.

We got back at about one A.M. I'd run sixteen hours. Nothing happened.

Gail was upset because she didn't know I was going. She didn't know when I was going or where I was going. I don't trust anyone. It was my life and I was driving with three million dollars and I didn't want anybody to know that I was going to drive all the way to Calabria.

In the middle of that first morning, Iovinella had come to Gail, asking her to sign an indemnity for ordering police to hold off on accompanying Chace. He said the police were working on the principle that it was a kidnapping and, accordingly, staying out of it. So she knew what was afoot, although she didn't know the details and she didn't want to know. Early the following morning, when Iovinella told her that Chace had attempted a drop without success, the accumulated tension of five months exploded. She went wild and Chace did too. In his customary fashion he said only, "I gave her a bit of hell," and blamed her for everything. When they had stopped shouting at each other, she was still able to exclaim, "Poor man." Their relationship was symbolic of the unlikely alliances forged by this affair.

Gail:

Iovinella came to the house and I signed a paper saying to the effect "No police interference." Iovinella and I were in touch throughout the day. "Have you heard? What's going on?" I got very nervous when it got late and called him. He called me right back, and said that he had just spoken to Chace. He was in the toll gate entering Rome with the money. The drop had not been made. I tore into him, "Why did Chace wait? Why did he wait till he got all the way back to the last toll gate to call?"

When Chace called me, I screamed, "My God! Why didn't you tell me before?" He was wild. He shouted, "I don't trust you! You're the fault of everything that's gone wrong in this whole kidnapping. Women shouldn't get involved in things like this. You've messed up everything. You should have told me what you were doing. I was in a very dangerous position, and you made it worse by ordering the police to stay out of it."

He was hysterical. I said, "You're frustrated by not being able to make the drop. I understand. Maybe they did this run so they could find out how long it would take. They aren't fools."

He said, "I can't believe you ordered the police not to protect me. You blew it. This whole kidnapping is your fault. You're the one who's delayed everything."

"Whether you are protected or not didn't make any difference, and if you knew that you weren't being protected why did you go on with it anyway? And when did you know? Did you find out at the toll gate? Or did you find out just now? If you did, how could it have been my fault?"

"Now I know what kind of woman you are. If your son dies, you're going to blame me. I want a letter from you saying you won't hold me responsible for whatever happens and that I've comported myself in a proper fashion throughout this business. I know the kind of person you are. You and your father. If something happens to Paul, you'll take me to court and blame me." He screamed at me, "You're nothing but trouble!"

By the time he'd finished, I was in tears, destroyed. I couldn't figure out what in God's name had gone on. I said, "Fletcher, I'll write you a letter. Don't get excited. You've had a long day. I've had a long day. Maybe there were mistakes made, but here we are right at the end. Let's not blow it by fighting."

Fortunately for all of us, Fifty didn't call until eleven that night, so I was able to tell him that a man had left at eight o'clock yesterday morning. "He did exactly as you told him, he went to the point where you told him, he didn't get a signal, it began to snow and, having so much money in the car, he turned 'round and came back." Fifty said the kidnappers were all really mad at me, screaming and yelling and carrying on. I said, "I don't know what happened. I promise you, I guarantee you that the man went. The money was in the car. It's all perfectly regular. I signed a paper to make sure there was no police interference. It was all straight."

Suppose the kidnappers had called earlier. I wouldn't have known what to tell them. They would have thought we were really doing a number and they would have cut off Paul's other ear.

The next day the papers said "the drop had been made" and reported that police had set up to film it. Of course, anything that was reported in the paper at that time was likely to be nonsense. I said, "I really have nothing to say," which usually means "yes." We wanted them to think the drop had been made, but it hadn't.

Two more days went by. Both sides were bruised by the failure of the first run and each was highly suspicious of the other.
Chace (notes):

The next two days I talked to them several times giving them hell for why they didn't stop me. At first they didn't believe I'd made the run. They didn't realize that Gail wasn't knowledgeable about the details. They said I hadn't made the trip. I gave them hell, told them about the snow, what I'd seen, the different villages. They came back and said, "I guess you did. It was a bad night, wasn't it?" So they backed off and got all friendly and said, "Let's try again." I said okay but I refuse to drive all night. If you don't stop me by such and such a time I'm turning back, to hell with you. I'll drive down the road at the speed you give me and when I get to a certain time I'm coming back, and it's your problem, not mine. I'm not going to keep driving through Calabria in the middle of the night."

I told Gail, "Okay. I'll do it again but no questions. You don't ask me any questions. It's going to be done. You just keep out of it."

I made the second run with Mr. X. Again, I told the police to stay out of it. Follow me but don't louse it up. They assured me they wouldn't. Driving down the road Mr. X and I were doing a very careful check of cars that passed us and passed us again and I identified the police in a plain car stopping and looking at a bridge in Solerno. I'd seen him pass me in a blue Alfa Romeo, assumed they were cops, identified them—blue and white car. So they were in the offing, being very discreet, staying out of the way.

After we passed Naples we increased vigilance, Mr. X kept descriptions of drivers on a yellow pad, tracking cars that passed us. One car went by twice, the driver took a look at me so I told Mr. X to take down his description. Then the same car passed with a different driver. We were in business. He went by several times then pulled into a gas station ahead of me. I went into the station and pulled in behind him. The driver got out, and turned his face away. I was surprised he hadn't seen me drive up behind him. I got a good look at him and he went off to the restroom in a hurry. I checked his car, I didn't see any sign of hardware and he had three empty suitcases in the back—leather suitcases, pretty good quality. As I was doing this, the service station attendant came. He was obviously wondering what the hell I was doing. I waited for almost ten minutes. The driver stayed out in the washroom watching me so I went my way. No sign of the police car.

I was toodling along at 2:30 P.M., going slowly, minding my own business, keeping alert, smoking my pipe. If it had gotten dark, I probably would have put my pipe away and had my hands free and watched what was going on. I figured I had at least two or three hours to go before anything happened. We were completely relaxed. Gravel hit the windshield. It was the signal. I didn't think I was going to be stopped until dark. It happened. There was no way anyone could have known where they were going to do it unless they were a member of the kidnap gang.

I stopped. We were off the *autostrada* on a curving road. As we were going 'round the corner gravel hit the windshield. I slowed down and saw movement, people.

I was driving slowly, when a bowlegged type, rickets, all Italians have rickets down there, came out with a gun in his hand and a handkerchief over his face waving his arms.

I stopped and got out. He kept waving his gun around, telling me to back up. I told him I was going to give him the money, and to be calm and stop waving his gun. I took my pipe out of my mouth, blew some smoke at him, put my pipe back in, and looked at him; he lowered his gun. I turned as his friends were crashing through the underbrush. I think there were three of them but I couldn't make it out. A guy moved at me a little and I told him to stay where he was. He did. I put it at the edge of the road and then I drove off.

I went back to the apartment I was staying in, and phoned the police and told them to bring over all the photographs of all the people they suspected of being in the kidnap gang. They came over and laid the photos on the kitchen table and I picked out of a whole deck, two men that I had seen that day. I said, "Those are your men." They were the Malevito brothers, Saverio and Vincenzo. Very tough guys.

I told the police everything that happened, spoke to them for two hours.

In Gail's telephone conversation with Fifty, they seemed like estranged lovers.

Gail:

Fifty called me after the drop. In many ways he was really so nice. He said, "I don't have to call you and I really shouldn't be calling, but I want you to know that it's all right and we have the money."

I said, "Is everything okay? You've got the money. Is my son all right? Please give him my love. When are you going to let him go?"

He said, "It's going to take time. Please trust us and please be patient."

I said, "Come on. Why? You've got the money. Please don't do anything." There was this whole trust thing. At that point I believed him.

He said, "Trust us. Obviously we have certain things we must do. Give us the time to do them and as soon as I can . . ." And I said, "Will it be tonight, tomorrow, when?"

He said, "I can't tell you when it'll be, but as soon as we can organize ourselves, we'll release him to you."

15.

Paul's release was a complicated exercise carried out in the dead of night.

Paul:

About seven, they led me from the tent. They had kinda dressed me up. It shows you the Italian mentality, isn't it incredible? They had flannel pants on, new little shoes, blue socks, a white shirt, thick white sweaters. They had expensive clothing, way into that sort of thing. Italians are like that; you have to be at least presentable when you go home. It was snowing, imagine, a hundred miles north of Africa, it was all snow and ice. The snow was high. There was a cliff right in front of us.

I'm sure it was only a five-minute walk, but they made me walk around so it would look longer. They turned me around and around. I was still weak from so much loss of blood. It took so long to walk a kilometer; it took three hours. I couldn't see anything, they made me wear one of those ski masks with the hole for the face, over the whole neck, but they turned it backwards.

They all said good-bye. Five or six of them, Piccolo and VB1 weren't there. I think they'd been with me so long; they were scared I would recognize them. One of the guys told me, "Now, don't talk. Promise not to talk."

They put me in a car. It was all very organized. "You guys pick him up, then you keep him, you guys let him go . . ." It was more serious than one thinks. They drove me for, like, seven hours. I slept. I really slept. I bet it was really only forty-five minutes. They just went around and around.

They had patrols. They were more organized than the police. They had systems, incredible systems. They got me and let me go, then caught me. The car would go for a mile, then it would stop and the car would meet another car. Then they would talk and say okay. Then a car goes ahead with us behind. If something goes wrong, they'd wait at the exit. It was like five or six cars—Morris Mini, and an old Alfa 600. You see, they knew that they were really looking for me. The hills were full of police.

At this point they had the money, and they were scared to die. They had families, and they had been paid next to nothing. Maybe seven thousand dollars. I think that some of them must have some sort of debt with some guy. This guy brings them under his thumb, they have to do what he says. One of them didn't even know my last name.

They talked with the guy at the toll gate. They paid for the ticket with me right there, right in front of him. I was not even lying on the floor, the seat. It wasn't dark; it's all neon there. They were joking with him, like, yeah we'll see you later. That's it. They're all the same.

They changed cars again about five minutes from there, on the side of the road. A Fiat 1100, those old Fiats. All military people have them; most of the government cars are like that.

They never went off the *autostrada*. They made U-turns, going back and forth. But you see it doesn't matter, the *autostrada* was deserted. Two kidnappers went to phone my mother. They told her that she could find me exactly here, or there. So she drove out. These were new guys. They were not from the south; it's impossible to be from the south and not have an accent.

Gail remembered the call.

Gail:

Fifty called me at eleven-thirty and said, "You'd better hurry. You'd better get in the car right away, because at one-thirty this morning, we'll be releasing Paul at such-and-such a place."

I said, "One-thirty? It's going to take me a long time to get there. The weather's horrible. How's he going to be?"

Fifty said, "Don't worry. We'll give him blankets. We'll tell him what to do. He'll be told to wait there for you. Can I tell him you're coming?"

"Absolutely."

He also threatened me. He said, "Don't come with the police and don't talk. There are a lot of things you're never supposed to say. No matter where you are in the world, if you turn us in, we'll get you, all of you. Please hurry. It's cold."

"Please tell Paul I'll give our family whistle, and not to be afraid to just come down when he hears it."

I immediately called Iovinella. He didn't want me to go. I knew what they were thinking. They were sure Paul was going to be as dead as could be. We argued about who was going to go. They said, "We'd rather you didn't go." And I said, "I am going to go and there's no question about it. But who's going to go with me?"

Lou obviously wanted to, but it wasn't possible. I panicked. I said, "Can't Chace and I go by ourselves? If you want to come some other way, okay, but can't we be in separate cars? I promised I wouldn't come with the police."

Then the big problem was how to get me out of the house because there were press all over the place outside my door. We made plans for me to go up ladders, over rooftops, down drainpipes, and out alleys and finally the d'Almeidas said, "If someone could just take her out the front door like she's going out. Then we'll dash off and meet at a certain place. From there, we'll decide what to do."

So this friend of mine took me down and got me out the door and shoved me into a funny little car, took me to a private residence, where Iovinella was. There were lots of police there. I told them, "I'm going." They said, "Okay. If it's not good, can you take it?" We left. Chace came with us in Iovinella's car with another car following.

The moment Paul had been dreaming of for five months had finally arrived.

Paul:

The one who wasn't driving said, "Don't talk, or else we'll cut your tongue out." The other driver said, "Maybe we shouldn't let him off, he'll talk. I promise you in six months, he'll talk."

They stopped and let me out. There was a cold wind and it was night. There were enormous blocks of ice on the side of the *autostrada*. There was a big concrete drain thing, a pipe. They lifted me over that, walked up the hill across a field or something. They gave me blankets and a pack of cigarettes. That was really nice. They were going to give me fifty lire, but they didn't.

I said to them, "Don't worry after me, guys, I won't say anything. I won't incriminate you."

He said to me, "There's a guy watching behind, so don't turn around; wait ten minutes, take off your mask. Your mother will be here in a few hours."

He went to get in the car with the other guy and then turned back and gave me his coat. I felt great. I wasn't scared. Not at that point. They were much more scared than I. But they kept their word, men of honor.

I heard the car start, the shifting of gears, first, second, third. It was a strange feeling. It was like a huge weight taken off me, twenty pounds on first, twenty pounds on second, twenty on third.

I got up, took the mask off. It was dark.

I walked down across the field and up the *autostrada* to a gas station. There was a phone there but I didn't have any money. I asked a soldier who was outside for a *gettone*. He refused. I went in and asked to use the phone. I didn't have any shoes on and my head was all bandaged up. There were about three people inside and they just looked at me and didn't say anything. I obviously freaked them out. They wouldn't give me anything, so I left.

I walked on down the *autostrada* through a tunnel to some houses, knocked on doors, nothing. That was such a downer, you know? My God, after all this, I have to come back to this indifference? Really cold. I walked up a mile and lay in the middle of the freeway, looking dead. A few cars and people stopped, but then they'd go again. An ambulance passed me. Exasperation. I left the *autostrada* on the turnoff to Lagonegro.

Finally a truck stopped. I told the driver, "I'm Paul Getty."

He said, "You are, aren't you?" Then he drove off.

Once again Capt. Martino Elisco, the carabinieri officer who had led the unsuccessful storming of the house where Paul had been kept, was called into the case. Captain Elisco was stout, with a smooth, round face, large teeth, and small feet.

He was in charge of a carabinieri station in Lagonegro, a small, impoverished hill town built on two sides of a gorge, four hundred kilometers south of Rome.

Elisco:

In Lagonegro the people are very poor and very quiet. There is virtually no delinquency to deal with, no bar fights. There used to be crimes of "honor" in the area, but even they have died out, apart from sheep rustling, I deal almost all the time with robberies. The Getty kidnapping put Lagonegro on the map, unfortunately.

I was patrolling the area until about two in the morning. We knew that somewhere the boy was being released. They had told us in Rome earlier in the evening and I had been cruising up and down the *autostrada* through fog and snow, but I had seen nothing and went home to bed.

I was sound asleep when I was called at two forty-five and told that Paul had been spotted at the bus shelter south of the carabinieri garage. I dressed and drove my new blue Alfa Romeo to where the truck driver said he saw Paul. There was sleet falling and heavy snow before that. Lagonegro looked like a German village under the snow. There was the boy, trembling badly, soaking wet, with no shoes.

Paul climbed into my Alfa and we drove to Lagonegro. I told him, "You know, nobody thought that you were kidnapped, until just now."

"Yes, that's what makes me so sad."

"Do you know how much was paid?"

"No," he said. I told him and asked him if he knew who paid. "No." I told him it was his grandfather, his family. "Oh, that's all right," he said. "They'll take it out of my inheritance."

The carabiniere's office is across the piazza in the Old Town. The captain led Paul past a little shrine with a couple of candles in the wall and up three flights of gray marble stairs. Carabinieri with thick black mustaches and crisp khaki uniforms looked on with reserve.

Gail's route to this office was circuitous.

Gail:

We arrived at the place on the *autostrada* where we'd been told Paul would be waiting around four in the morning. It was still dark. It was freezing cold and we didn't know where we were, whether we were at the right place or not. The kidnappers said they would leave someone with him. I actually thought when I whistled or called and they heard my voice, these people would shove him forward. And that would give them time to disappear. I believed it. I was a fool. Obviously they weren't going to be sitting there waiting. We searched around, looked in all the concrete culverts, expecting to find his body stuffed in one of them. Nothing. It got lighter and lighter. They broke into the house opposite, to see if he was there, and finally they sent one of the cars on down through the tunnel south to see if anything could be found.

I thought maybe he had hidden himself under a tree or fallen asleep. He was alive. There was no question in my mind. He was just up there on that hill somewhere. Finally the police were getting fed up. They said, "We're really wasting our time here."

Chace said, "Before we go away, let's just think about this a little bit. If you were a young boy and you had been held for five months and four days, would you sit on a hill because they said to wait for your mother? I wouldn't. I don't know this boy, but from what I hear there's no way he'd sit there. I'd get out as soon as I could."

I didn't want to leave this place, because I somehow felt if I left . . . I said, "Could we just do one more look, please? Let's all look around. We may find something." One of the men from the *squadra mobile* climbed over the wall in the area by the fence, went up a little, and came up with a blanket and a blindfold, holding it above his head, dancing and shouting. We got back into the second *squadra mobile* car, with Iovinella driving. Now we knew that he had been here, all we had to do was figure out if he'd gone north or south. They sent the two cars we had with us off in opposite directions, one north, one south, to see if we could find him.

Meanwhile, Paul was being well looked after by some extremely curious carabinieri who each wanted to get himself in the photograph with the boy.

Elisco:

Back at the station, I was amazed how good his physical condition appeared to be, standing without any shoes in the freezing road for six hours. We called the doctor. He came and gave the boy a shot of tranquilizer while my wife cooked him a meal and I gave him some clothes—a sweater and a pair of pants. But I have small feet and I couldn't find any shoes in the station that would fit him.

Gail was still floundering around in the snowstorm.

Gail:

We drove south on the *autostrada* because we had to drive south anyway; we headed that way when we stopped. We saw a carabiniere's car and we asked if they knew anything. The carabinieri don't care for the Roman *squadra mobile*. They're very defensive. All they would tell Iovinella was, "Yes, he's been released. He's been taken somewhere and we do have a report that he's all right."

They wouldn't tell us where he was. "Can you give us an idea where he is?" They told us, "Well, if you'll come to such and such a place, maybe they'll know something." There was a fight between the carabinieri and the *squadra mobile*. The carabinieri spoke with another car on the radio and were told nothing had happened, or that maybe somebody had been taken to Potenza, that maybe we should go there and check. They told us, "All we can tell you is that the boy is in the hands of the carabinieri, but we don't know where."

We turned around and we went north to a funny little carabinieri station and they didn't really want to say anything. Nobody knew anything. "Oh yes, he's all right. We have him, everything's fine." Chace said, "This is the boy's mother. She wants to see her son. Where is he?" Then they said, "Well, he's in the Carabinieri Due station at Lagonegro." We drove to Lagonegro, the longest time I ever passed in my life.

Captain Elisco debriefed Paul as they waited and provided some understanding of why Paul had met with such rejection as he walked along the autostrada *in the snow.*

Elisco:

I determined that the boy was dropped off outside the tunnel three kilometers north of Lauria, on the *autostrada*. Around ten-thirty P.M., he entered the snack bar at the ESSO station. The people on the *autostrada* didn't pick him up because this is very close to Calabria and people don't like to get involved in anything. Also, this time of year, when the snow is falling, people take the lower roads. The *autostrada* is at twelve hundred meters and ices up, so there was little traffic anyway.

In the snack bar, Paul's appearance probably frightened the people. He was wet. His hair was cut short and he had a bandage hanging from his left ear. This probably deterred the truck driver also.

It was now about six A.M. The journalists started arriving within the hour and the boy's mother arrived at the barracks about seven forty-five A.M. to be met by fifty or so photographers. Then the TV people arrived from Potenza, with a lot of other curious onlookers.

Gail, Chace, and Iovinella at last arrived at Captain Elisco's office. There was no love lost between the squadra mobile *and the* carabinieri. *The* squadra mobile, *the crack Rome city police, regard the* carabinieri *as country bumpkins, and suddenly the shoe was on the other foot.*

Gail:

When we got up into the captain's office, it was like hell. There was pushing, screaming, yelling, photographers. The place was jammed. This was like eight in the morning, and everybody knew but us. There we were, the people that had done it all, wandering around in the hills, going through abandoned houses, and all the while the news had been on the radio. In Rome, Lou knew, the children knew, everybody knew except us.

At Lagonegro they somehow steered us through the crowd and took us up to the captain's office. We sat there waiting for them to bring Paul in, but it went on and on and the captain wouldn't let me see Paul.

It was like a dam breaking, watching the police fighting in their own office. They poured in and they were on top of us. It was really scary, the head of the *squadra mobile* and his assistant fighting each other and then the press. At last they brought Paul in. When we first saw each other all we did was hold on and cry, both of us. They wouldn't give us the decency of being alone. It made me so angry. There they were, gaping. They wanted a photograph of that, but there was no way.

Paul and myself, we were like caged animals in there while the press was out there fighting for their rights: "We have a right to take photographs." They'd been promised a photograph. The police had to push them out.

PRESS REPORTS OF DECEMBER 15

The meeting between Paul and his mother took place at 8:30 with a long embrace, which lasted 4 minutes. "At last it is over," said the boy in English, while Gail, weeping, caressed him and kissed him on the right side of his face, which was marked by a wound. She said to her son, "I always believed you."

Paul was sure they were giving him some kind of truth serum or some other nutty kind of stuff. I think what they probably did give him was a tranquilizer. You're not going to tell me that that little man in Lagonegro had a bunch of speed on him. But they certainly were trying to force stuff on him. It could very well have been Valium.

They turned it into a big social event. "Won't you have some tea or coffee?" Who wanted tea or coffee?

Chace at last came into his own. He was the hero of the hour. With his customary modesty he recalled:

They wouldn't release Paul. I said, "You're just trying to get all the publicity you can out of this. You're holding him and he needs to be checked in medically. I promise you, he's in bad shape and you're holding him because you want the publicity and I'm going to give that to the press."

The captain said, "Are you talking to me? I'm in command here in my station."

"Yes, I'm talking to you." I tapped him on the chest and said, "You've got five minutes. I'm going upstairs and in five minutes I'm coming down again with the boy and his mother. If you don't let us go through, I'm going to talk to the press."

I can look mean when I want to, and I looked mean. I knew in my own mind that I had him and was on top. I went upstairs and said, "Get ready. We're getting out of here." I put my coat on Paul and we walked right through the crowd of press, got in the car, and drove off.

I was in the front seat. I put Iovinella in the backseat with Gail and the boy. We laughed and we had an incredible ride to the city, rather fun, and a few of the press were passing us, taking pictures as they drove by.

When we got to the north end of the *autostrada* outside Rome, the press had put out these cones so all the lanes were closed except for one. They had a camera set up. I was using the radio. I had the other two squad cars behind us, so we were all compact. The press were right behind the two police cars. I told the driver to keep going, keep going, keep pushing. He pushed right through the crowd. We kept the windows shut.

Gail described the triumphant return of the Golden Hippie to Rome.

Gail:

The press did some incredible things. They had obviously paid off the people at the toll gates because it was all blocked when we got there. There were television cameras. Of course, when we got to Rome the whole place was blocked. The radio followed us from the time we left Lagonegro, they reported everything that happened, what we were doing now, where we were going, what the paparazzi were doing, they followed us all the way, right into Rome. There were even helicopters. People said it was one of the most dramatic things they'd ever seen or heard in their lives, the returning to Rome. We lost them when the police car behind us stopped in one of those very narrow streets and let us get away from the press, but when we went to the *questura*, there was more press.

The world had been following Paul's plight for five months and now that he was free, he found himself to be an international celebrity. Rome has seen its share of triumphant returns, but nothing quite as bizarre as this.

Paul:

So many people and TV lights and everyone tried to look at me and they shouted my name. The police took me out of the car and the crowd closed in. They made a way for me through the crowd and inside the *questura* there was a big elevator. It had wire like a cage when it closed. There were all these people pressing against the wire, all these faces looking in at me through the wire and as the elevator started up, this one man, his face was right in front of me, said, "*Ciao, Paolo.* Remember your promise to us."

Gail described the scene in Rome:

When they had finished questioning Paul at the *questura*, they smuggled us out the back door. Nobody knew we were going to a clinic. We walked right in. Lou was there and this Italian man from the clinic's board of directors, who organized the whole thing. Probably they had Paul tranquilized, which was why he wasn't hysterical.

Paul was sweet enough to ask me if Martine could come. "Anybody you want can come. You can have everything you want."

When Martine came to the clinic, it was very funny. The two of them really didn't have that much to say. She was terribly shy.

Martine remembered:

I was very afraid and nervous inside. I thought maybe Paul was completely down and distraught. I didn't know what I would find. When

I came in, I started to cry. Paul was completely cool. Of course we were happy to see each other, but he was cool in the sense of being really strong, very strong. He said, "It's okay, I'm fine."

The doctor came in and I went outside and I started crying again. Gail was very sweet. She took me in her arms.

It was in the clinic that Paul and I talked again about getting married. We agreed that we would have a big wedding. We made these plans. We were very excited. It was a way not to talk about what had happened, I think. He didn't have any clothes. Somehow they had all disappeared. So I went to that shop called Carmenila; all those kind of David Bowie clothes. I went there and got all the things together. I had the owner of the shop come with a whole trunk, and Paul picked what he wanted.

Newspapers around the world seemed to have more access than Gail imagined and where they didn't, they seemed to exercise their own imaginations. Perhaps Paul was telling them what he thought they wanted to hear and what would get them off his back. Either that, or the staff of the clinic was paid for information. The reports come into conflict with the account Paul gave to me, particularly the account of how his ear was cut off. Presumably this saved him from further and far more complex explanation.

He refused plastic surgery because he said he wanted people to be reminded of the price he paid for "their money."

GETTY REFUSES PLASTIC EAR SURGERY

Paul Getty III was in a private room in the Villa Carla clinic in Rome yesterday.

It was his first day of real freedom since he was kidnapped and held for ransom 158 days ago. . . .

Yesterday at the clinic he had with him his American mother, Mrs Gail Harris and a few friends. . . .

He walked doubled up at the clinic and had to be helped

up the stairs. He said this was because he had been kept so long in the caves where he could not stand upright.

Captain Elisco, of the Carabinieri, found Paul sheltering from the rain by a closed petrol station. Paul's first words were: "I am Paul Getty, Captain. Give me a cigarette."

POLICE WAIT TO QUIZ BOY IN FIVE-MONTH KIDNAP ORDEAL

Yesterday a police inspector and the public prosecutor called at the private clinic in Rome where Paul is staying with his mother, but were barred by doctors.

They said the Getty boy was "very disoriented" and in need of 'profound calm.'

Doctors said that when the words kidnap, hideout or car were mentioned the boy burst into uncontrollable shouting, "Why didn't you believe me from the start? I'm sick and fed up with it all."

Yet in calmer moments, sitting up in bed in blue pajamas, sipping Chianti with his mother in his £10-a-day private room next to the clinic bar, he says: "I have decided to change my life-style."

But he did say his kidnappers hit him on the head to stun him while they cut off his ear.

"They cut it off with a kitchen knife. They stunned me with a club, but when the blade cut the flesh I woke up. I felt everything. It was terrible. Afterwards they gave me several injections."

For a day or two they had privacy, or at least the appearance of it. Then the press discovered them.

Gail:

Everything was so tranquil at the clinic. Paul's room had a little sitting room and a garden, and I had a room of my own. Police guarded the doors. They didn't allow anyone up.

When the press finally found out where we were, they asked if they could have something on the television, anything. They certainly couldn't see Paul, but it was suggested that I do something saying he was all right and saying thank you. Did I have any desire to say thank you to anybody? That was a heavy scene.

They dragged me out at nine o' clock at night and there was every television camera, every photographer, everybody I'd seen through the whole thing. I had some pretty bad feelings, resentment, plus I was starting to finally fall apart a little bit. The Italian on the clinic board of directors took me to meet the press. I told him, "If you see me starting to go, grab my arm, do whatever you can to get me out. I'm on the edge."

Anyway, one thanked various people and I said a special thank-you to the newspaperman Paolo Graudi and the *Il Messaggero* man. It was so strange. They asked the most extraordinary questions, which of course I couldn't answer. They finally got me away.

We used to sneak the children in to see their brother. We had a special entrance going. Marcello, Martine, everybody was walking in and out. Each night somebody stayed, Marcello, Lou, or Philip. They stretched out on chairs in his room, and Paul was happy as a lark.

He was terribly protective of me, which I found strange. It was sweet, but it was strange, although Paul's always been that way with me. He didn't want to tell me anything about what he had been through and I didn't particularly want to hear it. He was really like a little boy. He just wanted to eat and have loads of orange juice. He just ate his heart out.

He was very neurotic about what was around him, who was there. Outside there were terraces and rooftops, and we had to do a whole number every night. I'd go 'round and check. He was terrified somebody was out there, coming after him. We had to be sure the doors and windows were locked.

The British press understandably focused on the local interest.

GETTY SENIOR PLANS FAMILY REUNION FOR HIS GRANDSON

Getty Senior has invited his grandson, now recovering in Rome, to Britain to spend Christmas.

Last night grandfather Getty said: "I am so very happy that the boy is alive. . . . He is very welcome to come home for Christmas, but if he needs medical treatment a visit early in the new year will be certain.

"His safe return is a birthday gift I will never forget." His birthday, December 15th, had just passed.

Despite earlier statements by the senior Getty that he would not pay "one cent" in ransom, fearing it would endanger his other 13 grandchildren; it was clear last night that he did contribute to the family fund.

16.

Paul recovered rapidly, even for a seventeen-year-old. Soon after his release he went to London to see his father. It was a disaster.

Paul:

When we left the clinic, we went to my mother's apartment. Martine was there every day. My mother was very nice to her. I was very shy. I couldn't speak to anybody. I was scared of people. When people came, I hid in the kitchen; I didn't want to see anybody. The paparazzi were so bad that we went to some friends of my mother's, Martine and I needed our own apartment and money to get a film together. They all convinced me to go to London to see my father. So I phoned him, and said, "I'm coming tomorrow." He said, "Great."

I arrived, dressed nice, white pants, white shirt, tie and everything. Derek came and said, "Wait here," and I must have waited four hours before he even came down. Nobody was there—just him—very strange, very strange. Finally he came down; by that time it was so strained. He said, "Excuse me, I was in the bath."

We went into his study. He has one of those video things [VCR], we watched some movies, then we ate. It was really nice as long as you didn't talk about anything to do with responsibility; it was okay.

I explained that thing about Victoria. He probably believed it because they weren't together anymore and he was pissed off with her. But I mean, he's just mad. We never got into anything heavy and then I said, "I need to get things together, I'd like to make a movie. Maybe you can help me." He said he wanted to produce a porno film, a two-hour porno film, a full-length feature.

I said, "My God, why don't you let me do something a little bit more intelligent?"

And he said, "No, I like this."

So we watched these things, you know, everybody fucking around—little movies they made at home, all these chicks. And then we got into this kidnapping. I mean it had to come out at one point. He then said, "You should tell me a little bit about the kidnapping."

I said, "I don't feel like it. We'll do it tomorrow when we have more time. My mother told me you believe that I did it."

He said, "Yes, I believe that you had something to do with it, I'm sure you did."

That's just one point too much. And really paranoid, Charlie. I mean, it's shocking. Just put yourself in my position. You just might blow your mind. You'd spent fucking five months, almost half a year with some gangsters, and you come back to this.

He said, "I know you have something to do with it, and goddammit, now I'm going to have to pay sixty thousand dollars a month." It was bullshit, he didn't have to. I flipped out, really furious. There was a knife. I wanted to slit his throat. And then I thought, Well, hold on, maybe he'll be nice now. Nothing, complete blank.

I started to cry. He said, "Why are you crying? What is there to cry about? Go up to your room. Leave tomorrow."

I slept upstairs. I hadn't been there since that acid trip. It was so dreary and dark. The whole upstairs was locked and I got this really scary thing, like maybe he had a corpse up there. I phoned my mother that night before two and said, "Get me away from here."

The next day he comes crying in my face and I was really heavy with him. Then he had Byron, the driver, take me to the airport. Victoria had this blue jean coat which I just adored—maxi, looks like so—and I took it with me. On the way to the airport we had to stop at somebody's house to pick up some books for my father. I had stolen this coat and I got to the house and the minute we walked in the phone rang. "Leave that coat." So I did. He sent me back to Rome with one pound in my pocket—one pound. Incredible.

When I got back to Rome, we went to Austria to [go] skiing, somebody had some money.

With his father's refusal to help him, Paul was thrown back into chaos. He was a celebrity, appearing to have everything, but in reality it was the opposite. He and Martine wandered aimlessly and soon the drugs reappeared, but this time it was heroin.

Martine:

We went to Munich for a while and then to Berlin, I wanted to show it to him. A taxi driver recognized us and asked for our autographs. In an Italian restaurant the owner said, "Ah, you look like Paul Getty. Let me see your ears to see if one is cut." They recognized us in all the restaurants.

We got a video camera and Paul filmed a little bit. The film was called *Berlin by the Wall*. It was just of Berlin, the people, the incredible sex shops. From Berlin we went back to Rome.

Ultimately, nine men, including two Mammoliti brothers, were arrested for Paul's kidnapping. There was a trial in Lagonegro.

Paul went as a witness; he was heavily guarded. Only two were convicted. Only $85,0000 of the $2.8 million were recovered.

Martine had been brought back into Paul's life by Gail.

Martine:

When I got pregnant, Gail invited us over to dinner, and she said, "Paul and I, we want you to have this baby. Paul wants it and he wants to marry you." She wanted to meet my parents and they came to Rome. She welcomed them, took them around, gave a festive dinner at her place, an old palazzo. She was very nice to us.

Paul and I had envisioned a huge wedding on the Spanish Steps in Rome with the most incredible dress. But nobody had any money and in the end, we got married in Siena, a tiny little country wedding in a field with all the journalists around us. We came outside the courthouse into the piazza. It was at night. There were thousands of people. They had come in buses. It was the biggest sensation that Paul, the Golden Hippie, now free, was marrying his girlfriend, one of the twins—"*Le Gemelli Del Momento*," the twins of the moment. Paul and I got separated by the crowd.

When we came back to Rome, it was a very difficult time. We didn't have money and the paparazzi were following us everywhere. Marcello, Paul, and I took a place above the Spanish Steps. Jutta was in Munich. Her friend, a refugee from the political movement in Germany, a bomb-maker, came to live with us. He was in hiding, and he had come from Afghanistan to Rome.

Marcello, Jutta, Paul, and I wanted to make a secret society, half political, half spiritual. We wanted to start an agency, like an art center, but it was all farce. Nothing was really serious. We couldn't pay the rent. We failed. We were all having a really hard time. There was nowhere to go. We were stagnating. The chapter in Rome was finished. Paul just couldn't be there.

We were living in a hotel, Residence Ripa, and Tina Aumont was living there too. As I remember she turned him on to heroin. He might have asked her, he had tried it before. We used to go to Paul's father's palazzo. It was rented out to a black model and her husband. I think she shot him up.

This was when I first discovered the syringe. Until then I thought, "Paul is just snorting, and he's going to pull himself together." When I saw the syringes, I knew it was a whole different level.

At this point Donna Long [Paul's aunt, his father's half sister] came to Rome. We all got together with Gail and talked it over. The whole family thought we needed to get out of Rome. In December, we went to America, to San Francisco. We found ourselves living with Donna, Paul completely strung out on heroin, and I'm eight months pregnant. We didn't know where to go. We wanted to go to L.A. Anne and Gordon gave us a thousand dollars and said, "Go find a house and settle down." So we went to Union Street and bought a sitar. Paul said he wanted to make a book, to make some money, so he can do something. He said he just wanted enough to live, so we came to see you.

EPILOGUE

It was three months after that breakfast at the Caffe Trieste when he asked me to write his story that I drove down to Los Angeles. Martine had had their baby, a boy, christened Balthazar. Paul had put off starting work on the book until then.

I found him and Martine living behind the Whisky A Go-Go on a residential side street that parallels Sunset Strip. I arrived at dusk. No one answered the bell, but the door was ajar, the house empty. In the sitting room, as in Rome, white predominated—the carpets, the upholstery, the drapes, the walls, the marble on the coffee table, a white azalea floating in a silver bowl.

Canned laughter and applause came from somewhere. In the back bedroom stood a crib, from it an infant stared up, wide-eyed, silent. He must be Balthazar.

I went to wait in the living room. When Paul and Martine returned, they weren't surprised by the sight of me. There clearly was other business afoot. Paul stood by the window, looking out into the street. Without turning his head he said, "Later. We'll have to do it later. I'm expecting this guy."

At last the doorbell buzzed. Paul quickly opened to a young man in a cowboy hat, paisley shirt, bell-bottom jeans, and pointy-toed cow-boy boots. They went into Paul's bedroom, closed the door. Martine looked at me; she said nothing. Paul was buying cocaine, I assumed. It wasn't surprising. In L.A. everyone did cocaine. It was de rigueur for the hip. The more coke put out, the better the party.

It was after midnight when the work began. This was going to be a difficult assignment, if not impossible. He was peripatetic, ram-bling all over the place, running down, taking a snort and getting revved up again. As much as I wanted to steer him to what I saw was the logical starting point of the story, I didn't interrupt. Let him go where he would, gathered what I needed. He said: "This book could be bad for me. The kidnapping brought me popularity. I love it, but at the same time I see that it's destructive, terrifying. You wouldn't know it here but in Italy I'm public property. I can't walk around in Rome. It's just so embarrassing.

"People like Jagger, they have it okay. They're properly insulated. I'm trying to make a film with Maria Schneider and I spoke with Alice Cooper about playing on a record. I only hope that what we're doing now will be the answer.

"There's gonna be so much information in this book that nobody will ask me any more questions, nobody will ask me for an interview.

"What they want me to do is go to school. All these years I never went to school and everybody bitched and said, 'Why don't you go to school?' So finally I've told them, 'All right, I'll go. I'll study math-ematics and physics.'"

Paul was admitted to Pepperdine University. I'm not sure how it was done. He hadn't graduated from high school.

He insisted I accompany him there on his first day. He drove a green MG sports car with a license plate, YARBLES—cockney rhym-ing slang for "marbles," meaning testicles. He got the word from *A Clockwork Orange*.

The Pepperdine University campus lies near Malibu, northwest of L.A., beside the Pacific. My memory is of a tall, impressive adobe tower rising up in the morning sun. Paul didn't seem to know where to go or who to see. It wasn't clear to me what we should do next. We wandered the hallways among throngs of purposeful students. As they passed, they turned to stare at him, with his boots and long green woolen cloak. He was a tall ship adrift, lost in the fog. His bravado was gone.

We went into a lecture hall and sat among students. Every eye turned to him. After half an hour, Paul leaned over to me and whispered, "We have to get out of here." So we did. We left, burst out of the building, foolish with relief. Paul's first day at university would be his last.

I wrote to his grandfather, saying it was no use to expect his grandson to go to college and behave like a normal boy. It was too late for that. I wrote, "Paul has already seen too much, done too many things. It seems to me that the only chance now to save him is to give him his money, give him the means to be creative, make something of his life, preserve it. He has inherited your speed of mind. He may be uneducated in a formal academic sense, but he is creative, determined, and his instincts are good. He may destroy himself with the money but he will certainly do so without it."

There was no reply.

Paul said of money, "It is just a measure. Money doesn't really have anything to do with it. I do everything, even without money. My name is a curse, such a curse. It's like *The Godfather*; it's a family trip, the Gettys."

We covered the ground slowly, gathering a fragment here, a fragment there, going over the same episode time and again, each time a new detail coming to light, to be put in place like a piece of jigsaw puzzle. We never began taping before ten at night and generally finished at dawn.

He would digress and talk passionately and at length about Gabriele D'Annunzio, Anna Magnani, Aleister Crowley, Rossetti, or the last days of Mussolini. These characters seemed to form an imaginary core in him. He praised, defended, and sometimes railed against what he saw as a misunderstanding or miscarriage of justice where they were concerned. It wasn't always clear where imagination took over from fact, but it was dangerous to underestimate his intelligence, to dismiss what he said. His wit was merciless and humor absurd. He loved Peter Cook and Dudley Moore.

He trusted no one and tested anyone who came into his circle. He would make some outlandish observation and, if the individual agreed with him, he would look at me and wink. He liked to tell the truth and watch your reaction. A sort of measuring device. Which isn't to say that he would always tell the truth. He liked to play with who he was and who people perceived him to be.

Yet when the sun shone he took an almost childish delight in the world around him. He was complicated, high-strung, and fragile and willing to try anything. Time after time I told him, "Oh, for God's sake, Paul, don't do that," and he would look surprised and grin.

Sometimes we changed our venue and went to stay in Malibu or Palm Springs. Sometimes he came north to Briones, the village by the sea where I had moved from San Francisco after the hills of North Beach had become too much for my legs afflicted with a slow-acting degenerative neurological disease. He was curious about it, about how it was for me. His empathy was genuine, as was his curiosity, and over these months we became fast friends.

He liked to go surfing when he visited Briones. I would borrow a wetsuit and a board for him and watch from the beach.

Once he flew up from L.A. with a cousin. I picked them up at the San Francisco airport in my Impala, an aging two-door hardtop. Duct tape covered holes in the front seat. The children had spilled a milkshake on the speaker cover in the dash, and the radio sounded fuzzy. His cousin, a fresh-faced, clean-shaven young man, razor-cut hair, chinos, and a sweater-vest, seemed startled. To break the ice I asked him what he'd been doing. He said he had bought a new horse. "My daughter's just come down for the summer with her Arab mare. What did you get?"

"A thoroughbred stallion."

I didn't see it coming. I asked, "Where do you ride?"

He shook his head "I don't ride. We flew him in from Kentucky." It was beginning to dawn on me. The cousin went on, "We'll probably ship him to Ireland. That's where we keep the horses during the European racing season. We have other stables for the French horses at Longchamp and Vincennes." One forgot the scale of these peoples' lives.

Paul and his cousin slept with the children in sleeping bags on the living-room floor. In the morning we all went down to Scowley's restaurant, where patrons must cook their own food. The coffee was already made. We took a table by the window. The cousin said he had to buy a paper and went to the village store. When he had gone, Paul at once leaned over to me and said, "We have to get out of here, he can't handle it. He lives in the Jockey Club."

There were half a dozen of us gathered at the bungalow in L.A. one night. The lights were low. The night was warm. We were sitting around, talking and listening to Pink Floyd. There was a variety of drugs; Paul preferred speedballs—heroin and cocaine.

Around midnight the doorbell rang. Paul opened and there was the famous face of Vanessa Redgrave. With her were two minders in dark suits who looked on in silence. Redgrave was then starring in the movie *Murder on the Orient Express,* and was appearing onstage in Los Angeles with Richard Harris in a Shakespeare production. They came into the living room and sat with us.

Paul was smooth, welcoming. She knelt on the carpet three feet from me and launched into an appeal on behalf of her Workers' Revolutionary Party. I don't recall what she said. The sight of her beautiful face, so near my own, the sound of her celebrated voice, the clear precision of her English, the sincerity of it, mesmerized me.

She had come for Getty money. Her audience watched her, fascinated. She kept her gaze low, spoke uninterrupted for five or ten minutes, and then Paul invited her into the kitchen. When they had gone, the rest of us looked about at one another. In a minute they came back, she thanking Paul and smiling graciously at the rest of us. When the door closed once more and they were gone, our little group whirled in their wake. I took Paul into the kitchen. "What made her so happy? What did you do?"

"I wrote her a check for ten thousand dollars."

"You don't have ten thousand dollars."

"It doesn't matter."

It didn't. Paul could write wallpaper. The family would cover his checks. It wasn't that he didn't have the money. It's just that they wouldn't *give* it to him. That's how he saw it, and as far as he was concerned, he had paid his dues.

In that way Paul was a traditional character, scion of a rich man, confident that his aberrant behavior would be covered over to protect the family name. It was at this time he introduced me to Gail.

When we sat down to work, the first question I asked her was whether she thought the affair had been a hoax. Her handsome face, the set of her jaw, the twinkle in the eye seemed undermined for an instant, then she said calmly, "I knew Paul hadn't done anything really wrong. He wanted to take care of me. Times weren't easy, but he wouldn't really hurt me, especially in that period. He just wouldn't. He told me too much, he came to me too often. We'd sit, the two of us, and talk and talk. He'd tell me his problems. He thinks his father isn't good enough for me. In his peculiar way, he has finally worked out that no one is. Perhaps it was an Oedipus thing.

"He wanted freedom. He was a hangover from the sixties, which had been about freedom. Adults were free and young people were free. The period of the early Beatles influenced a young boy, who was then given freedom because I felt he was really capable and I still feel it. Perhaps I didn't do all of the right things. But I was sure if I sent him off to some fine fat school to be controlled, he wouldn't have *one* but *twenty-two* nervous tics. He needed to be with older people. He's a very unusual boy. There are special things in Paul.

"I may be proved wrong, but I think he's going to be extraordinarily successful—and I don't mean in terms of money—in whatever he happens to do. He's unusually bright, an exceptional man. Certainly before he was kidnapped, he'd seen a lot of life. Was he able to cope with all that? Maybe he did funny things, saw too much at a young age, but he's got past it. He should. He was set up anyway. It seems obvious to me.

"People said I was involved. . . . I know the children's father said some very unpleasant things during the bad period and after it, but I somehow have to excuse him, because he's not really with us. When I saw him in London, he had great fantasies: 'It must have been so and so. It must have been this one. You could have been involved. You could have done it.' I told him, 'I don't need money. If anybody needs money, you do. I don't have a habit to support. If I do need money, I only need a tiny bit.'

"When Paul was fifteen, he went to stay with his father, a disastrous visit. He saw too much in that house and he was given too much. Victoria did or didn't give him 'something'; I imagine she did. When I see Victoria, I'm fairly civil to her, pleasant enough, I suppose, really, because I think I have to be. But when I do stop and think about what she did, I just want to kill her. I know it's great for a young boy to be initiated by an older woman and all that, but not your father's mistress, come on. I'm sure she would deny it, but I know it's true. He had a twenty-four-hour really bad trip on whatever it was that she gave him. I wonder how he's as fine as he is today."

I found backers for the project, film people. They provided me with seed money and with it I spent much of the following summer flying about the world talking to friends of the family, mistresses, servants, and policemen, gathering fragments of the whole. Finally there was Chace, the "controller." He would only see me if I had consent from Old Paul. I did and then flew to Charleston to find Chace living alone in an expensive little bungalow in a pine wood on Wadmalaw Island beside a slough in which floated a forty-foot yacht.

He was still adamant that Little Paul and Gail, as he put it, "cooked up the whole thing and then lost control."

I spent two weeks with him. Not that the interviewing took that long, but he made me call him from my hotel every morning, at which point he would tell me whether it was convenient for us to meet that day or not. Returning at summer's end to the house in Briones, I set about writing Paul's story. My backers, the movie people, constantly chivvied me for pages, but I could not bring the story or myself to life.

Once more I drove down to L.A. to see Paul. There was the usual scene going on, people drifting in and out, Paul avoiding them.

In the afternoon Paul and I went to get breakfast at a coffee shop on Sunset. We sat on stools at the counter. I told him, "I'm not going to write this story. It isn't going to do you any good. I'm sorry."

He swiveled on his stool and looked at me. He didn't seem surprised. "I've made an awful mess of my life."

"Don't say that. There's plenty of time to put things right." There wasn't, and somehow we both knew it.

Thereafter I saw Paul only now and then. On one occasion he drove up to Briones and we walked together beneath eucalyptus trees beside the lagoon, I leaning on a stick and only fourteen years his senior.

As we walked, he looked me up and down and asked, "What's it like?" It was as if he needed to know.

On June 6, 1976, almost exactly a year since I'd stopped work on Paul's book, Old Paul died. He was eighty-three.

Paul told me that his grandfather was found sitting in his armchair in his study, dressed in a dark suit. No one knew the extent of his wealth. His principal interests were said to be business, sex, and the collection of antique art, in that order.

For the next five years, Paul was adrift in the world. I saw little of him in these years. Slowly I lost the use of my legs and adapted to life riding the chair. I wrote a novel that was well received in Hollywood.

Martine was living in San Francisco with Balthazar and Anna, the daughter she had with Rolf Zacher and whom Paul adopted. Sometimes she came out to see me. She gave me what little news there was of him.

He was evidently in London, for we read in the newspapers that he had been caught with a woman one night in flagrante delicto on a bandstand in Hyde Park. Then he called me from the Chelsea Hotel to tell me that he and Patti Smith were going to be in San Francisco and would I have dinner with them. The pair of them, she aglow in the wake of her performance, he high on whatever it was, were excited and enthusiastic. They were a good match that night, very much a couple.

Then I heard he had been given the lead in a Wim Wenders film, The State of Things. *It was being shot in Portugal, all but the last scene, which was to be shot in L.A. I heard nothing more of him for a month or maybe two.*

Martine's memories of these days are what we have to go on:

We had a very open marriage. I am from the sixties and I never believed in a possessive relationship. At the same time I was jealous, but I was very connected to Paul. I always saw him as a big part of myself and Jutta, the three of us. One day we would pull through, and have our world and our vision realized. I had no idea how much I would compromise myself.

Paul and I thought of ourselves as together for the next six years, except that he was gone a lot. He lived in London for a while, in L.A. and in New York. We were "modern nomads," constantly moving, living on credit. I would go to Munich and renew myself. I went to San Francisco when Aileen, Gail's mother, died. We stayed with the grandfather, George, for a while. Then we all decided to stay in San Francisco with the kids and not be in L.A. while they were little.

At one point Paul came to visit me and the kids in San Francisco. He looked very bad. There were many, many times, over and over, every couple of months he would say, "I'm going to quit." But he never did. We went to Tosca's bar, and Paul put his arm around me and said, "We will be together when we're old. We will sit back and look at the mountain." It was one of his attempts at wanting to get straight, to change his life. He had his own vision that somehow it would work itself out and we would have our enlightenment. None of us had any idea how much was in store, how dark it would get, how much shadow there would be. If you fly up very high, you also fall very low.

At some point I realized I could not change Paul, all I could do is pull myself together. I was never a drug addict, but I certainly was crazy and irresponsible. It was all about being free, being an artist, and I thought our lives were normal. At the same time the addiction was real. There was time to put it back together. When I look back now, I don't know what I thought.

I think he couldn't change for several reasons. Paul had to work with facing his own dark side. He often behaved with no consideration, no scruples. I have these things in me, too. I can't just project it all on him. He went through a lot of shit; it was more difficult for him because he had it so easy. He could go through life, living fast and living on credit. In every sense—spiritually, financially, everything. There was so much accumulated. Often we can only change our lives when there is no option. Paul always had so many options. He had his painting, and his words, his writing, his charm and youth, but most of all he had his name, and all the power that went with it. He could get away with murder with no repercussions. He was practically freed of responsibility and consideration for anyone, but then one day was payday. Fortunately I have had faith, to have met Rainer, my guru in Munich, through Jutta, and there was an element in me that took my work with Rainer seriously enough to survive. The constancy of having my whole special family was why I eventually moved to Germany.

When he came back from Portugal, we were staying in New York on Long Island with Mick Jagger, and Paul tried to drown himself. He walked into the sea and Mick had to pull him out onto the beach. After that, we flew back to L.A. and he went into the rehab hospital.

I was living in San Francisco with the children and he was with friends. They took him out of the rehab hospital and brought him up here to see you.

I was awakened in the early morning of a gray dawn to see someone sitting on my wheelchair a few feet from my bed. It was Paul.

I wasn't surprised, or if I was, surprise was overwhelmed by the shock of how he looked. He was a macabre sight, ashen, bloated, almost as unrecognizable as a corpse dredged from the river. An awful image. An aura of malevolence seemed to surround him.

"Let's go outside," I said. He rose from my wheelchair, pushed it beside me, and helped me onto it. He told me, as we stood out on the deck in the dawn, "I haven't read your book, you know."

I shook my head. "It doesn't matter."

"It does. All my friends have done something, but I'm just a name. I can call up anyone in the world and they will meet with me, but only because of my name." He spoke quietly, tentatively, as if afraid of being overheard. Slowly we made our way up the ramp and into the house.

There, in the living room, sat his two companions: his old girlfriend, a rather large young woman, an apprentice opera singer, and a young Englishman, an old Etonian with a nose like the Duke of Wellington's and a chin like Prince Charles's. The young man told me proudly of how he had rescued Paul from a clinic in Los Angeles and they had driven up to see me at high speed. Paul did not join us for breakfast; he had gone into town. He came home in the early afternoon and collapsed in the back bedroom, drunk. I wanted to lock him in, to bar the windows of the room where he was passed out, and hold him prisoner. But it was beyond me, beyond any of us.

That night at dinner Paul was still asleep in the back. I sat with his friends, the two of them bright-eyed, enthusiastically recounting their adventures with Paul, the prize they had liberated from the re-hab hospital. They had no sense of what had come to pass, or what their real role was in all of this, no sense that they were facilitating something awful. I groped around for a solution, something to do. Paul had been in L.A. waiting to shoot the final scene of Wim Wenders's movie. Wenders was in Paris trying to raise more money. The three of us talked into the night around the dining-room table. We went to bed at two. I got up at five to call Wenders in Paris. I wheeled my way into the studio to make the call. Wenders himself answered the phone. I told him that he'd better get here quickly if he wanted his leading man in the last scene. As I was talking, Paul appeared through the French doors, looming over me unsteadily in the half-light, staring down, stony-faced.

I looked at him and said evenly, "There are better ways to kill yourself than this."

"I'm not trying to kill myself."

"Well, you're going to get terribly fucked-up."

They left in the late morning. Got back into a big Mercedes. When his friend asked me to sign a book for him, I wrote, "You're killing our friend with your kindness."

I watched them go and with a heavy heart slowly wheeled my way back into the empty house to find that Paul had drunk every drop of alcohol in the place, even the cooking sherry.

After he'd gone, I once more wished strongly I had kept him with me, or at least persuaded him, talked to him, done something more than I did.

Martine picks up the story of Paul's last discretionary days:

After you, he came to see us in San Francisco. His girlfriend said to me, "I want to marry Paul." Then he and I went to pick up the kids from school. In the car he said to me, "Don't ever say yes to a divorce. I just had to say it. I'm going down. I'm watching my own destruction, and I can't stop it. Just stay with me. I'm all over the place. I'm destroying myself, but don't say yes to any divorce." Paul and I had very different friends at this time. I was with Dennis Hopper and Sean Penn and my acting class, and Paul was with some nice boys who came across drugs, and they liked to party, but not like Paul. They were harmless, but not interesting to me. I met the girlfriend the first time they came to San Francisco and I thought she is a very nice girl, but she doesn't understand what's going on with Paul. It's come to a point where Paul is finished. He needs to go to the hospital. He doesn't make sense anymore. He was not even in his body. It was very poignant. I have this letter he wrote when he was in the rehab hospital. He wrote, "Today is my birthday. I am destroying myself. I miss my wife, I miss my children." He was very paranoid. He had this obsession with Aleister Crowley and black magic, just like his father. He said he heard human voices. He was very, very scared of these voices. He kept pushing his limits. In the end, it was just a question of "Is he going down by himself, or is he going to take someone with him?" When he was in a car or on a motorcycle, he was completely mad. I wanted so badly to understand him better, to be able to talk to him. It's very sad.

He looked so bad, I couldn't imagine that he was the person I had married. I really, really missed him. After he left, I cried like a little girl and I said, "I want my Paul back. I want my Paul back." I couldn't accept that something was all wrong, all wrong. My friend was there and she said, "You better wake up." I was in some deep emotional place that didn't want to see or believe what was happening, to understand anything. He was at the end. That night I had this awful dream that he had been kidnapped again, and brought into the swamps, and he was going down. I called Gail and I said Paul is in really bad shape, he needs to see a doctor. Then a couple of days later I was out with Baltha-zar and Anna and when I got back there was a message on my ma-chine, and it was Gail's voice and she said, "Come immediately, Paul is in a coma, he might not survive." He was only twenty-five years old.

It happened in his British friend's apartment after a party. They thought he was asleep and anyone who knows what happens with heroin overdoses knows that you must wake them up or they slip into a coma. They just didn't know what was happening. They didn't have a clue what to do.

After his Hollywood Bowl truffle had a sewage problem, Paul had left L.A. to take up residence in a house on a lake in County Tipperary, Ireland. No doubt the move was encouraged by the country's most favorable tax laws, but it also made it possible for him to make a rap-prochement with his father, who had embraced British culture so thor-oughly he had a replica of Lord's Cricket Grounds built on the fields of his country estate, Wormsley Hall. It also allowed Paul to spend his remaining summers with his mother in her beloved Tuscany.

One weekend I was up on Lake Shasta in a houseboat and, after we docked, the attendant in office called me over. There was a phone call; it was Gail. Little Paul had slipped into a coma. My son, James, now fifteen, took me, and we flew down to L.A. to see Paul.

We were going to say good-bye, I supposed. Paul was in Cedars-Sinai Hospital, a formidable fortress of a place. Gail met us as we came out of the elevator into a plush, carpeted room. She looked gray and tired. Her usual cheerfulness had turned somber. She seemed relieved to see us. She led us down a hushed, windowless corridor and opened the door to a private room, and there was Paul lying in bed on his back, head turned away from us, auburn hair cut short. He was connected up to lines hanging from IV bottles—a maze of them connected to arms and belly. He was being fed intravenously. There was the hum of electric pumps and the soft hiss of air, presumably being fed into his mattress. We stood looking down on him in silence, as though we were in a church.

I asked to be left alone with him. When the door was closed, I said to him, "You've done it now."

At the sound of my voice his head turned on the pillow to face me. It was a shock. His eyes stared at me blindly, like those of a dead fish, only more bulbous. His stare made the hair on my neck rise. A message was transmitted to me as clearly as if it had been spoken in my ear, "We've got him now. Why don't you fuck off."

I suppose it was the strength of my own imagination reflected back to me.

A moon had slipped from orbit, fallen from the sky, crashing into me. For surely he had been a moon, lit from some other source. When Gail returned, we left. James wheeled me back down the corridor. There was nothing to be said. We descended in a silent, empty elevator. Even James was silent. We went from the cool interior into the clammy heat and glare. It was a shock, this other world still here, still going on, unaffected.

The afternoon sky was washed out, evening coming on. Traffic was building, surging past us, oblivious, slowing, horns, engines blaring, swirling grit into the air to tear our eyes. As we went, the doubt set in, useless and persistent. When I had declined to write his book for fear it might discredit him, had I not denied Paul work, the very thing I had then thought might save him? It was going to be a long drive home, far into the night.

Some days after we got home there came a long, rambling letter from Paul's girlfriend. Her handwriting was as florid and generous as she:

> Charles dear friend,
> I liked meeting you, being at your house, talking to you and I very much want to see you again, to talk to you again and give you good news. But every day I call Paul's doctors and . . .

I let the pages fall to the ground as I read them.

Fragments, that's all any of it was—the speed of a mind, the intent, the ambition, the means, pieces never joined together, never made into a whole. That was the tragedy of it.

After this, I only saw him occasionally, when we went down to L.A. Sometimes we stayed for the night. Finally there came the meeting where once more he asked me to write this story.

I had been working on another book, a medical memoir, when all this happened. I went back and forth between this memoir and the book of Paul's story, so progress was slow on either hand. There was also the matter of my deteriorating health.

Gail, now seventy, had telephoned. I was in the intensive-care ward of a hospital near San Francisco. She said in that same cheerful voice, "Paul and I are in Squaw Valley. He likes to sit-ski." It was a surprise to hear they were in California, for Paul had already left L.A. and moved to tax-friendly Ireland. Martine said that he lived in a castle beside a lake. When I told Gail the work was almost finished, she paused, and then she said, "Well, you know how I feel, but we must respect Paul's wishes."

In April of 2003 came the news that Big Paul had died. He was in the London Clinic. I got the impression that he pretty much lived there.

He had planned a winter sail in the Caribbean aboard his yacht, the *Talitha G.* He invited the Matsons, sent his jet down to Devon where they now lived to pick them up and bring them out to join the party. At the last minute, doctors adjudged Big Paul unfit to travel.

He called the Matsons and told them to carry on without him, come and tell him of the voyage on their return.

He died while the *Talitha G* was at sea. Fiammetta Rocco wrote in London's *Independent* newspaper:

SIR PAUL GETTY [HE WAS MADE A KNIGHT OF THE REALM AFTER HE GAVE SO GENEROUSLY TO THE NATIONAL GALLERY], QUIET BILLIONAIRE AND PHILANTHROPIST, 18 APRIL 2003

"Paul is a much-loved figure," Prime Minister John Major said of Getty in 1994. "And when I say much-loved, I mean for what he is—not just what he's been able to give." . . .

Often anonymously, and without seeking anything in return, Getty became Britain's greatest private philanthropist, giving away well over £200m in the last 20 years. His best-known gifts were the £50m he gave the National Gallery in 1985, £20m to British Film Institute, £5m to St Paul's Cathedral, £5m to the Conservative Party, £1m to Canova's Three Graces, £1m to the Churchill Papers. He supported small projects over big ones and schemes that helped to rehabilitate prison inmates and young offenders, preserve old churches and small village cricket clubs, and help women driven by stress to self-mutilation. His J. Paul Getty Jr. Charitable Trust advertises itself simply as "Supporting Unpopular Causes."

His wife, the former Victoria Holdsworth, whom he married after a long friendship at the end of 1994, was a guiding hand into the outside world that Getty often found so frightening. . . .

When I read these words I realized Paul had not "got to his money" as Marcello had put it, but that Big Paul had spread his father's fortune across the land, just as Little Paul might have done if

Marcello had been right when he predicted that Paul would do great things for his generation. So, some suffering had been relieved, some peace and beauty restored just the same.

It was another two years before I could finish the book Paul had asked me to write when we had sat in the Caffe Trieste in North Beach, San Francisco. Voices freed at last from imprisonment in one closet or another for thirty years had a powerful and disturbing effect on me. It was like bursting into a silent cathedral wherein some barbarous deed had been done. What to do with it now? Who to send it to? If the words they had spoken had been a shock to me, heaven knows what they would do to those whose past they represented.

I thought of Balthazar, Paul and Martine's son, now thirty. He had for some time seemed destined to follow his father into the never-never land that lies beyond the overdose. But now he clearly had gotten over any drug issues and was busy with his family and his music and acting career. What effect would this story have on him? Wasn't it Little Paul's decision to let his son know these details?

I decided to send the typescript to Martine. She had been there when Paul had asked me to write this story, and had long urged me to put it down. She was in Los Angeles visiting her daughter, Anna, who had herself given birth to a daughter. She said she was about to return to Munich. I asked her to review the material in case there were things I had gotten wrong, mailed the typescript to her, and waited for the explosion. It came sooner than I expected. She e-mailed a day or two later:

> I am not sure what your aim is . . . you expose a lot of private things, at the same time you are this "special understanding friend." But in a clan like this, you can only be a "friend" if you

serve their interest, and certainly that isn't done when you make anything controversial public.

You unroll the kidnapping minutely, but seem too cautious to speculate.

I'm somewhat willing to come to see you. But the journey is an exhausting endeavor and as much as I like to see you, it must make sense to me and that it will add to the book. Please write to me your thoughts and what it is you are missing and would like to go after.

Found this little journal from the Rome-times a few days ago. It has a photo with you and me on our terrace in Rome with Anna on my lap.

With love,

Martine

I telephoned her at once. She sounded unhappy, doubtful, hesitant. It wasn't surprising. I reminded her this was a work in progress, that our discussion was part of the work, and invited her to come and set the record straight. I told her that I had been careful not to intrude, interpret, or speculate. These were not my words. This was not my story. The day after this conversation, there was another e-mail from Martine:

I feel that I was too harsh and projecting, I think that you are right. That I was distraught . . . and I am still. The book has put me in real upheaval and a lot of anger came up and you are the first one I hit on.

But I also think that you understand that it's part of a process and I'm even glad because I do feel I have to face my past, my "history" . . . and you present new information in my somewhat "idealized" version of it . . . let me know what you think and let's discuss everything further . . . I would like to cooperate with you in a positive way. . . .

I called her the next day and said that what struck me, and what I would like to know from her, is why her voice, apart from those times when I was with her in Rome, was missing once Paul disappeared and she had taken the first letter to Gail. Thereafter, there is no trace of her until Gail invites her to the clinic. I assumed that this was because when we were doing the interviewing, making the transcripts in '75, the focus was on Little Paul and getting his story, so hers had been eclipsed. She made no answer. Once more I invited her to come to see me and explain what had happened to her voice, why it had disappeared. It would be better if she came to where I was, escaping from all the other demands on her attention. She said she would come and postponed returning to Munich so that she could do so.

It was on a Thursday, a few days later, that she called. She said she would drive up on Friday morning and be with me in the afternoon so we could spend a day talking.

A winter storm was in progress, rain lashing the house, drifting across the lagoon, sometimes heavy enough to obscure the hills. Ducks flew about urgently into the wind.

Los Angeles was being hit by the storm harder than usual. There were reports on the radio of mudslides destroying houses. One such mudslide delayed Martine. She telephoned in the afternoon. She had taken the Pacific Coast Highway and was stuck somewhere south of Big Sur. It was dark by the time she did arrive.

I suggested we go to the studio. She pushed my wheelchair out of the living room onto the deck, sliding the glass door closed behind us. The rain had let up; the night sky was clear. From the marsh came the symphony of frogs. Down the ramp, across the wooden footbridge, to the studio we went, the two of us. Paul was in Ireland somewhere, Jutta in Germany, hopefully fast asleep, the both of them.

In the studio Martine and I sat across from each other, the reading lamp low so that its light rose from the desktop, illuminating her face softly, drawing the pair of us into its close circle. In that light the years dropped away; she was young again, as when I had first come to Rome. The light did not reach far into the darkness. I sensed Paul was there just beyond its edge, where he had stood the last time we were together here.

"What is it you want to know?" Martine chose her words carefully. I repeated my question: Why did her voice disappear immediately after the kidnapping commenced, reappearing only when it was over?

She talked quickly, earnestly:

Jutta is my great love, and no man could ever colonize us. We had each other, and Paul was like a third one. He was so intelligent, fast, so beautiful. Jutta and I wanted to create our lives as a "living theater" and we thought that Paul wanted the same, wanting to get out of the power structure of his family. We wanted to make, the three of us, movies, art. He told us about his father's castle in Marrakesh, and how fantastic it was. We had pictures of Moroccan castles on the walls. We decided we were going to have artists come and make films together. We had this whole fantasy. But it was more; it was a vision of this life we wanted to create. We wanted to help to create a female world in this sort of tough mafia world, and Paul was the one to help us do it. We had this vision of our "Island of Eternal Happiness."

At some point, when we were in love, Paul came to me and said, "I know the right people, I'm going to have myself kidnapped, then we can get a castle in Morocco." Jutta and I were afraid, but we thought it was more talk, like our vision of a different world. We needed money for our vision. At least, we thought we did. We thought, "We are the New World, the New People," and we were going to make something totally great and beautiful with the grandfather's money.

Like the young generation of that time, we were looking for Utopia, for a world of love. That was the aim, the cause, the Holy Grail for which we did everything. And as children of God, everything, we thought, was allowed.

Paul, coming from a very rich family, had on one side the lawlessness of the super-rich, but also on the other side the new lawlessness of the young quester. He was looking for the new world, and his tragedy was that he got caught between these two forces. He thought that with the means of the old world he could build the new world and cooked up the kidnapping. It was his tragic mistake thinking that with the money we could build our parallel world, "A World of Love and Peace." He didn't tell us much about his kidnapping plans, but whatever he told us, we sanctioned. We fell into the same mistake of thinking that any means justifies the end.

Paul wanted to find and be part of the new world. His father, and he is very influenced by his father, had done this already to a certain degree. He married Talitha, a golden hippie, left the old world and its confinements and responsibilities [working for Getty Oil, his four children, stepping into his father's shoes, etc.]. They went to Marrakesh, living a free life, and that's where Paul saw it first. Talitha and Big Paul also paid dearly for the same reason, not understanding that in order to live a new life you have to change yourself. I think that's why they got stuck in drugs that eventually destroyed them and my Paul even more, since he also wanted more and risked more.

He asked me to marry him the day he disappeared because he wanted to reassure himself, that his risk would be worthwhile and that I still would be there.

He is not the only one; many young people of that generation who wanted to build a new world got caught in this mistake. You cannot use the wrong means for the right cause. Also the RAF [the Red Army Faction, another name for the Baader-Meinhof group], who took up arms and went into the violent way of wanting to change the world, became tragic victims of themselves and lost their lives. The revolution eats her own children. You can only build a loving world with love, not by violence.

Only the Kommune 1 [a political group in Berlin and our idols at the time]—and that's where Rainer, our lifelong friend, comes in—understood deeply that before you change the world you have to change yourself. Within! And they did it, and that distinguishes them from all other political groups and that's why they were the "Heart of the Revolution."

Paul knew and understood that and he phoned Rainer a few days before he fell in his coma. They talked about it and Paul had a moment where he wanted to come to Munich to work with him, like we do. But it was too late. He could not stop his self-destruction. He did finally get out of the role that was assigned to him, but at the cost of his self-destruction. He still calls Rainer when things get serious and when he needs to get a perspective of his state of being.

We always thought we would work our way through the tunnel into the light. We, of course, had been taking acid. We really thought we were God's children. We could do anything, play any game, everything was maya, illusion. We saw ourselves as visionaries. We thought Paul was like us. We thought, "He understands, and he can provide it all." We were going to carry on the sixties.

But after Paul told us he was going to get himself kidnapped, things changed. They started to go well for us. We became a little bit known. After we made the *Cocaine* pictures, we started to get work. Paul didn't want to be kidnapped anymore, but they were following him. One night when we were in our apartment, he saw them standing out in the street, waiting, and he threw a chair at them from the window.

He asked me to marry him, then he disappeared.

When he had told us about his kidnapping, Paul had told us never to talk about it. So after he disappeared, we were in this dilemma. If we told the police all that had happened to us, about Ciambellone kidnapping us, they wouldn't take this kidnapping seriously, and at this point I thought it was very serious. If we tell what we know, then the gangsters would come and kill us, or they would kill Paul. We were really stressed. On one hand we knew the truth, but we didn't know if it would help the police and if we said one word too much, *boom*.

A man telephoned us and said, "We are journalists writing about Paul. He is on a boat. He is safe. We want to tell you that." I couldn't find any words. Then he asked, "What is the name of the boat?" We said, "We don't know, you are the one who said he is safe." He said, "Did you make those photographs with him?" He was talking about the *Cocaine* picture. This photograph is famous all over the world. I said, "We didn't get anything from this." He said, "This was a good idea of yours." Then he started to talk very tough with us, and he said, "We are police." And suddenly, there were like twenty police cars and they took us to the *questura* like we were criminals. They put us in separate rooms and shone light right in our faces. I knew that Jutta wasn't going to say anything, and Jutta knew that I wasn't going to say anything. They didn't know about twins. They tried several things. First, they said I arranged it with Paul, and he's somewhere on a ship, that we wanted to do it so our pictures would make money. Then they said it was politically related, because we had been in a Communist student organization in Berlin in the sixties, and we did it to buy weapons for the Red Brigade. They assumed we knew where Paul was. They shouted questions at us from the late afternoon through the whole night until early in the morning. It was exhausting. Especially with all the accumulated fear we had. They were finally nice and let us go and told us to stay in Rome.

So we stayed in Rome.

We became really known. We were in the papers. All the attention was very exciting, I can't deny it. Jutta was together with Mario Schifano, a very big, known, charismatic, beautiful artist. He lived in the palazzo of Dado Ruspoli. He was Jutta's great love. He was great friends with the whole Bertolucci crowd; they were very interested in making a film with us. We became in a way the hip girls. We were written about in magazines. We were the new type of women looking for new ways to express ourselves, trying to invent a different way of living. We came out of the sixties and we won, maybe not politically but in a cultural, self-finding sort of way. At some point Mario Schifano said to us, "You should get out of this whole Getty thing. You are popular, you are artists, you should have your own lives." He hated the Gettys. He got us a hotel and said, "You go into hiding, no reporter will find you." So we stayed in this grand hotel, in August, very huge. It was Ferragosto, so everyone had left Rome, and we were alone in this enormous hotel. We invited all our friends. Normally we didn't have any money, but Mario paid for it all. When he got the bill, he asked, "What's this?" and we said, "You feed us, you feed our friends." There was a great sense of community and friendship, and we are all one. Then Carlo Ponti called us into his office and wanted to make a film with us, but we were completely disorganized, not reliable. We wanted to be as free as possible, and when you're free you don't take any responsibility, make any commitment. Then we moved to the apartment where you met us, with the terrace.

After Marcello told us that they had found that burned-up body on the beach [the Chipmunk], we were really afraid. We were very afraid for Paul. We didn't hear from Gail and we didn't hear much from Marcello, until you came. You came at the time they found the body. We were living in this fear, with this kind of guilt, we knew all this stuff and we couldn't say anything. And at the same time the excitement of being personalities, somebody. We had very exciting lives, and I always felt very connected to Paul. But we weren't sure what was going on, maybe Paul was safe, maybe he had done it all and we were going to have our castle in Marrakesh. We thought perhaps he was free and the family had taken him away. Then we didn't hear anything about it except what was written in the newspapers. We had no clue what was going on.

Marcello knew about our vision, but he never mentioned it during the kidnapping. I didn't trust him one bit. Maybe he was harmless, but I always thought that he had got Paul mixed up with the *mala-vita*. He said he tried to keep Paul away from them.

Then one morning, in the winter, I went to the train station. I wanted to go to Germany to visit Anna, my daughter, and my parents for a couple days. I didn't tell the police I was leaving Rome. I purchased a ticket and waited for the train. I bought a paper and saw the picture of Paul's ear. I thought I was going to have a heart attack. I sat down on a bench. I was shaking. It seemed so unbelievably cruel. I thought, How is Paul going to survive this? How can anyone go through so much pain and fear and everything? I sat on the bench for a very long time. The train came and left and I went back home and laid down. I got very depressed. Still no word from Paul's family. We went to the Sorrento Film Festival in December. Fassbinder, he was one of the icons of the political movement in Germany, he was going to be there and he was going to make a film with us. While we were there Marcello called us and told us Paul is free and he wants to see us. Jutta and I said, "Let's pack up and let's go back to Rome." So we went up to our room and when we came down with our bags we met Fassbinder in the lobby. He wanted us to come with him. There was this instant. There was this feeling that we were choosing our future lives. Paul was free—Fassbinder was waiting. We decided to go to Rome.

Jutta and I are very defensive about Paul. He is part of us. We don't want to shed any bad light on him. But I think I have a kind of fantasy about him that I blend out the really heavy stuff. Because of what he was and the speed of his mind, one wanted him to be more than he was. He was like a promise. Morocco was disastrous for him. He was highly intelligent, highly sensitive. He wanted to be with his father, and what his father was doing was all wrong. He was neglected and spoiled at the same time. We were all in the same boat. We all paid a high price. Paul paid the highest price.

———

She fell silent, finished. I spun on. A pattern was forming in the mosaic. Munich, Munich, Munich. It had kept cropping up in both her account and Gail's. The Munich gang Gail said they had almost paid a ransom to. When she began talking about Paul organizing his own kidnapping to finance the art, it fit with my idea of what had happened, but now something very different was emerging and I looked at Martine anew. Had I been wrong? Was it the haywire politics of the sixties, the German Red Army Faction, the Baader-Meinhof? Was that what Little Paul, at sixteen, so sure of himself, had been swept up by—Kommune 1, Rainer Langhans [Martine's guru], Uschi Obermaier, Munich? Sex, the rejection of bourgeois values, it was all there. Had these people made a plan, released the idea into the world? They needed money; revolutionaries have their expenses. If it had been these people, they must have been surprised when they quickly realized, in Munich, there was suddenly and silently another player on the field, the Calabresi mafia, and that they were in a race for Little Paul, or rather his grandfather's money. The mafia had gotten to Little Paul first. He had been, as Bob Dylan put it, "a pawn in the game," nothing but a name, as he himself had said. Had he been a naïf caught between the old and new eras, cultures and criminals, Baader-Meinhof and Calabresi, the sixties and seventies, between the Beatles' *Sgt. Pepper* and David Bowie's *Diamond Dogs,* between *Easy Rider* and *A Clockwork Orange?* What chance had he, the son of those who imagined, as Fitzgerald said, that they were different, that wealth might also buy license to break natural law without penalty? No wonder the Munich group had been so persistent and the Calabresi had been so worried that the ransom would go to Munich.

Now I began to wonder if Little Paul had boasted to the Munich group that he knew people who would stage the kidnapping on their behalf and that he had then approached the Chipmunk, a Napoletano cigarette smuggler who in turn had approached his friend Piccolo, a bandy-legged Calabrian Lambretta mechanic connected with kidnappers. If, unbeknownst to anyone, Piccolo had sold Paul to the Calabrian mafia. Paul had then changed his mind, but it was too late. The mafia had already picked up his scent and were coming for him.

He had proposed marriage to Martine in Piazza Navona the night he disappeared because he knew they were coming for him; Martine herself had said as much. So even before it began it must have been a nightmare for Paul. He had been out of his depth, gotten it all wrong. Haves and have-nots became their opposites and thus they were one and the same; Little Paul had become caught between them, between left and right, have and have-not, between two parties who attached to money more strongly than to life itself.

The Calabresi had murdered the Chipmunk to cut him out of the deal. Piccolo was the villain, as far as I could see. He had betrayed them all. Paul had first recognized him as he had been carried out of the car in the beginning, identified him again at the cutting of the ear, and surely it was Piccolo, short, bow-legged, as Chace described the man, who had come out of the bushes, waving a gun when the money was handed over. Piccolo was there all along.

Looking upon Little Paul comatose in Cedars-Sinai hospital, I had assumed that it was my own inner voice I had heard: *We've got him now. Why don't you fuck off?* But just then came Martine's words. "He heard voices. He was very scared of them." And I suddenly found myself wondering whether the voice had some independent reality. In either case, I had no wish to linger in this realm, sucked at by darkness, no wish to lend my light to another, leaving myself in the dark. There could be no fathoming. There was no single truth.

Martine smiled. Now I knew. She had opened to me, revealed their secret. She was relieved. I felt ambushed and strangely exhausted. This was entirely unexpected: justifications, denials, revisions, these I expected, not a confession.

First I looked to place blame, but it was everywhere and nowhere.

His grandfather's great fortune gave rise to a sense of omnipotence. Paul had been raised this way. How can we blame Gail for standing by her son, a son for wanting his father's love, the desperate for turning to desperate means? The snake feeds upon the flightless bird. There is no blame.

"Should we go back into the house?" Martine said softly.

We left the studio back into the dark, across the footbridge. I felt Paul standing there just beyond the edge of the light, saying to me once more, "I am nothing but a name." Silently we went, Martine behind the wheelchair, rising above me more than I once rose above her, leaving Paul standing there alone in the dark.

She pushed my chair up the ramp.

Light from the living room lit the deck. Martine slid open the glass door and we went in. There was the aroma of cooking. Véro was in the kitchen. The room was warm. I knew Martine would not stay. "I have to see some other friends," she said. She had given of herself and wanted rest. We made some small talk. She was gracious. She had an assurance she had not had before. It fitted her well, making up for whatever the years had taken away. Then she went down the steps into the hall. The front door closed softly behind her. The sound of her car faded into the night. I remembered the sound of her voice over the telephone: "We would like to make some work with you." It had been done. The adventure was over. I heard Véro's step behind me and felt the wheelchair gently turning. "Let's eat," she said.

Martine e-mailed the following day:

> I'm glad that I came. It was a poignant visit for me . . . last night I sat in the hot tub under the stars for a very long time and, in a strange way, everything seemed good even though there were also sad feelings, a kind of mourning.

I'm happy I saw you and was in your house . . . it is full of memories and very connected to Paul . . . he was very much there last night.

I also enjoyed seeing Véronique, she looked very beautiful. Please give my love to her.

Much love and thank you so much,

Take good care,

Martine

I sent Paul a draft. Gail told me that Paul had the typescript read to him. She said it took three days. Martine told me that Paul had told her to tell me, "That's how it was."

Paul outlived his father by eight years. He died in his father's country house in England surrounded by family. He was fifty-four. He and Martine had spent his last summer together in Tuscany.

London's *Independent* wrote:

JOHN PAUL GETTY III: OIL HEIR WHOSE LIFE WAS OVERSHADOWED BY HIS 1973 KIDNAPPING

The sad and relatively short life of John Paul Getty III, whose severed ear became a grisly symbol of the wave of kidnappings that swept Italy in the 1970s, was proof that being a grandson of the richest man in the world was no guarantee of happiness.

Happiness? He had his moments: the farm on the Appian Way; Christmases in his grandfather's mansion; *A Midsummer Night's Dream* at St. George's; a picnic with Talitha and his father in the Garden of Eden; the gardens of Mamounia, where his boyhood innocence was finally laid to rest. Thereafter, forces that had been gathering were unleashed, and he and his beloved Talitha paid for whatever good his father did. Paul was knocked off his feet before ever he found them. What may be said for him is that he lived the life that was presented to him.

Long-haired Getty with wife Martine Zacher. (AP Images)

INDEX

Abate, Claudio, 130
Prince Moalay Abdellah (King
    Hassan's brother), 86
acid, 84, 202
    Big Paul's use of, 86
    Little Paul's use of, 114–18,
        120–21, 124, 269
A Clockwork Orange, 112, 115, 273
Agnelli, Gianni, 69
Air France drug dealers, 125–27,
    146
"A Last Confession" (Rossetti), 111
Algerian War of Independence,
    52, 53
Alpert, Herb, 92
Antonioni, 3
Aumont, Tina, 246

Baader-Meinhof Gang, 27, 33, 268,
    270, 273
Balaban, Bruce, 64
Banca Commerciale, 218
the Beatles, 14, 59, 252, 273
Becket, Thomas à, 111
Berlin by the Wall, 244

Bertrand, Olivier, 11–12
The Bible, 68
Big Paul. *See* Getty, Jean Paul, II
Bob (Big Paul's friend), 110
Bobby (Little Paul's girlfriend), 110,
    124
Boleyn, Anne, 59, 118
Botticelli restaurant, Rome, 25,
    28, 32
Bowie, David, 124, 273
Boyd, Rick, 19–20, 124, 131, 144
Brando, Marlon, 83–84
Bridges, Harry, 45
British Film Institute, 263
Bronson, Charles, 109
Brooke, Lionel, 76
Brooke, Victoria, vii, 76, 84, 87,
    263
    Little Paul's kidnapping and,
        153–54, 165–66
    Little Paul's relationship with,
        112–17, 121, 243–44, 253
    Pol's death and, 97–99, 101–4,
        106–7
Bruno (kidnapper), 190–91, 204
Buddhism, 110

Bullimore, Francis, 120
"The Burden of Nineveh" (Rossetti),
    111
Burroughs, Bill, 79–80
Byron (driver), viii, 118

Caen, Herb, 44
Calabresi kidnappers, 273–74.
    See also hoax/fraud speculation,
        Getty kidnapping
    arrests of, 244–45
    ear severance by, 35–36, 192, 197,
        199–211, 238–39
    false kidnapping claims and,
        149–50, 159–61, 182–85, 273
    fractures within, 168, 178–79,
        180, 187, 189–90, 195
    history of, 39–40
    meetings arranged with, 185–86,
        195–99
    negotiations with, 9–11, 18–20,
        33–38, 135–36, 144, 150, 152,
        154–61, 164–65, 166, 169–75,
        179–85, 190–93, 195–99, 203,
        204–11, 212–18
    ransom amounts and, 145–47,
        150–51, 157–58, 168–73, 175,
        206, 212–13, 215–16
    ransom drop made to, 180–81,
        191–92, 206–7, 213, 216–24,
        230
    release of hostage by, 225–29
    treatment of hostage by, 162–64,
        168–69, 186–90, 193–94,
        200–204
Canova's Three Graces (sculpture),
    263
carabinieri, 205, 229–30, 232–36,
    239
Castaneda, Carlos, 5

Castle, June, 54
Catherine of Aragon, 118
Cedars-Sinai Hospital, Los Angeles,
    260–61, 274
Chace, James Fletcher, vii, 177–78,
    253
    background of, 137–38
    ear severance and, 205–10
    hoax speculations by, 151–52, 159,
        167, 175, 254
    kidnapping investigation by, 137,
        139, 143–44, 149–52
    kidnapping negotiations by, 150,
        155–56, 158–59, 161, 164–65,
        166, 170–75, 179–82, 190–92,
        204–5, 207, 212–18
    Little Paul's release and, 227–28,
        231–36
    meetings with kidnappers and,
        185–86, 195, 196, 198–99
    ransom exchange and, 180–81,
        191–92, 206–7, 217–23, 274
Chace, Patsy, 137
Cherchio, Jerry, viii, 62, 154
    Big Paul's drug use and, 103–4,
        107
    kidnapping hoax speculation and,
        167
    Pol's death and, 99–100
Cherchio, Ruth, 62–63
Chevalier, Maurice, 53, 87
the Chipmunk (kidnapper), vii,
    162–63, 168–69
    kidnapping plot origins and,
        273–74
    murder of, 34–35, 178–80, 274
Churchill Papers, 263
Churchill, Sir Winston, 79, 83
Ciambellone, viii, 28–31, 124–26,
    146, 152, 269
cocaine, 81

Big Paul and, 85–86, 100
Little Paul and, 112–13, 125–27, 130, 248, 251, 269–70
malavita and, 28–32, 41, 126, 146
Cocaine pictures, 130, 269–70
"Cockney Pauline," viii, 114, 120
Conservative Party, United Kingdom, 263
Cook, Peter, 250
Cooper, Alice, 248
Cozzi, D. O., viii, 39
Crisi, Marcello, vii, 4, 22–24, 41, 124, 134, 136–37, 138, 245, 263–64
    fraud, 25–26
    Getty's release and, 240
    kidnapping, 161
    Mafia, 125–28, 189, 271–72
Crowley, Aleister, 110, 249, 259
Curtis, Tony, 109

Daily Express (London), 11
Daily Mail (London), 11
Daily Telegraph (London), 11
Daley, Ed, viii, 185
d'Almeida, Ann, 57, 64, 228
d'Almeida, George, viii, 57, 64, 113, 154, 177, 228
Daniel (Little Paul's friend), 127
D'Annunzio, Gabriele, 249
Della Ratta, Luigi, viii, 144, 151, 155–56, 165, 166, 176–77
    Little Paul's release and, 214–15, 227, 234, 237, 240
Derek (Big Paul's minder), viii, 166, 242
Derek (Old Paul's manservant), viii, 120

Devret, Danielle, viii, 128, 131–32, 136, 144, 147
    kidnapping suspicions, 11, 19, 129–30, 144, 148
Diamond Dogs, 124, 273
DiRobina family, 57
Distinguished Service Order (DSO), 137
La Dolce Vita, 56
drugs/alcohol
    acid, 84, 86, 114–18, 120–21, 124, 202, 269
    Big Paul's use of, 47–48, 71, 75–76, 85–87, 97, 100–104, 106–7, 117, 147, 253, 268
    cocaine, 28–32, 41, 81, 85–86, 100, 112–13, 125–27, 130, 146, 248, 251, 269–70
    heroin, 12, 99–102, 107, 109, 111, 117, 147, 244, 246, 251
    Little Paul's use of, 108–9, 112–18, 120–21, 124–28, 244, 246, 247–48, 251, 253, 255–59, 269
    opium, 75–76, 85–87, 97, 101, 103–4, 106–7, 111
DSO. *See* Distinguished Service Order
Dunaway, Faye, 112
Dylan, Bob, 36, 273

Easy Rider, 124, 273
Elisco, Martino, viii
    Getty's release and, 205, 229–30, 232–35, 239

Faisal, King (of Saudi Arabia), 57
Faithfull, Marianne, 84
Fantasia, 112

Fassbinder, Rainer Werner, 272
FBI, 183, 207
Fellini, 56
Fifty (kidnapper), vii
    kidnapping negotiations by, 34,
        135, 150, 157–58, 169–72,
        181–82, 184–85, 192, 203,
        205–7, 210–11
    Little Paul's release and, 227
    ransom-hostage exchange and,
        221, 223–24, 227
FitzGerald, Desmond, 74
Fitzgerald, F. Scott, v, 273
Fonda, Jane, 89
Fonda, Peter, 89
Forrester, Jack, viii, 53–54
Fox, James, 1–6, 260–61
Fox, Véro, 1–6, 275–76
Franco (kidnapper), 191
Frankenstein, 130
Freeman, Bob, 13–14, 16, 130
Freud, Sigmund, 146

Gandolfo, Mario, 149
Garbo, Greta, 119
Getty, Aileen (daughter of Big Paul),
    56–57, 58, 166, 234, 240
Getty, Anna Zacher (stepdaughter of
    Little Paul), 27, 247, 255, 260,
    264–65, 272
Getty, Anne (wife of Gordon), 246
Getty, Ariadne (daughter of Big
    Paul), 56, 58, 166, 234, 240
Getty, Balthazar (son of Little Paul),
    vii, 5, 260, 264
    birth of, 247
Getty, Gail Harris (mother of Little
    Paul), vii, 24, 75–76, 112–13,
    255, 276
    background of, 45–49

custody issues and, 166–67,
    176–78, 215
Della Ratta's relationship with,
    viii, 144, 151, 155–56, 165,
    166, 176–77, 214–15, 227, 234,
    237, 240
ear severance and, 205–10
hoax speculations associated with,
    9, 11, 18–19, 135, 140–42,
    151–52, 159, 167, 175, 252–54
Jeffries' relationship with, 71–72,
    94–95
kidnapping negotiations by, 9–11,
    18–20, 33–38, 135–36, 144,
    150, 155–56, 164–65, 180–83,
    195–99, 205–10, 273
letters from kidnappers to,
    138–42, 145, 151, 160, 169,
    174–75, 196, 266
letter to Nixon by, 215
Little Paul's relationship with, 6,
    20, 70–72, 92, 93–94, 108–10,
    122, 152, 244, 245, 252–53,
    260, 275
marriages of, 45, 47–48, 60–66,
    71, 94–95
overdose/stroke of Little Paul and,
    1, 3, 6, 260–61
press's portrayal of, 142, 147–49,
    155–56
ransom exchange and, 180–81,
    191–92, 206–7, 216–24
release of Little Paul and, 226–28,
    230–41
Getty, George (son of Old Paul), 49,
    153
Getty, Gordon (son of Old Paul), vii,
    1, 45–47, 53, 77–78, 246
Getty, Jean Paul (Old Paul), vii, 6
    background/family history of, 14,
    17–18, 33, 44–46, 49–55

Big Paul's relationship with, 48,
49–50, 52–55, 57, 60–62, 66,
77–78, 119, 153, 155, 212–13
death of, 254
kidnapping investigation by,
137–39, 147–50, 151–52
kidnapping ransom and, 20, 33,
37, 152, 156, 158, 170–71,
207, 211–13, 215–16, 230,
241
Little Paul's ear severance and,
211
Little Paul's relationship with,
52–53, 55, 59, 66, 118–21,
210–11, 241, 249
Little Paul's release and, 241
marriages of, 14, 45, 46
museums funded by, 24, 118–19
son's lawsuit against, 77–78
Getty, Jean Paul, II (Big Paul, son of
Old Paul), vii, 165
alcohol/substance use by, 47–48,
71, 75–76, 85–87, 97, 100–104,
106–7, 117, 147, 253, 268
birth of, 46
children's births and, 44, 56–58,
81, 84, 96, 98, 123, 153
custody issues and, 166–67,
176–78, 215
death of, 262–63
kidnapping/ransom negotiations
and, 37, 135–36, 145, 150, 152,
154–55, 170–71, 181, 210–13,
215–16, 230
Little Paul's ear severance and,
210–11
Little Paul's relationship with, 2,
67–70, 87–90, 93–95, 108–18,
121, 152, 154, 210–13, 242–44,
253, 259, 260, 268, 272, 275,
277

marriages of, 45, 47–48, 50,
60–66, 71, 75, 99
Morocco lifestyle of, 33, 79–90
Old Paul's relationship with, 48,
49–50, 52–55, 57, 60–62, 66,
77–78, 119, 153, 155, 212–13
philanthropy by, 263
Pol's relationship with, 11–12, 17,
66, 68–70, 73–76, 78–90,
96–107, 112, 147
youth of, 45–47
Getty, Jean Paul, III (Little Paul, son
of Big Paul), vii, 8, 277. See also
kidnapping of Little Paul
art fraud by, 25–26, 151–52
Big Paul's influence on/
relationship with, 2, 67–70,
87–90, 93–95, 108–18, 121,
152, 154, 210–13, 242–44,
253, 259, 260, 268, 272, 275,
277
biography interviews given by,
247–52
birth of, 44, 48, 58
Brooke's relationship with,
112–17, 121, 243–44, 253
childhood, pre-kidnapping, of,
58–60, 66–72, 87–96, 102–6,
108–24
children of, vii, 5, 247, 255,
264–65
Cocaine pictures by, 130, 269–70
college attendance by, 248–49
death of, 276–77
drug use by, 108–9, 112–18,
120–21, 124–28, 244, 246,
247–48, 251, 253, 255–59,
269
film by, 244
health of, 1–6, 55, 65–66, 95,
259–62

Getty, Jean Paul, III (*continued*)
  kidnapping hoax speculation tied
    to, 11, 18–20, 26, 140–42, 144,
    175, 253–54, 267–70, 273–74
  Lang's relationship with, 67–68,
    70–72, 91–92, 94
  malavita ties to, 25–33, 124–27,
    140, 152, 175, 272
  marriage of, 41, 245, 255–56,
    268, 269, 274
  mother's relationship with, 6, 20,
    70–72, 92, 93–94, 108–10,
    122, 152, 244, 245, 252–53,
    260, 275
  Old Paul's relationship with,
    52–53, 55, 59, 66, 118–21,
    210–11, 241, 249
  overdose by, 259–62
  paintings by, 23–26
  Pol's death and, 96, 100–102,
    105–6
  post-kidnapping state of, 241,
    242–46
  self-kidnapping references by, 127,
    129, 267–69, 273
  suicide attempt by, 257
  Zacher's relationship with, 4–5,
    32–33, 41–42, 124–28,
    237–38, 240, 242, 244–46,
    255–56, 267–69, 271–72, 274
Getty, Mark (son of Big Paul), 56,
  58, 123, 166, 234, 240
Getty, Sarah C. (mother of
  Old Paul), vii, 46
  trust fund of, 50, 77–78, 207
Getty, Tara Gabriel Gramophone
  Galaxy (son of Big Paul), 81,
  84, 96, 98, 123, 153
Getty, Teddy (wife of Old Paul), 14
Getty, Timothy (son of Old Paul), 55
Gibbs, Christopher, 84, 87

Ginsberg, Allen, 79–80
Glin, Knight of, 74
The Godfather, 43, 249
Graudi, Paolo, 149, 240
The Great Dictator, 109
The Great Gatsby (Fitzgerald), v
Greer, Germaine, 105–6
Gurdjieff, G. I., 5

Halsey, Brett, 64
Hammer, Armand, 176
Harris, Aileen, viii, 45, 177–78, 213,
  255
Harris, George, viii, 45, 177–78,
  207, 213, 256
Harris, Richard, 251
Hassan, King (of Morocco), 86–87,
  89
Hazelwood, Jay, 79–80
Hearst, William Randolph, 69
Heatherton, Joey, 182–83
Henry VIII (king of England),
  118–19
Hepburn, Audrey, 56
heroin, 111
  Big Paul's use of, 100, 117, 147
  Little Paul's use of, 244, 246, 251
  Pol's use of, 12, 99–102, 107, 109
"Hey Jude," 105
hoax/fraud speculation, Getty
  kidnapping
  by Chace, 151–52, 159, 167, 175,
    254
  Cherchio ties to, 167
  Getty, Gail, ties to, 9, 11, 18–19,
    135, 140–42, 151–52, 159, 167,
    175, 252–54
  Little Paul, ties to, 11, 18–20, 26,
    140–42, 144, 175, 253–54,
    267–70, 273–74

by police, 140–42, 148, 152, 175,
    270
Zacher and, 18–19, 140–42,
    267–70, 273–74
Holdsworth, Victoria. *See* Brooke,
    Victoria
Homage to Catalonia (Orwell), 20
Hopper, Dennis, 259
Huston, John, 68

Iacovoni, Giovanni, vii, 20, 33, 36,
    149
    ear severance and, 208–9
    kidnapping negotiations by,
        34–35, 150, 157–58, 159–61,
        164–65, 167, 169–74, 181,
        184–85, 195–96, 198, 204,
        218–20
    ransom delivery and, 218–20
Ichazo, Oscar, 5
Independent (London), 263, 276
Intento, 214
Iovinella, viii
    Getty's release and, 227–28,
        231–36
Italy. *See also* Calabresi kidnappers;
    malavita
    drug laws in, 12, 100–101
    kidnappings, historical, in, 39–40

Jagger, Bianca, 131
Jagger, Mick, 84, 129, 131, 248, 257
Jeffries, Lang, viii, 62–65, 66, 109
    Little Paul's relationship with,
        67–68, 70–72, 91–92, 94
    marriage of, 71–72, 94–95
John (Little Paul's minder), 1–5
John, Augustus, 12
John, Elton, 109

Johnson, Sue, 131, 136
J. Paul Getty Jr. Charitable Trust, 263
Jung, Carl, 5

Karim, Aga Khan, 39
Kathy (Old Paul's cook), 120
Keller, Hiram, 98, 127–28
Kennedy, John F., 58
Kerouac, Jack, 80
kidnapping of Little Paul. *See also*
    hoax/fraud speculation,
        Getty kidnapping
    arrests in, 244–45
    ear severance in, 35–36, 192, 197,
        199–211, 238–39
    events leading up to, 129–32
    execution of, 132–35
    hoax/fraud speculation related to,
        9, 11, 18–20, 26, 37, 41,
        129–30, 131, 135, 136–37,
        138–42, 144, 148–49, 151–52,
        159, 167, 175, 179, 253–54,
        267–70, 273–74
    hostage release in, 225–41
    kidnappings, historical, and,
        39–40
    letters from hostage/kidnappers
        in, 138–42, 145, 151, 160, 169,
        174–75, 192–93, 196, 266
    living conditions of hostage in,
        133–35, 138, 144–45, 162–64,
        168–69, 186–90, 193–94,
        200–204
    meetings, with kidnappers, and,
        185–86, 195–99
    negotiations during, 9–11, 18–20,
        33–38, 135–36, 144, 150, 152,
        154–61, 164–65, 166, 169–75,
        179–85, 190–93, 195–99, 203,
        204–11, 212–18

kidnapping of Little Paul (*continued*)
    parties claiming responsibility for,
        149–50, 159–61, 182–85, 273
    press coverage of, 9–11, 16–20,
        35–38, 40–41, 135, 137,
        141–42, 147–49, 155–56,
        173–74, 181, 208–9, 211, 217,
        221, 228, 233–41
    ransom amount fluctuations in,
        145–47, 150–51, 157–58,
        168–73, 175, 206, 212–13,
        215–16
    ransom exchange in, 180–81,
        191–92, 206–7, 213, 216–24,
        230
    release of hostage in, 38
"Knockin' on Heaven's Door," 36
Kommune 1, 269, 273
Korean War, 137
Krupp, Arndt, 85

Lagonegro, Italy, viii, 229–36, 244–45
Lambton, Lord Tony, 74, 115–16
Langhans, Rainer, 256–57, 269, 273
Lanza, Mario, 100
Las (dog), 104
Leary, Timothy, 5
Lewis, Fiona, viii, 112–13
Lexington and the Ants, 114
Little Paul. *See* Getty, Jean Paul, III
Logue, Christopher, 102
Londonderry, Lord Alastair, 74, 76
Long, Donna Getty (sister of
        Big Paul), 46, 166, 177, 246
Lovin' Spoonful, the, 89
Luau Club, Rome, 62, 99, 152

Maccarelli, Sergio, 175
Madonna Dell Etna, Italy, 188

The Magic Christian, 59
Magnani, Anna, 249
Magritte, 70
Major, John, 263
malavita (criminals), 99, 125–129,
        189, 218, 271–72. *See also*
        Calabresi kidnappers
    kidnapping of twins by, 28–32,
        40–41, 43, 126–27
    Little Paul's ties to, 25–33,
        124–27, 140, 152, 175, 272
Mammoliti brothers, 152, 244
Mamounia Hotel, Marrakesh, 79,
        83, 86
Margaret, Duchess of Argyll, 120
Mario (chauffeur), viii, 110, 156,
        184–85, 190
"Marrakesh Express," 86
Marrakesh, Morocco, 109, 144,
        271–72, 276
    Big Paul's palace in, 69, 79–90,
        267–68
Masone, Fernando, viii
Matson, Norman, 49–50, 262–63
McInnis, Martin, viii, 77, 207
McKno, Fraser, 58, 156, 177–78, 218
Meers, Nicolette, vii, 79–88, 101,
        102–3
Il Messaggero, 16
    kidnapping coverage by, 141, 149,
        174, 192–93, 205, 207, 209, 240
    severed ear and, 205, 207, 209
Midsummer's Night Dream, 59, 276
Mohammed, Si (house guardian),
        82, 88
Momento Sera, 17
Moore, Dudley, 250
Moore, Roger, 89
Morgan, J. P., 14
Morrissey, Paul, 128, 130, 131
Murder in the Cathedral, 59

Murder on the Orient Express, 251
Murray, Phil, 57
Mussolini, Benito, 249

National Enquirer, 41
National Gallery, London, 263
Negri, Pola, 6
Nero (lion), 120
Newsom, Bill, 111–12, 155
Newsweek, 10
The New York Times, 10
The Night Watch (painting), 54
Nixon, Richard, 215
Notre Dame, 92–93, 95–96

Obermaier, Uschi, 273
Old Paul. *See* Getty, Jean Paul
Olmstead, Remington, 129
O'Neil, Kevin, 131
On the Road (Kerouac), 80
OPEC (Organization of Petroleum
    Exporting Countries), 137
opium, 111
    Big Paul's use of, 75–76, 85–87,
        97, 101, 103–4, 106–7
Organization of Petroleum
    Exporting Countries. *See* OPEC
Orwell, George, 20
Oufkir, Mohamed, 86–87, 90

Paese Sera, 149
The Panic in Needle Park, 114
Parkes (Old Paul's valet), 120
Patrick, John, 103, 105–6
Peccinotti, Harri, 12–13
Pedro, Don (Getty family priest),
    198–99
Peelaert, Guy, 124

Penelope (Old Paul's assistant), 54
Penn, Sean, 259
People, 41
Pepperdine University, Malibu,
    248–49
Philip (Little Paul's friend), 23–24,
    123, 177, 240
Piccolo (kidnapper), vii, 133, 145,
    187–90, 196, 226
    ear severance by, 201
    kidnapping plot origins and,
        273–74
Pierry, Judge, 78
Playboy, 128
Playmen, 12
Polanski, Roman, 13–14, 129, 131
police, Roman
    ear severance and, 207–10
    Getty's release and, viii, 227–28,
        231–36
    kidnapping hoax speculation by,
        140–42, 148, 152, 175, 270
    kidnapping investigation by,
        139–42, 148, 152, 175
    ransom drop and, 218–23
Pollock, Jackson, 70
Pol, Talitha, vii, 66, 69–70, 75–76,
    78–80, 82–83, 85–90, 111,
    119, 268, 276–77
    background of, 18, 68, 73–74
    child of, 81, 84, 96, 98, 123, 153
    death of, 12, 17, 33, 96–107,
        112–13, 121, 123, 147
    heroin use by, 12, 99–102, 107, 109
Ponti, Carlo, 271
Presley, Elvis, 86
press
    Big Paul's death notice in, 263
    ear sent to, 35–36
    Getty, Gail, portrayal by, 142,
        147–49, 155–56

press (*continued*)
  kidnapping coverage by, 9–11,
    16–20, 35–38, 40–41, 135,
    137, 141–42, 147–49, 155–56,
    173–74, 181, 208–9, 211, 217,
    221, 228, 233–38, 240
  Little Paul's death notice in, 276
  Little Paul's release and, 228,
    233–38
  Little Paul's wedding and, 245
  post-kidnapping Getty stories by,
    238–41

Red Army Faction (RAF), 27, 33,
    268, 270, 273
Redgrave, Vanessa, 251–52
Rembrandt, 54
Rentzel, Lance, 182
Richard (Little Paul's friend), 109,
    124
Rimbaud, 110
Rocco, Fiammetta, 263
Rock Dreams, 124
Rockefeller, John D., 50
Rockefeller, John D., III, 51
Rolling Stone magazine, 41–42
Rolling Stones, the, 89. *See also*
    Jagger, Mick
Roman Holiday, 56
Romeo and Juliet, 59
Roosevelt, Franklin D., 44, 79
Roosevelt, Teddy, 50
Rork, Ann (mother of Big Paul), viii,
    17–18, 45–49
Rork, Sam, 46
Rossetti, Dante Gabriel, 249
  house of, 12, 69, 79, 110–11
Ruddy, Al, 43
Ruspoli, Dado, viii, 87, 97, 100, 107,
    270

St. George's Prep School, Rome,
    59–60, 93, 276
St. Laurent, Yves, 89
St. Paul's Cathedral, London,
    263
Sallopaco, Italy, 194, 204–5
San Francisco Chronicle, 9, 48
Sarah (Big Paul's friend), 110
Sarah C. Getty Trust, 50, 77–78,
    207
Schifano, Mario, 270–71
Schneider, Maria, 17, 248
Scorpio Rising, 109
Scott, Gordon, 63–64
*Sgt. Pepper's Lonely Hearts Club
    Band,* 273
Shimonova, Carlo, 130
Sinatra, Frank, 86
Smith, Patti, 255
Sorrento Film Festival, 272
squadra mobile (police)
  ear severance and, 207–10
  Getty's release and, viii, 227–28,
    231–36
  kidnapping hoax speculation
    by, 140–42, 148, 152, 175,
    270
  kidnapping investigation by,
    139–42, 148, 152, 175
  ransom drop and, 218–23
Stalin, Joseph, 79
Starr, Ringo, 59
The State of Things, 255
Steadman, Ralph, 102
Sticky Fingers, 109
Stockholm syndrome, 182, 196–97,
    223–24
Styron, Bill, 57
Summers, Owen, 11
Sunley, Mr. (Little Paul's
    headmaster), 59

Talitha G. (yacht), 262–63
Taylor, Mrs. (Little Paul's nanny), 49
Il Tempo, 149
Thynne, Lord Christopher, viii,
    73–76, 97, 102
Time, 50–51
TIP (Turn In a Pusher), 93
Tomasini, Amber, 64
Trash, 130
True magazine, 10, 16, 22, 40–42

VB1 (kidnapper), vii, 188–89, 226
VB2 (kidnapper), vii, 189
Vejak, Aron, 116
von Bülow, Claus, 66

Wall Street Journal, 59
Warhol, Andy, 128, 129–30, 131
Wenders, Wim, 255, 258
White, Stanford, 48
Whitman, Lily, 79
"Wild Horses," 109
Willis, Bill, 79–82
Winkelmann, Jutta, vii, 4, *8,* 38, 70,
    245, 256, 266
  background of, 27–28
  interviews by, 14–17, 20–23, 27
  kidnapping/assault of, 28–32,
    126–27, 269
  Little Paul's disappearance and,
    134, 139–40
  Little Paul's relationship with,
    32–33, 124–28, 255, 267,
    271–72
  pictures by, 130, 269–70
Woolsey, Cardinal, 118

Workers' Revolutionary Party, 251
World War II, 137

The Yellow Rolls-Royce, 59

Zabriskie Point, 3
Zacher, Martine, vii, *8,* 38, 70, 163,
    275–76, *277*
  background of, 27–28
  children of, vii, 5, 27, 245, 247,
    255, 264–65, 272
  interviews by, 14–17, 20–23,
    27–34, 36, 130–31, 134,
    139–40 237–238, 244–46,
    259–60, 267–74
  kidnapping/assault of, 28–32,
    40–41, 43, 126–27, 269
  kidnapping hoax speculation and,
    18–19, 140–42, 267–70,
    273–74
  kidnapping letter delivered to,
    138–40, 142, 266
  Little Paul's overdose and,
    259–60
  Little Paul's relationship with,
    4–5, 32–33, 41–42, 124–28,
    237–38, 240, 242, 244–46,
    255–56,
    267–69, 271–72, 274
  Little Paul's release and, 237–38,
    240
  marriages of, 27, 41, 245, 255–56,
    268–69, 274
  pictures by, 130, 269–70
Zacher, Rolf, 27, 255
Zajac, Jack, viii, 57